CONTENTS
NUMBER 40 SPRING 2000

D1806206

Culture/China

NEW FORMATIONS

EDITOR:
David Glover

GUEST EDITORS
Stephanie Hemelryk Donald
Harriet Evans

REVIEWS EDITOR
Alasdair Pettinger

EDITORIAL ASSISTANT
Alyson Pendlebury

EDITORIAL BOARD:
Timothy Bewes
Laura Chrisman
Jeremy Gilbert
Cora Kaplan
Neil Lazarus
Mandy Merck
Scott McCracken
Bill Schwarz
Judith Squires
Jenny Bourne Taylor
Wendy Wheeler

ADVISORY BOARD:
Ien Ang
Angelika Bammer
Tony Bennett
Jody Berland
Homi Bhabha
Victor Burgin
Lesley Caldwell
Hazel Carby
Erica Carter
Iain Chambers
Joan Copjec
Lidia Curti
Tony Davies
James Donald
Simon Frith
Stuart Hall
Dick Hebdige
Colin Mercer
Edward Said
Renata Salecl
Gayatri Chakravorty Spivak
Valerie Walkerdine

New Formations is published
three times a year by
Lawrence & Wishart
99a Wallis Road, London E9 5LN
Tel: 020-8533 2506
Fax: 020-8533 7369
Website:www.l-w-bks.co.uk/
formation.html

ADVERTISEMENTS:
For enquiries/bookings contact Vanna Derosas,
Lawrence & Wishart

SUBSCRIPTIONS:
For 2000, subscription rates to Lawrence & Wishart
are, for 3 issues
UK: Institutions £70, Individuals £35.
Rest of world: Institutions £75; Individuals £38.
Single copies: £14.99

CONTRIBUTIONS AND CORRESPONDENCE:
Send to:
The Editor, *New Formations*
Dept. of English, University of Southampton
Highfield, Southampton SO17 1BJ

BOOKS FOR REVIEW:
Send to:
Alasdair Pettinger
Scottish Music Information Centre
1 Bowmont Gardens
Glasgow, Scotland G12 9LR

Prospective writers are encouraged to contact the
editors to discuss their ideas and to obtain a copy of
our style sheet.
Manuscripts should be sent in triplicate; experts in
the relevant field will referee them anonymously.
The manuscripts will not be returned unless a
stamped, self-addressed envelope is enclosed.
Contributors should note that the editorial board
cannot take responsibility for any manuscript
submitted to *New Formations*.

ISSN   0 950 2376
ISBN   0 85315 9254

Text design and setting by Art Services, Norwich
Printed in Great Britain at the University Press,
Cambridge.

NOTES ON CONTRIBUTORS

Tony Ayres (cover image) is an award-winning Australian film-maker and scriptwriter. He has worked on television and in the independent film sector. His work includes *The Long Ride* (1994), *Ghost Story* (1997), *The Violent Earth* (1997), *China Dolls* (1997), *Mrs Craddock's Complaint* (1997), and *Sadness* - an adaptation of William Yang's autobiographical monologue(1999).

John Cayley is a London-based poet, translator, publisher and bookseller. His work is much concerned with writing in networked and programmable media. He has taught at the University of California, San Diego, where he has been a Research Associate of the Centre for Research in Computing and the Arts (CRCA).

Stephanie Hemelryk Donald is senior lecturer in media at Murdoch University, Australia. She has published *Public Secrets, Public Spaces: cinema and civility in China* (2000), *The State of China Atlas* (1999) (with Robert Benewick), and co-edited with Harriet Evans *Picturing Power in the People's Republic of China: Posters of the Cultural Revolution* (1999).

Harriet Evans is senior lecturer in Chinese at the University of Westminster and senior research fellow at the Centre for the Study of Democracy. She has written *Women and Sexuality in China: dominant discourses of female sexuality and gender since 1949* (1997), and co-edited *Picturing Power* with Stephanie Donald.

Gay Hawkins is a senior lecturer in cultural and media studies in the School of Sociology, University of New South Wales. She is the author of *From Nimbin to Mardi Gras: constructing community arts* (1993).

Katie Hill is completing a doctoral thesis on the cultural politics of contemporary Chinese art at the University of Sussex.

Tamara Jacka is senior lecturer in Chinese Studies at Murdoch University. Her research interests are in social and political change, gender relations and rural-urban migration in contemporary China. She is the author of *Women's Work in Rural China: change and continuity in an era of reform* (1997).

Tseen Khoo is working as a policy and projects officer at the University of Queensland Graduate School, Australia. She has published articles about Asian-Australian literary politics and feminism. Tseen is currently co-editing a collection of essays about Asian-Australian cultural production.

Jo Law (images) is a freelance photographer, film-maker and multimedia artist working in Perth, Western Australia.

Greg Kwok-Keung Leong (images) is an artist and writer working in/from Tasmania

Pamela Leung (images) is an artist working in London.

Richard Read is senior lecturer in art history at the University of Western Australia. He publishes on word-image relations, the history of European art theory and contemporary painting-in-film, and is completing a book on modernist debates in the early career of Adrian Stokes.

Shu-mei Shih teaches literature and on film from Taiwan, China, and Hong Kong, as well as literary theory and Asian American studies at UCLA. She is the author of *The Lure of the Modern: writing modernism in semicolonial China, 1917-1937* (2000) and *Visuality and Identity: cultural transactions across the Chinese Pacific* (in progress).

Sarah E. Stevens is a doctoral candidate in East Asian Languages and Cultures at Indiana University, with a minor in Gender Studies. Her research focuses on gender and sexuality in twentieth century Chinese literature and culture. She has presented papers at major American and international conferences. Her dissertation examines the social construction of female sexuality in Republican China (1911-1949).

Wanning Sun is lecturer in media at Curtin University of Technology, Western Australia.

Souchou Yao is lecturer in Anthropology at the University of Sydney. His research and teaching focuses on the overseas Chinese, and the social formation of aesthetics and cultural representation in Chinese societies. He is the author of *Confucian Capitalism: discourse, practice and 'Chinese Business'* (2000).

Audrey Yue is lecturer in cultural studies at the University of Melbourne. She writes on postcolonial Hong Kong cinema, Asian media, diaspora cultures, new technologies and queer theory. She has published in *Asian Journal of Communication, Meanjin, Inter-Asia Cultural Studies, Multicultural Queer* (1999) and *The Horror Reader* (2000).

EDITORIAL

Stephanie Hemelryk Donald and Harriet Evans

The title of this special issue, *Culture/China* is as elusive in its possible meanings as it is general. It indicates broad fields of interest and experience, but does so without any suggestion of how they might be defined. It draws on but challenges the well-known formulation, 'Cultural/China', initially associated with an article by Tu Wei-ming published in *Daedalus* ten years ago. The term 'Cultural China' is commonly associated with an underlying political and ethnic centrism, according to which different practices of Chineseness are collapsed into a homogeneous and regionally fixed notion of 'Chinese culture' as a unifying signifier. *Culture/China* sets out to critique and explore some of the ideas associated with this earlier term, without any necessary reference to them, through a collection of essays about different experiences and representations of 'Chineseness'. Our juxtaposition of terms suggests a process of re-evaluation, of re-appropriation, as well as of acknowledgement. Tu's concept is inimical to the positions expressed in this collection. Nevertheless, the fact of the concept, and its organising power, cannot be dismissed out of hand.

Culture/China is then in many ways a political project which acknowledges - without engaging in - controversies of ownership and location. Where one reader might see the discrete words of the title as linked, even mutually supportive, others will identify one or other ... *culture* ... or ... *China* ... as the key to understanding its framing of the essays that follow. The term suggests links and divides, it invites reflections on the areas of the imagination where the notion of 'cultural China' might have some meanings. It neither identifies nor excludes, hence it can incorporate in its meanings the variety of migrant and settler experiences of people of Chinese ethnicity. It can also countenance the problematics of Chineseness without culture - without language, without ethnicity in some circumstances. Tu Wei-ming's coining of the term 'cultural China' in the late 1980s was a statement of economic and political centrality in the context of a centred Confucian version of being Chinese outside China.[1] As Ien Ang has argued, the trouble with any centre is that it immediately needs a periphery in order to function.[2] In Tu's version of 'Cultural China', the periphery consists of those who determine multiple ways of being in and out of cultural China at the same time.

Negotiations with China, with Chineseness and with the politics of not *being* Chinese - in whatever sense one may understand that - inform the essays here. Those negotiations are investigated as they work through cultural forms: language, the Internet, television, metaphor, food, painting, fashion and film. Finally we return to the geopolitical centre and diasporic periphery

1. Tu Wei-ming, 'Cultural China: The Periphery as Center', *Daedalus*,120(2): 1-32, 1991; see also Audrey Yue/Gay Hawkins in this issue.

2. Ien Ang, 'Can One Say "No" to China' , *boundary 2*, vol 25, no 3, 1998.

of the mainland, the state of China. The domestic politics of periphery are discussed in relation to women, and to internal migrants in particular. Cultural China does not come out as a liberating concept in these arguments, although it retains some currency as an organising trope in reflection and debate. The question of who may speak to and from such a space is unresolved. The concerns around assimilation versus annihilation, fearfully realised in Indonesia in 1998, can be spoken through and against 'cultural China'. The antagonisms of politics and style experienced between nation states: China, Singapore, Taiwan and proto-national claimants; Hong Kong and again Taiwan can be complicated by the supposed ties of 'cultural China'. Yet cultural China can also remind the supposed multicultural societies of the world that dominant cultures arrest the development of their constituent others. In those cases, Australia, Indonesia, Malaysia, the USA and the UK (and China itself) are some of the examples that emerge here, cultural China (s) still have a role to play.

LA CHINE IN CULTURE/CHINA

Stephanie Hemelryk Donald

Next comes the response, the artist, the artist's creation - the attempt to name, recognize, and instigate change through his or her creative expression. But the artist's creation is not the end of the process, as it is often thought to be. The process continues as members of the community experience the release, the inspiration that allows them to enflesh the message and begin activating change in their own terrains.[1]

The 'enfleshment' of the message that Májozo advocates as best practice in public art is both a demand for the political in aesthetic production, and a recognition that the political is not the job of the artist alone. The artist must develop a keen eye for the contemporary moment whilst giving space for the observer to enjoin with the aesthetic in an agenda for change. The idealistic ambition of Májozo's position is attractive, but it also raises questions when applied to the politics of diaspora and settlement. Does the meaning of politics in art arise through 'recognition' or through 'enfleshment' and is a common class or other identity assumed by the terrains of action?

In this analysis of three contemporary Australian artists - Greg Leong, Tony Ayres and Jo Law - I suggest that the condition of hybridity and its artistic formations cannot be factored through identity alone, but through multiple recognitions of political position and emerging alliances. This approach acknowledges that random but determined synergies of proximity and pleasure are crucial factors in the development of the political address of aesthetic objects and texts. The thread that runs through these brief analyses and the works themselves is that the artists' project of expression is played through as *chine*. The concept of *chine* is borrowed from Jean-Marie Floch's work on modern marketing.[2] He uses the dictionary meanings of the word to name the processes of design that result in composites and unexpected patterns. His own composite draws on the *Petit Robert* definition, which offers primary and secondary meanings. First, the verb *chiner* comes from a Chinese textile process, the practice of: 'alternating colours on the threads of a warp prior to weaving the cloth, in such a manner as to end up with a design once the weaving process is complete'.[3] Second, it means to seek out a good bargain, or to tease mercilessly - as a hawker might 'tease' (or cheat) a customer. So *chine* in Floch's analysis of Habitat and Ikea (and the prime *chineur* Terence Conran) comes to mean something like 'browsing', but doing so with desire or lust for emotional experience. Commercial *chine*, Conran's kind, builds up a syntagm of meaning through accumulated objects. Many of these objects hover on the cusp of authenticity, nostalgia and

1. Estella Conwill Májozo, 'To Search for the Good and Make It Matter', in Suzanne Lacy (ed) *Mapping the Terrain: New Genre Public Art*, Bay Press, Seattle Washington 1995, pp88-93, p91.

2. The concept of *chine* is developed through Jean-Marie Floch, *Identités Visuelles*, Presses Universitaires de France, Paris 1995, pp145-179. Translation by Alec McHoul and Pierre van Osselaer, *Visual Identities*, Cassell, 2000, (forthcoming).

3. *Ibid.*

4. *Ibid.*

practical elegance. They are *found* and then *designed*, 'a very specific ... collection of signs taken from contemporary material culture'.[4] It works well as a description of the logic of accumulation in a Conran influenced middle-class household. There is an extension of Floch's coinage however that works to explain the logic of aesthetic accumulation in the cultures of diaspora. This extension could be abbreviated as *political*, implying an inclusion of publics as well as individuals, and of diachronic contingencies as well as claims on existence.

Political chine in artistic production weaves alternating colours into a text of difference, but not necessarily one that can be understood in terms of identity. The compulsion to claim identity through hybrid formations allows that there has been a pure antecedent and that the collation of purities has combined into something altogether more interesting. With *chine* as both the process and the outcome of artistic production and spectatorship, the unexpected and the contemporary take priority. In the terms of this issue, in the world of *chine*, culture/China only exists in the active imaginations and embodied recognitions of the artist and her public.

5. The title of Greg Kwok-Leong's 1999 exhibition of Australian textile objects.

'REMEMBERING CHINESE'[5]

An embroidered red robe, an embroidered green robe, the characters for double happiness (*shuang xi*): and the artist's coined characters for double sorrow (*shuang bei*); Pauline's superior shoes (the 'Mother of Australia'), and shoes for the 'Queen of Australia': these garments of woven silk are shimmeringly stylish, and extraordinarily sexy. They are the some of the textile objects of Greg Leong. Kwok-Leong uses Manchu and Han styles of clothing from the late nineteenth century to play games with Australian politics in the realms of multiculturalism and sexuality. He also uses them to tell us of his love for his multiply displaced Australian-Chinese-Hong Kong-Australian mother, Jeanne, and to declare his own passionate investment in gay Australia. He seduces himself and his audience with detail and texture, with intricacy and fetishism. He plots and weaves his way though to the surface of satirical art with a grandeur of imagination that baffles the political senses at first sight. He writes of his own work as 'symbols and transferred metaphors' designed, highly designed, to:

> Speak strongly of a) the political and socially accepted oppression of minority groups, b) the fashion expression of superior/inferior social roles, and c) the aesthetics of minority, sexual taste ... The resonances of history are seldom clearly explained or are able to be interpreted in only one definitive way. Hence if a pair of Manchu shoes reference elaborate be-jewelled footwear of the Empress Dowager Cixi, the cultural transference strategy I use demands a conceptual and linguistic leap from Chinese Empress Dowager to *Chinese Australian Queen* (a queen of

Australia) - or for that matter, another sort of queen, Pauline Hanson, the self-proclaimed 'Mother of Australia' ...

Similarly, in the case of bound feet, for what is considered by the contemporary world as cruelty to women, one might substitute the historical oppression of gay people in Australia on one level, and the current undercurrent of blanket racism against Asian Australians on another.[6]

6. Greg Leong, 'Notes on *Remembering Chinese*', 1999 tour.

Leong's work sets up his political stall with a particular hybrid glamour. It is self-proclaimed identity-art and a reclamation of cultural Chinese 'things' from his imagined past into an experienced Tasmanian present. I wish to refer Leong's work to a more random sphere of production, however, where identity *as such* is unlikely, except in its *necessary emergenc(i)es in moments of political constraint*. Leong is literal *chineur*. He weaves ideas and images, words and colours with a deliberation that might seem to deny any possibility of random result. Such delicacy and careful documentation both beside and *within* the work (Leong makes sure to translate all the texts printed or sewn onto the cloth) points to a clear statement of identity as an Asian-Australian in 1998. Nevertheless, the wonder of the work lies in the way that an accumulation of finessed detail *surprises* us with its power. At first, such ritualised garments of ancestry pleasure their audience, drawing us into the sensuality of experience which helps us browse with *desire* or *lust*. On second sight, there is the frisson of recognition of signs (Hanson's head, the juxtaposition of the celebratory colour red and the *double sorrow* coinage on the garments and 'shoes for bound feet', the portraits of Leong's family, and a tender biography of his mother). Finally, the accumulation of detail is a syntagm of experience, and only in that very extenuated sense does the work describe identity. Its political origins do not account for the whole of its aesthetic narrative, but their presence in the weave of the fabric (sometimes literally in Leong's objects) marks the work as an address to public action as well as a statement of the defiant self.

The Manchu-style 'superior' shoes that Leong made for Pauline Hanson, the evil genius of Australian politics in 1998, the self-proclaimed 'Mother of Australia', of course, have not been delivered to the woman herself. Leong's work is not the kind of gear that you ask an actor or a performance artist to wear down the street, or on the steps of the Senate in Canberra. It is much too special for that kind of 'enfleshment'. But the shoes sit in galleries begging the question: what would we look like if *she* were wearing us? What would *she* look like if she dared to slip us on in a moment of self-aggrandising complacency? Would her body resist the appearance of the hybrid? Would she change once and forever by the naming of the shoes as shoes for feet, and by the recognition that Asian-Australian shoes are made for *her* feet in particular? Would we suddenly notice the affinity between her sexual attraction for the disaffected male ex-Liberal Party (one of her constituencies

'Pauline' photo courtesy Greg Leong: 'Mother of Australia - Pauline's Superior Shoes

in 1998?), and the girlishly decorated slippers of the terrifyingly powerful Empress Dowager? In seeing that glimpsing likeness would we then see the hugeness of Cixi's status in history and remember with ridicule Hanson's bid to be 'Mother' to the Australian nation? Májozo believes that the public artist must 'recognise' and 'name' *change*. Leong repeats the self-appellation of the need for change, inviting her to step into the shoes of the 'Mother of Australia'. In so doing his work challenges her Oedipal call to the political desires of Australian manhood with the elegant seduction of hybridity. Leong's *chine* is a syntagm of desire that makes unexpected links between identity and identity politics, but also with the textures of pleasure, the associations of painful politics and sex appeal, and his love for his mother. In some tangential way, these garments resonate with the carefully stitched memory quilts sewn for AIDS victims by their lovers and friends: they are textured documents of anguish felt in the individual heart and in the collective memory of the immediate present.

SEDUCTIONS OF GRIEF

In 1999 Tony Ayres directed a documentary of William Yang's theatrical monologue *Sadness*. The film takes us on two journeys, one through the landscapes of northern Queensland to trace Yang's family roots and the other through the years of the AIDS plague amongst the gay community in Sydney. Yang addresses us directly for much of the film, with stills and his own snapshots to progress the collection of memories, which are the signs of his Australia. The dominant and enduring image is that of his mother, who died in the early 1990s. Although this monologue is 'about' Yang, and 'about' being gay in Australia, it is also a *chine* of grief - for his mother and for old and new family losses. The film's progress is ritualistic, in which the main theme is one of the invited recognition, naming and expurgation of sorrow. Audiences are 'enfleshed' through the steady pace of the monologue and the collected juxtapositions of 'found' images and spoken memories and their 'design' for the screen. The threads of this syntagmatic browsing are threefold: we are invited into the bricolage of old memories (specifically the gossip around the murder of a great grandfather by a stockman) to take our pick - all are picturesque and gothic at once; we are allowed to share in the journeys of death recorded by Yang's photographs of stricken friends; and we are taken home to meet his mother. Her face organises us as a mother should. We see the lines of her expression in the concentrated beauty of Yang's own age. Our pleasure is her pleasure: in a last journey to meet relatives up north, in her children's love, and in her place in the Australian landscape. This Australian ancestor-mother is also a Chinese mother, and as such bears the public face of the discriminated. *La chine* teases again, how does the pleasure of catharsis lie in the weave of love affairs, friendships and family hurts? How much of this sadness is Yang's, and how much is in the fabric of Australia itself? Is this one of those objects that takes flight in shared terrains?

The eponymous heroes of *China Dolls* (1997)[7] are the drag queens of Australia, and particularly those that are already feminised in White Australian gay culture, the Asian Australian queens.[8] Moving from the seriously powerful to the seriously sexy, from Cixi and her shoes to the China Dolls and their masquerade, the performance of femininity by the

7. *China Dolls* was made for the ABC and Film Australia. It won the Director's Award for best short documentary at the Washington International Gay and Lesbian Film Festival, and an AWGIE for Best Public Broadcast Documentary.

8. The issue of feminisation arose from three papers at the '1999 Asian Australian Identitites Conference' (ANU, Canberra 27-30 September): Peter Jackson, ' "That's What Rice Queens Study!" White Gay Desire and Research on Asian Homosexualities', Tony Ayres' presentation of *Sadness* and Audrey Yue's talk on *Fruit Salad: Asian-Australian Cinema, Asian-Australian Modernity.*

'China Dolls', courtesy Tony Ayres and Film Australia

*'China Dolls',
courtesy Tony
Ayres and Film
Australia*

drag queen becomes another kind of ridicule, not of the feminine nor of the self, but of those who assume that the structure of their desire controls the gender of another person. Tony Ayres puts on his make-up for the film (see picture above): his film, his make-up, his *design* of the *found* sexuality of his self. Ayres was brought up in Western Australia (he now lives in Melbourne), Yang's family came from the north, Leong works in Tasmania.

These are old-fashioned places, in so far as the young leave to find urban freedoms elsewhere. Yet these are the landscapes that *la chine* pulls into focus, in erotic play between the found and the designed versions of the objects of life in 'this' place at 'this' time.

THIS PLACE AT THIS TIME

Jo Law is a film-maker and photographer working in Western Australia.[9] Her 1997 photograph of a bus stop outside the Immigration building in Hennessy Road, Wanchai, Hong Kong captures and exceeds the bricolage of Floch's original *chine*. Advertisers dress Hong Kong models in Spanish clothes, and say 'Cheers' with a can of San Miguel. San Miguel is the beer that the British drank from bottles in London bars in the selfish eighties. Every bottle was served with a slice of lime squashed into its neck. They probably said 'Cheers' too. But here we are in Hong Kong in 1997, in the midst of the handover to Tung Chee-hwa's leadership of the second system of Chinese Government. He is smiling from another ad, adjacent to the San Miguel text 'Another Hong Kong miracle!!' (*Xianggang qi ji, yi guan chu se*). The magazine that his head graces is called *Zhong* translated here as *Chinese* but it can also mean simply *China*, another useful ambiguity in the circumstances. The catchphrase of the magazine is printed in English: 'the talk of global Chinese'. Law's photograph embraces the incisive certainty of an advertiser's cultural politics, and the realpolitik of the event. *Zhong* is the talk of global Chinese, but the Hong Kong of this photograph is sitting on the cusp of the periphery and the centre. Another 'Hong Kong miracle' is the hope and the text of these ads and of the handover itself. The ' very specific … collection of signs taken from contemporary material culture' at this particular bus stop are the threads of a weave from which no clear

9. Film works available for view: http:// www.imago.com.au/ photonics/Movies/ Movies.html

'Bus stop', courtesy Jo Law

design has yet emerged.

Jo Law took this photograph as a visitor to Hong Kong. In her film *The Green Green Grass of Home* (1995) she performs her status as a citizen of Australia. The film consists of several takes of Jo standing in streets, and on sidewalks, in two areas of Perth: Nedlands (an up-market area around the University of Western Australia) and Northbridge (the Soho of metropolitan Perth). She stands and shouts at passing cars 'Go Home! Go Home! Go Home!' Eventually, tired, she goes to her own home and shuts the door on the camera behind her. Jo mimics the neurotics of the racist who doesn't allow that citizenship is the institutional token of being at home, but then she returns to herself and slams the door on the passing stupidity of strangers.

The claims on existence that all these works represent are strongly attached to the logic of accumulation and to the density of the material object. The pleasures of unexpected proximities and contingencies invoke in the artist and the spectator – the makers of culture - a diasporic consciousness that exists alongside the knowledge of settlement. At its most poignant the art of culture/China is also its most political. It drives in a stake for the logical and accumulative hybridity of citizenship and belonging within this settler society, this place at this time.

Thanks to Tony Ayres, Jo Law, Greg Leong, and Alec McHoul for access to their work.

'A STRANGER TO YOURSELF: WAYS OF BECOMING AN OTHER'

John Cayley

AN INTERVIEW/DISCUSSION WITH YANG LIAN

Yang Lian (**YL**) is a Chinese poet and writer, currently resident in London, UK. He is the author of numerous collections in Chinese and has been translated into many languages. In English, his most recent books are *Where the Sea Stands Still: New Poems*, (Bloodaxe, Newcastle 1999) and *Non-Person Singular*, (Wellsweep, London 1994). Further collections are in preparation from, amongst others, Green Integer Publications, Los Angeles, CA. In China a two-volume collected works was published in 1998. Major collections have also been published or are forthcoming in German, from Ammann Verlag, Zürich.

John Cayley (**JC**) is a London-based poet, translator, publisher and bookseller. Currently his work is much concerned with writing in networked and programmable media. He has translated extensively from Chinese poetry, has written on Chinese and Ezra Pound for *Agenda* and *Paideuma*, and provided notes on Chinese references for William Cookson's *Guide to the Cantos of Ezra Pound*. Recently, he taught at the University of California, San Diego, where he has been a Research Associate of the Center for Research in Computing and the Arts (CRCA).

JC Yang Lian, we will begin by talking about this notion of 'cultural China' as it is purveyed by latter-day Confucianists such as Du Weiming. I understand that you have a strong objection to this notion of cultural China, and would like you to elaborate.

YL Well, to me it seems that this concept is confused and unsatisfactory. I say confused, since, rather than simply speaking of Chinese culture - culture based on the Chinese language, or on forms of thought which emerge from the Chinese language - this concept focuses on whatever is culturally 'China' and I ask myself, 'Where is the China to which this concept refers?'

JC Well, one way to look at it is to say that this 'China' is being defined in cultural terms, as a culture, as oppose to a socio-political entity, as opposed to a place and a politics.

YL To me, the 'China' of cultural China pretends to represent or establish a political identity. When you use 'China' in this phrase it first indicates

China within its determined borders, a land, and also what China has been in the past.

JC   So China for you is defined primarily in historical and political terms?

YL   Yes: a history from which a state emerges and defines a politics. But the problem is that this notion of 'China' is one that has greater prominence outside China than it has within its own borders. Its use in 'cultural China' seems to me to be part of an attempt to create an illusionary land, an illusionary state which shares and bases itself on 'Chinese culture'.

JC   And basically you object to the use or appropriation of 'China' - and what you see of an extension of the state's influence - to culture which exists beyond China's borders, in the diaspora?

YL   Yes. I'm saying that the evocation of 'China', the attempt to institute this illusionary 'land', involves the establishment of a central power, a complete social and cultural system which implicitly accepts 'Chinese culture' as part of a state ideology. This system exists in an illusionary land where people can simply rely on it for their cultural identity ...

JC   and positions in the structures of power ...

YL   ... Yes, those structures are important. My question remains: 'Where is this land? Where is this state?' The reality today is that there is 'China' in the People's Republic, China in Taiwan, China throughout the diaspora. If this word 'China' already represents something which is disparate and dispersed - politically, socially, culturally, in every way - then there is no way to hold it together with one idea or one image. So what is this identity which derives from 'cultural China'? It has already ceased to exist.

JC   I want to take this a little bit further, knowing something of you and your work. You've raised the spectre of these breaks and divisions within the idea of 'China' that make it a sort of impossibility, but I'm sure that, in your own work, you would take these back further. So that, for example, the culture of early south and south-western China, the culture, say, of Qu Yuan and the *Chuci* (*Songs of the South*), which is clearly distinct from what you might call the northern or north-eastern orthodoxy, drives and operates within your work, life and culture. Presumably this also creates problems for you with any unitary idea of 'China' or 'Chinese culture' in so far at this is dominated by the northern, Confucian or orthodox culture.

YL   I've always seen Chinese culture as disparate, with a major division between 'official culture', often conceived as 'traditional' and closely tied to a state ideology, such as Confucianism on the one hand and, on the other a wide variety of alternative cultures, like the southern *Chuci* tradition or the many popular, folk art traditions. Even in ancient times, there was no unitary Chinese culture at all, and none of the great writers of the Chinese past - Qu Yuan, Tao Yuanming, Li Bo, Du Fu, - worked by following the prevailing cultural orthodoxy. Rather, they selected and adapted materials from whatever was on offer, to build, so it seems to me, their own cultures. And I have to say that I see my own work in the same way. I continue a tradition which attempts to build a *personal* Chinese culture, not some instance of a hollow, unitary Chinese culture.

JC   I see. Before we go on to talk about your sense of the individual as a builder or maker of culture (with the implication that this is of greater significance than some external or state-sponsored delineation), I want to question you a bit further concerning culture and the Chinese diaspora. There is clearly some sense in which this diaspora is, meaningfully, 'Chinese'. I just want to ask you: to what extent do you believe that your problems with Chinese culture are shared by other dispersed Chinese people, especially, of course, your colleagues, other writers and intellectuals?

YL   Well, I think that's the very reason that this concept of 'cultural China' has been put forward. Anyone who is a part of the Chinese diaspora has a clear problem, one of finding a position for themselves between China and the West. They feel the pressures of western culture and fear assimilation and the loss of Chinese identity which that entails. So they create something that is more concrete than abstract Chineseness, something, in my view, that pretends to be more like a country which can exist in their imaginations and serve as a foundation, an illusionary land where they can nonetheless 'dwell' and preserve their distinctiveness.

JC   Well, I have to put forward a small objection here. Say you compare this situation to my own as a Canadian living abroad in the UK. I'm simply an Englishman displaced by colonial and imperialist adventurism, whereas a person of the Chinese diaspora has a genuinely problematic relationship with a very distinct culture - one which is admittedly not unitary. Nonetheless, the strength of the attachment or attraction to this centre of cultural gravity is remarkable and, surely, significant, when you compare it to Western experiences.

YL   Yes, but my point is that I don't want to use these two phrases, 'Chinese Culture' and 'Cultural China' interchangeably. My argument is directed against 'Cultural China', which, for me, is a non-existing concept. It's the same type of problem which we continue to have with 'traditional Chinese culture'. The problem in both cases is that people are looking for a complete, 'finished' notion, a 'land' in which they can dwell and to which they can give their allegiance, so as to say, 'I belong to this idea'. In fact, this is precisely what happened, for example, during the Cultural Revolution, and in traditional Chinese society - whenever the government upholds a state ideology and cultural regime and forces its people to accept it, to follow it; while taking away the right of the people to question it, and to create it. This is a one-way system, and 'Cultural China' seems to me the same. You may be born into traditional Chinese society, but if you do not accept 'Cultural China' you are not Chinese, you are not someone who is allowed to hold a Chinese identity.

JC You see it as making culture concrete or determinate in way it shouldn't be.

YL Yes, I'm afraid, when I hear this phrase, I feel like I'm face to face with a new government, employing traditional Chinese forms of power, where identity and citizenship are within the gift of the authorities. If I agree with these authorities of 'Cultural China' then I am Chinese; otherwise I am not. But Chinese culture is what I am struggling to create, creating every day - whether or not I am 'in exile' from 'Cultural China'.

JC And you are not so much disturbed by the problems within the notion of 'Chinese culture'?

YL No, not so much ...

JC It's something you live with, or help create, or ...

YL Yes, what I want to say is that I am clear about the underlying nationalism, a nationalism that is contained within the phrase 'Cultural China' and which is being used to cancel individuality, to cancel the individual's contribution to the culture.

JC Let's talk now about the relationship of the individual to the culture. You see 'Cultural China' as defining or predetermining the relationship in a negative way, as a sort of prescriptive cultural 'citizenship'; whereas you prefer a Chinese culture where the individual is a participant or co-creator.

YL For me there are two notions here: individuality and cultural identity, but they are not contradictory, they are and they should be interrelated and interdependent. Without individuality - every person's creative thinking - any so-called cultural identity is a dead thing, because it is fixed, over-determined by the past; something which people come to only later and are obliged to accept or to follow. For me - in strong contrast to how I see the inclination of 'Cultural China' - the main energy behind the culture has to be the individual; the root of the culture is its openness to the energies of the individual.

Thinking about 'Cultural China' reminds me of the mainland in the 1980s, when we first had the opportunity to reconsider what had happened in China, culturally, under the Communist Party. We couldn't restrict our thinking to the obviously political: what was bad about Mao or the Gang of Four or whatever. We went on to discover a close correspondence between the so-called 'new' or 'revolutionary' power of the Communist regime and the traditional power structures of imperial times. Both systems of state control coerce the individual into giving up their own thinking, their own languages, their rights to question the state ideology, with - broadly - Maoist Marxist-Leninism substituted for Confucianism. In simple terms, my writing and the work of my colleagues has been dedicated to changing this situation.

JC   Yes, I can see that the individual (whatever that may be) has a very important role to play in your thinking, in bringing culture to life - as an irreducible problem for state-sponsored pre-determinations of culture. But what about the alternative emphasis? Agreed, you cannot have a cultural identity without the participation of individuals - but, as you admit, the relationship is one of interdependence - the individual is unable to make a contribution - has no way of acting or being - without a specific culture in which to make it. Perhaps 'Cultural China' is to be read, not as a traditional subordination of the individual, but simply a cultural redefinition of 'China' which invites individual participation; 'China' is something which the culture will (re)create.

YL   I said the relationship was one of interdependence, and I can see culture as contributing to the determination of 'China', but for this to happen the basic motive, energy must derive from a living culture, and by a living culture, I mean a culture which allows into itself the energies brought to it by successive generations of individuals, so that the culture may grow, develop and change - like life.

JC   At this point, I'd like to ask where you expect these new energies or sources of impetus to come from, especially in view of your own individual experience. Since you are an example of a writer who has been exiled, who now lives abroad and has experienced significant influences from the West and western literature in particular. Would you say that these outside influences, these border-crossings are necessary? That they give you the necessary degree of desire to make the culture new, to change it, to remake it?

YL   Basically, I feel that the important thing is the energy which the individual brings to the culture, meaning the questions which the individual has formulated from their experience, *whatever* that may be, and poses to the culture as a challenge to its preconceived ideas.

Before I started to write my own poetry, I had such experiences. When I was sent to the countryside in 1973, I had to face the fact that official publications were lying about the situation. What I knew from personal experience was completely different from what I read in the newspapers. Propaganda during the Cultural Revolution completely dominated the media, telling us only of a happy life which all of us led. But the facts of the lives in the little village where I was sent; the situations of my family and myself were completely otherwise. From that moment I began to ask myself what was the truth, and found myself unable any longer to accept the public lies. This was also the moment when I began to try to find words - a language for my own experience - and to record it in notebooks, as the earliest beginnings of my poetry. And the work is continuous from that moment up to the present. Now these poems are, in a sense, a part of Chinese culture, or a growth or development of Chinese culture which arose from my personal experience.

JC   You seem to be saying that the poetry arises precisely at the moment when you come into conflict with, what?, the 'Cultural China' of those times?

YL   Other writers with similar inclinations and I were trying to divert cultural activity away from such fixed ideas, down to a deeper root which is in language. We basically found ourselves needing to make a new language based on our experience ... This is difficult ...

When I use this word experience, it is also 'within' the language, we can't talk of anything - thoughts, feelings, experience - without there already being a language in which to put them. But when I say that we made a language for ourselves, I mean that we left behind the ready-made concepts and ideas given to us by public discourse and attempted to open the language to our own inclinations and desires, to our own feelings. The language, for me, at that time, had been closed ...

JC   But was it completely closed? Even at that stage, didn't you have Qu Yuan and the *Songs of the South*? Didn't you have some access to translations of western literature? I mean during this time when you started to write. Or did you start to write before you felt these influences?

YL   I say it was closed because, for example, Qu Yuan long predated this dominance of a state ideology.

JC   I'm only asking whether you had read Qu Yuan at this point, and western literature in translation?

YL   Yes, I had.

JC   So, in a sense you seem to be saying that your poetry arose from a direct conflict between an imposed language of the state, and a potential language of your own experience. But I'm putting it to you that there were already other influences in play (both from within and from outside 'China'), and that they were also 'within' language.

YL   As I said before, I had experienced such influences. However, when I read Qu Yuan, Du Fu and others, for me, they were not part of any fixed culture or alternative culture, they were creators of living culture, makers of cultures which are open to their own particular experience. Culture is never a closed box, the culture can be opened up by such individuals when they have a strong inclination to express themselves in language, and then the culture has the opportunity to break away from the constrictions of a state-sponsored orthodoxy, while incorporating the personal. Nonetheless, the individual must acknowledge some determination by and understanding of the tradition. When I talk about a living tradition, this already includes - it must be based on - energies deriving from the personal; and when we talk about a modern individual, this must encompass a special understanding of the tradition which precedes him or her. Hence the interrelationship between tradition and the individual. And in my own writing, I believe that I must engage the full complexity of these relationships.

JC   From what you say I get a strong notion of a dominant official culture, against which you struggle or into which you interpose the individual re-maker of a 'living' tradition. But, addressing these issues in the present context, I want to make a problem for you by asking, 'What is this thing that does the struggling?' From what you say, I still get the impression of an individual who is primarily determined by their personal experience. And I'm not sure whether such individuals - 'empty' or 'original' individuals - exist. The individual is always determined by manifold experiences and cultures, whether dominant or subordinated. In your writing, I think there is evidence of this, despite your apparent allegiance to the energies of a purer individuality. One of the attractions of your writing is that it incorporated a rich display of China's early south-western cultures.

YL   Yes, I have access to these materials from traditional Chinese culture, and from western culture and from my own experience, but I believe that I then have the freedom to make a selection or a choice from all of these different things, based on whether they are 'right' - it's hard to put it otherwise - whether they are able to help me understand my life. So, in this case, I'm not talking about a 'pure' or 'original' or 'empty' person or individuality, but nonetheless I want to retain my right, everybody's right, to select from the cultures which surround them, not the other way round, to have official cultures chosen for them.

JC   And just to bring the discussion back to earlier points, you're saying that the notion of Cultural China, doesn't allow you this freedom, because it demands your allegiance.

YL   Yes.

***

JC   I want to go on now, since I feel we should talk a little about language. There is continuity, because language is clearly important to you, language is the material with which you work. You work with Chinese, an integral, constitutive part of Chinese culture. Perhaps you could say something about how you use this material, when you are living, now, outside China, in the geo-political sense. Your work is in Chinese. How do you, for example, incorporate 'non-Chinese' influences into your life and work? How do you maintain your 'freedom' and exercise your 'rights' - as you say - when you are compelled or choose to use Chinese for your work?

YL   Well, in fact, I have been chosen. In each language there are limits and possibilities. So whichever language you were born into, you still must fight or play against those limits and possibilities. Chinese was the particular language within which I was born. This language is closely bound up with my memories and experiences, and even my sense of reality. This is an instance of culture determining the individual, as you were saying. When I try to make sense of my life today, as a Chinese poet living in the West, it means that I must make an extra effort to understand the Chinese language; to try and identify its special characteristics, to discover what is the particular way of thinking which is based on the nature of the language; what is the difference between this language and its ways of thinking, compared to other languages and other ways of thinking. Then, after I have uncovered a number of these differences, I must try to find out what attracts me to Chinese or rather, what are the problems of Chinese. All these thoughts and explorations bring me back and force me to further question myself, the Chinese language, my own language, and Chinese culture - not only my culture but 'our' culture that extends from the past.

JC   You mentioned that, in part, you were searching for things which attracted you about Chinese, as well as problems with Chinese. Would you like to say something about what does attract you to Chinese, now that you have been able to investigate it from 'outside'?

YL   Basically, these two impressions are rooted in one thing, the special characteristics of the language which we normally distinguish by way of linguistics, pointing out, for example, that Chinese grammar must be understood in very different ways than those suggested by the traditional grammar of western linguistics. But you don't want me to go into those sort of details, do you?

JC   No, perhaps I can get at it like this: when you write in Chinese, what is it that you enjoy about it? Can you think, for example, of a type of experience about which it is easier to write in Chinese?

YL   No, I don't ever want to say that it is 'easy' to write about anything. In fact, I feel that my language has made it even more difficult to make poetry - for myself and my generation of poets. We confront this great tradition of poetry, and it is such a heavy and difficult burden for us. There were so many great poets of the past, and their works prove that the language has such beauty and such special poetic powers. On the other hand, when we began to write, we were facing this same poetic tradition as one in which formal characteristics had been closed and fixed until the beginning of this century. Then after the May Fourth movement (1919), poets had attempted to open up these closed forms to the new 'modern' experiences of the Chinese people. However, since 1919, influenced by the troubled history since that time, and particularly the later advent of the communist period, a new language of Chinese poetry has remained undiscovered. That was the situation when my generation began. As we started to write, developments in poetry were very closely tied up with the various spontaneous demonstrations which took place from 1976 onwards, finally culminating in the tragedy of 1989. But nearly all of the poetry associated with these events was in traditional forms. The people, the participants in these events, had no way to express themselves, poetically, in a new form or language of poetry. This was the big challenge which I identified for myself, and which many other poets also engaged - how to open a poetic language for these experiences. This still exerts a great pressure on us as we write. Afterwards, living, 'outside' ...

JC   Go on, that's precisely what I'd like to hear about ...

YL   When we came out from China to the West, the knowledge which we slowly acquired about western language and literature - this was very important for the process of making comparisons with the Chinese language and its poetry. These differences became a primary source of interest, and helped to locate what, for me, was interesting about the Chinese language. I wanted, somehow, to develop the potential of Chinese poetry on the basis of these particularities. The energy for this development comes from my attempts to express myself in this language itself. Without this energy and the subsequent developments, poetry would simply be a game or a pretence. When a change in language is deeply related with something I want to express, then finally we have a Chinese poetry which is a contribution to what I would be happy to call 'my' Chinese culture. At such a moment, I can see the difficulties of this process - how language sets out from its delineated shoreline, and moves closer and closer - in the midst of a daily struggle - to my own 'way'. This is what really interests me.

JC   I would, again, have a problem with seeing what it is moving closer to. Where are you? You are a person, an individual having experiences of a certain kind, between traditional Chinese culture - extending into the constructed, state-sponsored culture of twentieth-century China - and Western culture and its literatures. And you are developing your individual language in these circumstances, as you put it, moving closer - my question is - to what? I can't really imagine an answer for this, because it seems to me that the language is constructing you as you remake it. It's already as close to you as anything can get.

YL   I don't want to say that the language is making me. It's a matter of mutual influence, like the Buddhist conception of existence - it's not that the nature of existence is empty, but each moment there is a temporality or contingent existence. Our life is a cycle, but each life is a temporary existence. So why I speak of this 'living culture' is because it moves and changes with each person's struggles. The language may have its particular characteristics, but these relate to and derive from each person's usage, at every moment ...

JC   These are philosophical and ethical questions about your own and a particular individual's relationship with language, but if you are talking about literature and culture, then you must also talk about things such as cultural value and 'achieving' a poetic language, achieving a new poetics. This is clearly, in your context and in the context of Chinese contemporary writing, a problem. I have no doubt that you are seriously engaged with this problem of trying to recreate a Chinese which is properly literary - and I know you have 'colleagues,' there are other serious poets. On the other hand, compared to what I know of contemporary poetic writing in the West, I do not see, in China - to the same extent - a search for a new language in the technical or artistic sense, a new poetics, a new way of writing poetry. Until you have a culture, growing within these three opposing cultures, what have you got?

YL   I have to say that I want to achieve a personal, developed writing, and that implies culture. I want finally to arrive at that.

JC   So you have to look after your own problems first?

YL   Well - agreeing with you - language is so deeply inscribed within ourselves and our culture. So, when I question myself, it's the same thing as questioning Chinese. Since my 'self' is somehow so deeply rooted in the language. When I try to write a poem, of course I try to express myself, but more importantly, the poetry is an attempt to reach the limits of language - certainly the limits of past language. Poetry is an attempt to develop new sentences, news ways of expression, new possibilities in language, and my 'self' can only be expressed in these new forms and potentials.

JC   This I understand, but once you've created this new language, you need to have created it in such a way that other people can use it. Isn't that the case? Other writers have to be able share it ...

YL   Well, not ...

JC   They have at least to be able to read it ...

YL   But on the other hand, for example, up until the present there are not so many people able to read Qu Yuan's poems.

JC   I don't think that's the same thing. That's something which holds for any writing, but ...

YL   What I'm trying to say is that if you create something which is for yourself but which is reasonable, possessing a coherent existence, that implies, it seems to me, a potential for others. Well, of course, it's possible that others may have difficulties with the work. We will always be called difficult poets. People take time to be able to make use of the new potential.

***

JC   OK, let's move on now and take up an example. I will try and say it the way I see it and you can tell me how it relates to what you have just said. We'll use, as we planned, the example of Ezra Pound. We are considering the western appropriation of a Chinese poetic. What I want to look at is not this much-debated appropriation, but how it has fed back into Chinese letters; in other words, how you see what Pound did, and how that has affected your language, your contribution to the development of a poetic language for contemporary Chinese. To relate this to what I was asking above: you may tell me, 'This is what I did with Pound', but other writers also did something with Pound. Did that lead to some sharing of poetic resources, introduced into the language by, say, a group of writers? And is that, in your view, a proper development of the language?

YL   In my view, what Ezra Pound (*mis*)understood, or imagined concerning Chinese language and literature is not really the important aspect of what he achieved. Well, his introduction of Imagism and his 'ideogrammic' interpretations of Chinese characters had a certain importance, but, for me, what was much more important was an indication of his way of thinking about a strange culture, a strange knowledge, a strange tradition. He didn't, I guess, try that hard to understand these things themselves, he tried, through these strange things, to come back to himself, to open himself to those influences, trying to find what was interesting for himself, for his own writing and poetics.

This is why Eliot called him, not the 'discoverer' (*faxian*) but the 'inventor' (*faming*) of Chinese poetry (see Eliot's 1928 introduction to Pound's *Selected Poems*). For me, this invention allowed him to take us back to the root of poetry, closer to the root of the poetry than other, more technical or academic approaches. Such approaches try to understand *that*, but he tried to understand *this* (YL points to his 'self').

JC   So you don't see whatever Pound thought about Chinese as being 'Chinese' *at all*? You just think of it as being 'poetic'?

YL   Yes, firstly poetic. Misunderstanding in translation is always present, and if we were too afraid of misunderstanding, then there would never be any work of translation. Pound found a way - which you might call 'higher misunderstanding' - to open, perhaps even to break open, this wonderful ancient Chinese poetry, which because of its highly strict form, is all but impossible to open. This form was so well constructed that there is no way to bring the language out from the form, even if you created another 'perfect' western form to contain it - once extracted, it would already be totally different. So Pound made these crazy, let's say, 'free' versions, to recreate the poems in terms of an English poetics and I think that, for me, this is the best, or the only, way to bring these wonderful Chinese poems into other wonderful English poems.

And to get to your question, there are many of my colleagues, who, until today, have tried, technically, to follow certain of Pound's ideas concerning Chinese poetry, for example, an analysis in terms of Imagism. In practice this means that they play around with a few simple images within a simple syntax, in a sort of basic algebra. They do this to add something a little unusual or surprising to their work, to make an impression. However, they forget Pound's extraordinary way of thinking; he attempts to find a totally different way to open language up and give it a new dimension. This is also what I was trying to do, for example when I was still in China in 1985, finishing the group of poems, 'In Symmetry with Death'. These were sixteen poems which were reincorporated into a single structure, using topics and themes from Chinese history and mythology as structuring elements, arranged symmetrically and designed to 'meet in a middle' which consists of four ironic, darkly humorous, slightly ridiculous prose pieces. Only in these four prose pieces is there any use of the first-person pronoun and the present tense - a personal, everyday reality - bringing the historical, mythological and other cultural references up into the present and what is happening to myself, today. I was selecting from the whole conspectus of

Chinese history, but for myself, as if I was creating a personal Chinese history. After I wrote this, I had the opportunity to read Pound's so-called 'Chinese Cantos' and suddenly I found him using the documents of Chinese history in an absolutely free way. There was no order or chronology, no history in an ordered, progressive sense; there were only the fragments of history, rearranged and structured by Pound's own hand. That is what really struck me. Here were totally different poets, writing entirely for themselves, but in some mysterious way meeting at a deeper level. That is what I really appreciated from reading Pound.

JC   I can see what you are saying, but that meeting never happens without a great deal going on, in the way of technical - poetic in this case - systems and procedures. It's not that Pound has an innate or intuitive understanding of, say, his Chinese materials, but he has engaged with them, used them, appropriated them, cut them up, mixed them, turned them into new language. I don't see it as being a sudden, mysterious meeting. I see in it the operation of a great many processes and procedures.

YL   I don't think that our position is very different from Pound's, and in fact we are carrying on from him. We are Chinese poets, meaning that we write in Chinese. Pound was writing in English making an attempt to understand Chinese language and materials. In the same way, we are trying to understand what is contained in Chinese culture and the poetry of the past. It's the same problem. We have to bring what we find into our own ways of writing, and to use them in our own way. In fact the centre of our world, of our culture, should always be ourselves. Perhaps, the difference between Pound's position and ours is that it is easier for us to forget this point. For Pound it was very clear. He knew that he was at a distance from his nonetheless fascinating Chinese materials.

***

JC   Let's make a leap now. Again, I can see what you are saying, but I'm also thinking that precisely one of the interesting things that happens here is the confrontation with something which you, as a writer, are prepared to use, but which is undeniably 'other'. There is no way that Pound wasn't aware that he was confronting something about which he, basically, had very little understanding. He had built up a whole range of ideas and conjectures. I want now to talk about a specific experience of yours, which you have described to me before. After you had come to the West and your work was translated, you said to me that this had made you write, and begin to think about writing, in a different way. When you are translated, you are confronted in a supremely practical manner, with another writer who is, as it were, using your words, taking them and making them into English; and you are watching this happen. I see this as very similar to what Pound did with his Chinese materials. He was doing it himself, for himself, but on the other hand I think that he was confronting himself with another language.

YL   I think Pound's is a more interesting case, since he is re-fashioning his imagination and his knowledge of China and Chinese, as the other of himself.

For Pound and myself or any poet who has some experience of translation, it can be like borrowing another eye to see yourself. This is very interesting. At the beginning, I found it quite funny, because when I talked to my translator, I recognised the words or line under discussion, but their interpretation was really quite different to one's own understanding. Often translators seemed to discover something new which even gave me a new understanding of myself. That was the most interesting aspect of this process for me - to read myself by way of another tongue.

JC   Did you, then, experience a desire to begin to use language in a different way, because of this, because of what you understood of this process?

YL   When any Chinese poet writes in Chinese, we use the language unconsciously, without thinking about the grammatical resources built into the language: for example, a verb in Chinese may not be explicitly inflected for tense, and plural or singular in nouns need not be specified. We just write the line without considering this. We arrange the images and leave it to the reader to make sense of the tenses and numbers according to shared knowledge and context. But when the poem is translated, then all of these questions are at issue and you realise that you have been unconsciously relying on characteristics of the language which are peculiar, in this case, to Chinese. The first reaction is one of surprise. You thought you knew this language so well, but it's not that you knew it well, you only knew its surface, the skin of the language; you didn't know what was its flesh, its bone, its blood, what was its life, why this language is special. Then, after this moment of strangeness and surprise, you more and more realise that this language's special characteristics were what really work to control your way of thinking, not only your own way of thinking, but that of the culture and tradition. And this is the great surprise or the great gift which translation gives to a writer. So today, when I sit at my desk and aim to write a piece of literature in Chinese, I always have the idea, the challenge of how deep I can go to try and reach the special resources of the language I'm using. Can I develop something special in this piece because of those potentials or limits, or will I simply use the language as before?

JC   Hasn't it also made you write in a different way? I'm thinking now of your recent formal experiments, where you analyse characters and chop them up in a way which is, perhaps, like playing serious literary games with letters in certain types of western concrete or visual poetry?

YL   Poetry is always somehow like a play or a game, but I always strive to play a game that is necessary, since it's not only a game of words, it's poetry. I mean the form must go together with some special content, relating one to the other. For example, this last group of poems you mentioned, from the new collection, 'Concentric Circles', this consists of three groups of poems based on the constituent elements of the single character for poetry. Within each group seven characters were also chosen as relating to one or other of the three elements, so as to finally reach the word, 'poetry'. The three groups are conceived as building a world within, in fact, one word. And poetry, for me, is the world built from language, although this language must be continually developed, in order for the poetry and its life to emerge, similarly, in continual development.

JC   But this analytic process - do you see it as something which you've done? Or it is something which comes from Chinese itself? Or does it spring from any western influences?

YL   I understand what you're getting at. Firstly, it is the possibilities or potentials of Chinese itself. Basically, this is deeply rooted in the nature of the language. But then, I'm unaware of other Chinese poets who have done things like this. This proves that even though the nature of the language has such potential, without the individual poet, and his or her special ideas, it's not necessarily the case that this potential will be realized in poetry. This is why the individual poet's - his or her ideas, desires and rhythms - are also important, along with influences from the West and from elsewhere 'outside', because they provide points of reference, for example. A lot of other writers - for example, James Joyce - made experiments with language - not necessarily the same types of experiments - in other languages and cultural traditions.

Again, it is a way of thinking (as with Pound) which provides the inspiration. When I read *Ulysses, The Waste Land, The Cantos* - especially when I saw those characters in the Cantos, I knew that Pound didn't really understand the language, but, again, it was an inspiration to see how a poet can derive energy from another culture, and take it back into his or her own language, feeding roots of another culture in order to create something new.

Internet, Memory, and the Chinese Diaspora - the Case of the Nanjing Massacre Website

Wanning Sun

1. Anthony Smith, 'Towards Global Culture?', *Global Culture: nationalism, globalisation and modernity*, M. Featherstone (ed), Sage Publications, London 1990.

2. James Clifford, 'Diasporas', *Cultural Anthropology*, vol. 9, no. 3, 1994, p308.

3. See: http:// www.cnd.org:8023/ nmjmassacre/ index.html

Talking about memory and identity in the formations of the diasporic public sphere means confronting the inevitable paradox between a national culture, which, to use Anthony Smith's words, is 'particular, time-bound and expressive', and a global culture, which is de-territorialised and 'memoryless'.[1] If one way of looking at the diasporic public sphere is to consider it a space whereby diasporic members seek identification 'outside the national time/space in order to live inside, with a difference',[2] then questions need to be asked as to whether or how well nationalist discourses serve those people now living in the trans/postnational condition. Consider the following paragraph from a letter to the editor in a Nanjing Massacre site in 1995 to commemorate the 50th anniversary of the Japanese War:

No matter how much conclusive evidence we have of the aggressive intentions of the Japanese people, many people still consider what I say to be raising a false alarm. Although today these people can ignore the clear and looming dangers, continuing to live and work in peace, when the day comes that our nation once again is conquered, there will be nothing we Chinese will be able to do to wipe away the humiliation and suffering of being an enslaved people ... Wake up! If you do not make a determined effort to strengthen our nation, we will soon be confronted with the death of our people and the destruction of our ancient civilisation.[3]

In terms of rhetoric and theme, the letter could very well have been written by someone living in war-torn China half a century ago, at the time of the Japanese occupation. It is clear that a distinctive narrative of the 'imminent death of the nation' in the history of modern China finds its way to this cyber-narrative of the Nanjing Massacre. The familiar trope of fear of losing one's freedom and sovereignty - effective in raising the national consciousness and patriotism in the face of foreign invasion, sounds hollow and ill-fitted both in temporary and spatial terms. For these readers and writers, how is it possible to say who is the 'we'? that constitutes 'our nation' and where is it? If 'we' refers to Chinese who mostly hold Australian or Canadian passports or American green cards and whose offspring may hardly speak Chinese - what action should 'we' take when 'we' 'wake up' to the danger facing the 'nation'?

Here we see an intriguing process, whereby cyber-identity, supposedly memory-less and de-territorialised, is grafted onto the Chinese government's version of China - a nation united by a common past and defined by territorial borders. It also points to the disjuncture between a displaced, fractured materiality of migrants and their ways of imagining 'our nation', which operate according to a spatial and temporal reality that precedes their displacement and fracture. Migrants may become more possessive on issues of national sovereignty than their country fellows at home, in spite of the fact that for these migrants, a peopled and territorial nation called 'China' is becoming increasingly imaginary. Contrary to their material identity, which is partial, contradictory and strategic, their discourses of the nation tend to be totalising and firmly anchored in traditional notions of place and time. It is somewhat ironic that in trying to come to terms with increasingly fragmented material reality, the diasporic imagination is maintaining some kind of strategically essentialist discursive position which corresponds with the People's Republic of China's official discourse of the nation.

This example testifies to an important point that Appadurai makes about the formation of a post/national imaginary. Although post-national movements challenge the monopoly of the nation-state as guardians of national identities, they are nevertheless trapped in the linguistic imaginary of the territorial state due to a lack of a separate repertoire of images, idioms and symbols. For Appadurai, this seems to constitute the contradictory nature of diasporic subjectivity: 'Displacement and exile, migration and terror create powerful attachments to ideas of homeland that seem more deeply territorial than ever'.[4]

It is here that the relationship between historical memory and new technology becomes crucial. The internet may provide a forum for such powerful attachments to be maintained in spite of time and distance, but it may also have slowed down or prohibited the formations of diasporic imaginaries which may more adequately address the needs and desires arising from myriad forms of fracture and displacement. The question, therefore, is: to what extent does this global cultural form - technical, timeless and placeless - enable or inhibit the articulations of post-national 'nomadic subjectivities'?

The relationship between history and nation is a complex one. Contemporary politics of nation-states may see it as necessary to suppress or even erase memories of some collective trauma. However, suppressed memories do not simply disappear. They are simply dispersed yet still capable of being mobilised in the attempt to form a new community. Pointing to the importance of historical memory in community building, Duara suggests that historical conceptions of political community have relied on a process of radical 'Othering' and that these processes are kept alive in historical memories and periodically re-enacted to 'mobilise the new community'.[5] Communities are formed not through the invention of new cultural forms and tradition, but through the hardening of boundaries - the privileging of a particular cultural practice as the constitutive principle of

4. A. Appadurai, 'Patriotism and Its Futures', *Modernity at Large: cultural dimensions of globalisation*, University of Minnesota Press, Minneapolis 1996, p177.

5. P. Duara, *Rescuing History from the Nation: questioning narratives of Modern China*, The University of Chicago Press, 1995, p51.

6. S. Turkle, *Life on the Screen: identity in the age of internet*, Phoenix, London 1995.

7. For cyberspace and race, see C. Bailey, 'Virtual Skin: Articulating race in cyberspace', *Immersed in Technology*, M. A. Moser (ed), The MIT Press, 1996; for cyberspace and gender, see D. Haraway, *Simians, Cyborgs, Women: the reinvention of nature*, Routledge, New York 1991.

8. H. Naficy, 'Exile discourse and televisual fetishization', *Quarterly Review of Film and Video*, vol. 13, no. 1-3, pp85-116.

9. D. Kolar-Panov, 'Video as the diasporic imagination of selfhood: a case study of the Croatians in Australia', *Cultural Studies*, vol. 10. no. 2, 1996, pp288-314; also see S. Skribis, 'Making it tradeable: videotapes, cultural technologies and diasporas', *Cultural Studies*, vol. 12. no, 2, 1998, pp265-273.

10. A. Mitra, A. 'Diasporic Websites: ingroup and outgroup discourse', *Critical Studies in Mass Communication*, vol. 14, no. 2, 1997; also see A. Mitra, 'Nations and the Internet': the case of a national newsgroup, 'soc.cult.indian', *Convergence: journal of research in new technologies*, vol. 2, no. 1, 1996.

the community - be it common history, race or language.

This paper is concerned with the relationship between history, new technologies, and the post-national imaginary. I wish to unravel this complex relationship by asking a range of questions: What is the role of new technologies in sustaining a sense of identity in the diasporic contexts? In what ways is diasporic identity formation dependent on shared histories? How is history constantly tapped to construct an identity of dispersal and displacement? In addition, in what ways do new technologies enable these new subjectivities to articulate a desire and pleasure of belonging? Furthermore, are there new forms and strategies of narrating the (post)nation, which are inspired and enabled by the new technologies, or are new technologies simply reproducing the existing narratives?

The last question is particularly pressing. Much has been written about how electronic media have transformed our understanding of temporality, spatiality and a sense of who we are as individuals.[6] Critical studies point to the materiality behind the virtual reality: both in terms of gender and race.[7] Naficy's work on the uses of video images of trauma and torture by the Iranian diasporic communities is relevant,[8] and so is more recent work on the ways in which Croatian ethnic communities use VCR technology for the purposes of reproduction and consumption of nostalgia.[9] However, not much thought - with the exception of Mitra's work - has been given to whether or how the new spatiality and temporality of cyber-technology transform our ways of imagining our diasporic identity.[10]

CHINA - A PLACE TO LEAVE BUT NOT TO FORGET

The size of the mobile population worldwide is increasing. It consists of refugees, migrants, guest workers, transnational intellectuals, scientists, and illegal aliens. These people deal on a daily basis with, not only the question of 'where do you come from' but also the question of 'where is your home'. For the diasporic, unrestrained by ideas of spatial boundary and territorial sovereignty, these questions are raised and answered at both the personal and collective levels. Global population movements are producing a growing tendency for bounded territories to give away to diasporic networks, nations to transnations. Due to these shifts, patriotism, often problematic, is now, as Appadurai puts it, not only increasingly 'plural, serial, contextual and mobile', but more importantly, 'susceptible to transformation, in theory and in practice'.[11] In arguing for a 'democratic cosmopolitanism', a goal for an 'emerging international civil society', Bonnie Honig points to the necessity of myth in political movements of transnational nature as well as the effectiveness of the strategy of mobilising existing narratives and other cultural resources.[12] The implication of these arguments is clear: study of the formations of post/national imaginaries needs to consider diasporic yearnings and subjectivities in discursive spaces, as well as post-national movements and organisational activities of migrants. Werbner's inquiry into the south Asian settlers in Manchester suggests that the diasporic public sphere remains 'a sphere of illusions' because of the 'futility' of 'highly localised, parochial battles' among the diasporic members.[13] I want to suggest, through a case of a particular Chinese diasporic group, that such illusoriness of the diasporic public sphere may also be a result of the fact that diasporic imaginaries are somewhat trapped in a discourse of place and time which is *national* rather than *post-national*.

Alongside of these post-national movements and migrant organisations, members of diasporic communities are increasingly active in seeking the means to reconnect with the homeland that they have, voluntarily or by force, left behind. This is certainly the case with the Chinese scholars, students and business people who left China for the West prior and since 4 June 1989. Since the 1980s, and particularly since 4 June 1989, many young intellectuals left China for political, educational, and economic reasons; most of them went to the US, Canada, and Australia. Although these expatriates, political dissidents in particular, may still be critical of the Chinese government, they have by no means stopped identifying with China. In fact, the relative political stability and the economic boom in the years since 4 June 1989 have enabled these expatriates to travel freely to China, where they have found various professional or business opportunities.

In other words, this group of people find themselves in a complex situation facing many members inhabiting the diasporic public space. On the one hand, their professional competence and relative security in social-economic terms may afford them a comfortable, or even a cosmopolitan life style. On the other hand, they may still be operating in a national space - be it the US, Canada, or Australia - whereby their racial difference, 'foreignness' of accent, or simply what Ghassan Hage calls 'a third-world looking' exteriority place them in a space of marginalisation on a daily basis and often in mundane yet profoundly alienating ways.[14] This in-between position renders many diasporic people susceptible to what Appadurai calls the 'anguish of displacement' and the 'nostalgia of exile' . In the case of this group of former mainland Chinese, absence increases their desire to see China taking a more assertive position on the international stage. Indeed, as some Chinese living in the West often remark, they have become more 'Chinese' since leaving China.

The desire of these people to maintain some kind of connection with China can be seen in their regular consumption of cultural products from mainland China. A good example is the popularity of Chinese television drama series among the mainland Chinese now living overseas. These drama series are initially screened on the Chinese state-owned television, some local and others national. Within weeks of their screening in China, video copies of these marathon-length drama series, such as *Yearning (Ke Wang)*, or *A Beijing Native in New York* would find their way into the video shops in Chinatown in the major cities of the world where there is a sizeable community of Chinese students. The viewing of these Chinese texts among

11. A. Appaudurai, *op. cit.* p176.

12. Bonnie Honig, 'How foreignness "solves" democracy's problems', *Social Text*, vol. 16, no. 3, 1998, pp1-27.

13. Pnina Werbner, 'Diasporic Political Imaginaries: a sphere of freedom or a sphere of illusions?', *Communal /Plural: journal of transnational and cross-cultural studies*, vol. 6, no. 1, 1998, pp11-32.

14. Ghassan Hage, *White Nation: fantasies of white supremacy in a multicultural society*, Pluto Press, Sydney 1998.

the diasporic often goes together with other communal activities, such as chatting in Chinese and cooking and eating Chinese food. Some of these dramas are in fact made with the participation of Chinese expatriates.

For a collectivity to form a sense of identity, two things are necessary: a shared memory of the specific events which have significance for the entire population; and an access to the cultural forms which enable these memories to be continuously refreshed and articulated. In the case of many diasporic communities, the issue of coming to terms with the local-global nexus is more urgent, if not desperate, since their identities are premised upon a nationalism without a nation, a sense of loss, or lack, which makes them more jealous of whatever cultural resources that they still possess. The result is an inevitable sense of displacement, manifesting itself as a portable 'memory bank' . The bank, which stores memories of shared histories of national events, traumas and tragedies, is carried in the diasporic (sub)consciousness, regardless of how dispersed and displaced the diasporic body can be. Therefore, the central issue here is: if the construction of nationalist discourses relies on both the powerful emotions of patriotism and the everyday comfort of 'feeling at home', how does a group of people removed from the country and 'home' maintain this 'nationalist' feeling?

CND - A VIRTUAL COMMUNAL HOME

Three factors suggest that a good place to look for some answers to this question are the website pages maintained by the former Chinese scholars and professionals now living in the diaspora. First, diasporic Chinese communities are increasingly strong forces to be reckoned with in the plethora of contending Chinese identities; secondly, their double 'outsider' position - marginalised in their host countries in racial terms and in their homeland in political terms - creates in them a desire to negotiate a new space in which to assert their Chinese identity, hence the value of the portable Chinese memory as potent materials; thirdly, scholars and professionals affiliated with academic and professional institutions of their host countries (US, Canada, Australia, Japan, Europe) are more likely than their counterparts in mainland China to possess the access and knowledge of new computer technology, including the internet. These factors come into play, making the enactments and mobilisations of certain cultural memories about China's past in these pages a significant phenomenon to study.

One of the most prominent sites maintained by this particular diasporic group is the Chinese News Digest (CND), a news distribution organisation in the computer network. Founded by a group of Chinese students and scholars in the US and Canada in 1991, CND readers can be found in all continents, in 63 countries and regions including Mainland China, Taiwan and Hong Kong. Since 1996, CND has developed from the original English service to CSS (Chinese Students and Scholars) in the US and Canada, into a customised news and information distribution service for readers in

Canada, Europe, the Pacific, the US, and China. In addition to the English regional services, the CND-Global section provides, three times a week, China-related news of interest to all readers around the globe. CND also disseminates the first network-based Chinese language periodical, *Hua Xia Wen Zhai*.

Since 1995, CND has been officially registered as a non-profit organisation under the name of China News Digest International, Inc., with headquarters in the State of Maryland, USA. In 1996, CND obtained its tax exemption status approved by the US Internal Revenue Service. As CND entered its 9th anniversary in 1998, it still claimed that CND would maintain its voluntary and non-profit nature and would continue to aim at providing news and other information services to readers concerned primarily about China-related affairs.[15]

15. See: http;///www. cnd.org

CND editors estimate that the total number of CND readers is around 150,000, although the exact figure is unknown, since many people access CND publications via other sites and print-out copies rather than CND's mailing lists. As a community-based free service, CND is maintained by some 40 active volunteers who are 'mostly overseas Chinese students and scholars', who according to its editorial board, spend on average 20 hours a week to keep the services running. The editorial board constantly encourages its readers either to donate money or offer voluntary work. When asked what attracted them to work for CND, the Board of Directors say, 'Not the money - that's for sure, since there is none. As a volunteer-based organisation, CND never questions a volunteer's motive to help, but volunteers are either established professionals or students working on their graduate degrees'.[16]

16. See: cnd-board@cnd.org

Many diasporic groups in the contemporary global context use the internet for community building. Mitra's study of the Asian diasporic websites highlights the tension in addressing in-group visitors and out-group browsers. He identifies an array of textual strategies - format, language, images and links - in negotiating the problem of plural address. Similar issues and textual strategies apply to Chinese diasporic sites. The distinction between intended audience and casual browsers is made primarily through the differentiating use of language. Many sites use only Chinese and even among the Chinese visitors, the choice between simplified Chinese (GB) and traditional Chinese (big5) further distinguishes Chinese who are migrants from the mainland, and Chinese who live, or migrate from, outside China. In addition, certain subject matters may strike resonance amongst one particular group of Chinese who share similar historical experiences, but not with others. For example, anecdotes and jokes about how fate played tricks on individuals during the Cultural Revolution are clearly intended for, and more intelligible to, mainland Chinese who migrated since the economic reform in the 1980s.

A further technologically derived difference is maintained between those who can use and have access to Chinese software, and those who do not, as GIF allows those who do not have Chinese software to read Chinese as images rather than as data. Hence, a seemingly simple choice of the language each time you access these sites has a ritualistic dimension of self-identification - answering the inevitable question: where do you come from?

The use of images in these pages also plays an important role in allowing diasporic members to live with a split identity. *Feng Hua Yuan* is a very popular electronic magazine in CND maintained by Chinese professionals and students in Canada (FCSPC). Unlike the American based *Hua Xia Wen Zhai*, literally meaning 'Chinese reader's digest', the literal translation of *Feng Hua Yuan* is 'maple flower garden'. The name operates on dual symbolism, maple being the symbol of Canada, and 'hua', which means 'flower' but also 'China'. The creativity of this symbolism of a dual allegiance, which negotiates the tension between 'where you are from' and 'where home is now', is further evidenced in magazine's logo: the image of maple leaves on top of the Great Wall.

'THE SPECTACLE OF DYING' - THE NANJING MASSACRE MEMORIAL

Apart from regular news bulletins and supplements (*Zengkan*), both in simplified and traditional Chinese, of essays and literature written by Chinese writers, CND also maintains a number of permanent virtual museums of the three most profoundly traumatic events in twentieth century China: the Nanjing Massacre, the Cultural Revolution, and the 4 June 1989 Incident. An important component of these sites is visual, in the form of photo archives providing 'documentary' accounts of violence and atrocities which the official Chinese history has shunned from - as in the case of the Nanjing Massacre - or suppressed - as in the case of the Cultural Revolution and the 4 June Incident.

CND began its 1998 Global News Bulletins with a special issue on the author of 'The Rape of Nanjing', the No. 1 book on CND's Virtual Bookshelf. The special issue includes a feature story about the book - claimed to be the first English book ever written on the account of the 1937-1938 Nanjing Holocaust. This is complemented by an exclusive interview with the author Iris Chang, a 29-year old American Chinese freelance journalist, a feature story on the publication and distribution of Chang's book, and messages to the Discussion Group. Website visitors, mostly overseas Chinese, and some Westerners, praise Chang for her work and express their rage at the Japanese atrocities.

What does it mean for the CND visitors when they find themselves, intentionally or not, taking a trip down memory lane in the nation's traumatic past? If nations are imagined through narration and, as Anderson points out eloquently, communities are to be distinguished not by their falsity or authenticity, but by the style in which they are imagined,[17] then what do these sites say about the internet as a tool for the national imagining of certain communities? I would argue that, in their bid for a collective virtual address these sites resort to the most repressed collective memories of China's twentieth century history. This new space of Chineseness is a virtual communal home to many Chinese, and as such is necessarily fraught with

17. Benedict Anderson, *Imagined Communities: reflections on the origins and spread of nationalism*, Verso, London 1983.

ambiguity and tensions - fact versus fiction, truth versus narrative, virtual versus real, image versus reality, self versus Other. Painful as they are to recall, the trips down these virtual memory lanes compensates the estranged visitor - both in the geographic and cultural sense - with a kind of pleasure of belonging, and of having one's Chineseness affirmed through an act of articulation or participation. In this sense, these sites testify to the arguments pointing to the potency of cultural memories associated with shame, trauma and humiliation as an active agent for the softening and hardening of the self/Other boundary.[18] In other words, trauma and memories of atrocities become perverse catalysts for a post-national pride and consciousness, which is useful for purposes of collective identification.

18. Lucien Pye, *The Spirit of Chinese Politics*, New Edition, Harvard University Press, Boston 1992.

To unravel these complex issues regarding the relationship between history, memory and new technologies, I will pursue the analysis of the on-line Nanjing Massacre Memorial, a permanent historical archive maintained by CND. To justify my choice of the case study, first of all, I need to question why CND has created this particular website from the many themes/subjects/events it could have selected, for after all, the history of modern China has been full of violence and trauma. The privileging of the Nanjing Massacre over colonial wars against the British (the Opium War), civil wars with the KMT (nationalists), and competitive international war with the Americans (the Korean War) shows that it is Japan that has served as the archetype of otherness for the Chinese nation. The Japanese military invasions and atrocities carried out during WW II have been most frequently constructed in the nationalist and anti-imperialistic discourses in modern Chinese history. Unlike the 'British' or the 'Americans', the 'Japanese', cast in the image of a historical enemy, appeals to the widest array of Chinese communities, including those in Taiwan, Hong Kong, Southeast Asia and Oceanic countries. Furthermore, unlike the website on the Cultural Revolution and the 4 June 1989 Incident, which seem to consolidate a sense of community among the diasporic Chinese from PRC who had lived through these periods, a website on the war against the Japanese invasion, half a century ago, may serve to soften the boundaries between various Chinese diasporic communities in terms of origin, dialect group, generation, as well as social-economic position, and at the same time harden the boundary between Chinese and non-Chinese communities. In other words, by practising both inclusion and exclusion, this website signals, firstly, the formation of a new diasporic Chinese identity which for particular political, historical and psychological reasons remains wedded to a 'nationalist' discourse of China, and secondly, the desire of this particular diasporic group to seek a more culturally based identification with other diasporic Chinese communities by mobilising a historical national trauma capable of emotional engagement across the broadest identification of Chineseness.

It thus can be seen that the project of maintaining the Nanjing Massacre website undertaken by these ex-patriots from the PRC is an ambitious one, for its politics of identification seems to operate on a yearning which is both cultural - a desire deriving from a general self-awareness of being Chinese - and nationalist, which is more politicised and localised. This is made even more complex by the fact that this nationalist project, which has its emotional anchorage in mainland China, is in contest with the PRC's official memory of Japan.

Analyses of the PRC's official media representations of Japan suggest that the CCP uses a strategy of cultural diplomacy in playing two themes alternately in its treatment of Japan's past, namely cultural affinity and war guilt.[19] Although conflicting events, such as the textbook and the Yasukuni Shrine issues are frequently reported to signify Japanese historical indebtedness to China, they seem to have been aimed more at the international community to win foreign moral support and to pressure the Japanese government. Throughout the 1980s, the Chinese government's desire to secure cheap government loans from Japan resulted in the Chinese government consistently discouraging its people to deal with the emotional trauma of events like the Nanjing Massacre in an organised, cathartic manner. This explains why sensitive topics such as the Nanjing Massacre were treated with caution and detachment, if not shunned in the official narratives. The appearance of the commercialised media sector in China in the late 1980s provided important alternative perspectives from which the Japanese war atrocities were remembered; however topics such as the Nanjing Massacre which had the potential to unleash powerful emotional responses were still not dealt with.[20]

The politics of how to come to terms with collective traumas is also closely linked to the (im)possibility of representation of language and technology in the remembering process. Reading representations of the Jewish Holocaust, Juchau points to the importance of a history which 'acknowledges its fragmented construction, which points to its gaps and absences and its silences in representing the past'.[21] She cautions us that historical representations tend, ironically, to forget three things: the process of rendering the past into a present account, is inevitably characterised by an intrinsic lack, an absence of the originating moment or event. Historical discourses often adopt an 'unquestioned and undefined position', and the 'we' is seldom identified or placed in a social, moral and political context. Furthermore, the narrative of the past events is often driven not so much by truth as by desire, and is concerned not so much by the past but by the present. Such a history, argues Juchau, is necessarily awkward - showing 'seams and lacunae that fracture many historical representations'- and non-cathartic, since it needs to 'testify to its own limits of expression'.

'Remembering' deploys language to represent death, and confronted by the profound madness and catastrophic scale of deaths of, for instance, the Nanjing Massacre, language is found wanting and gives way to the profusion of images, or what Juchau calls the silent 'spectacle of dying'.

To appreciate the madness and scale of catastrophe conveyed in the website of the Nanjing Massacre, it may be useful to visit its main menu:[22]

19. W. Sun, 'People's Daily, China and Japan: a narrative analysis', *Gazette: the international journal for mass communication studies*, vol. 54, no. 1, 1995, pp198-207.

20. W. Sun, 'Love Your Country in Your Own Way: Chinese nationalism, media and public culture', *Social Semiotics*, vol. 8, no. 1, 1998, pp297-308..

21. M. Juchau, 'Forgetful memory: the Holocaust, history and representation', *The UTS Review: cultural studies and new writing*, vol. 2, no. 2, 1996, p70.

22. See: http://www.cnd.org:8023/njmassacre/index.html

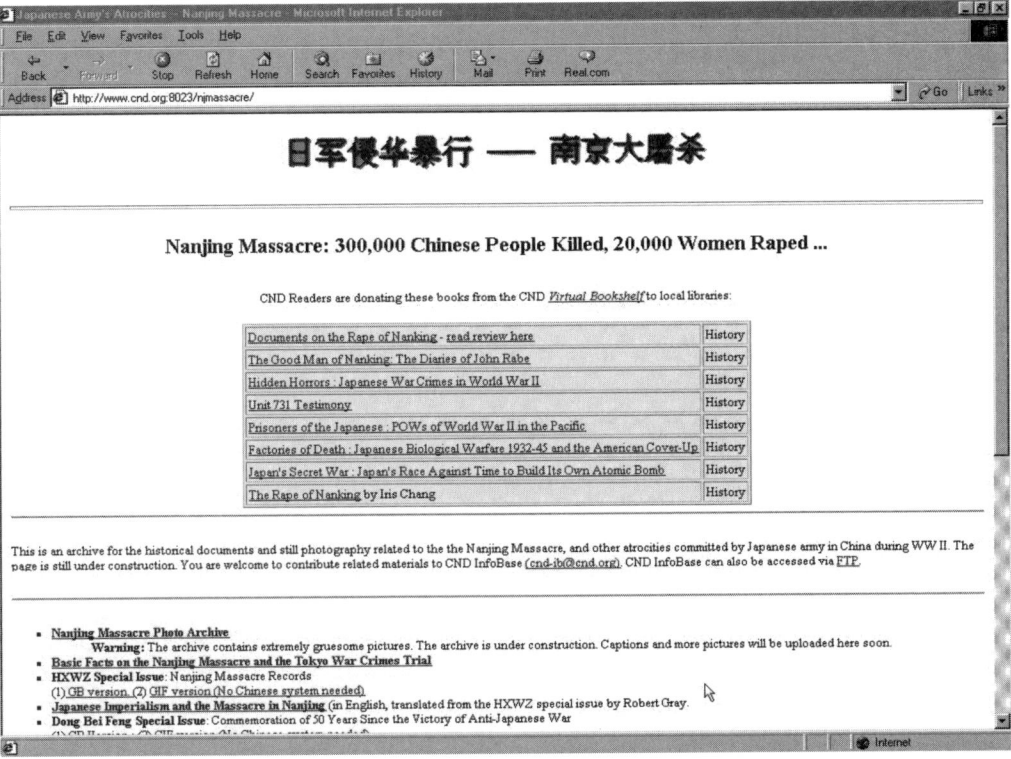

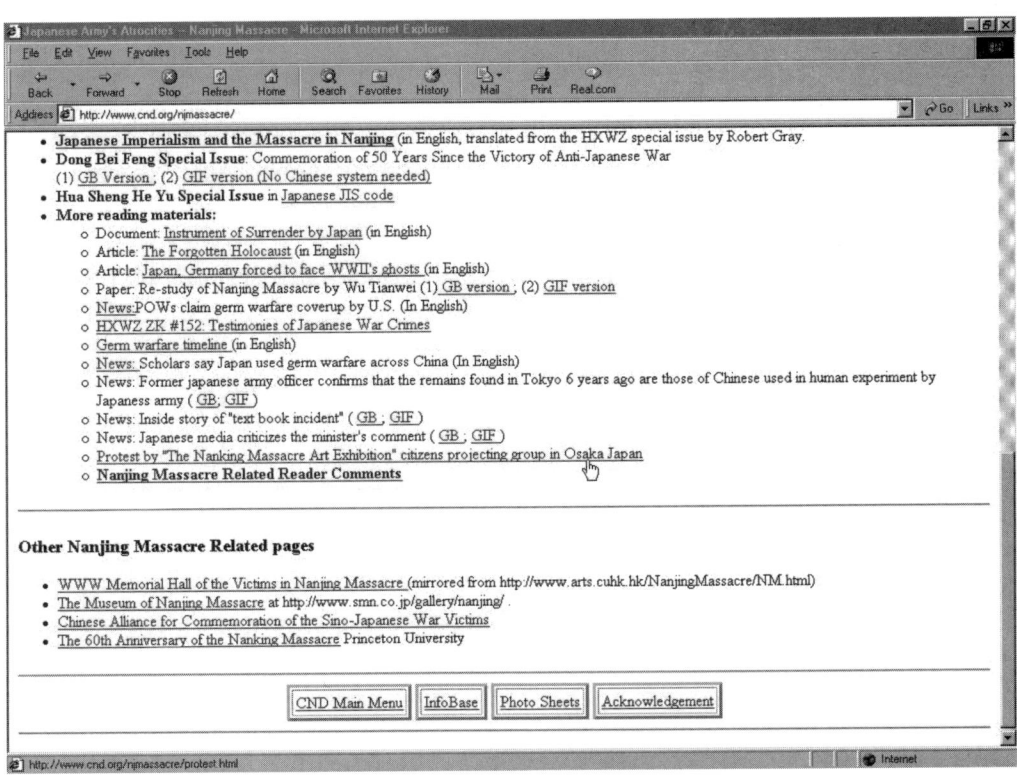

The items in this menu merely provide a list of starting points, whereby visitors can connect to a plethora of other related sites. The route of each visit could be different and unpredictable and is often navigated by whims and desire. Nevertheless there is a certainty about visiting these sites: no matter how long one lingers and how widely and randomly one roams, one is likely to return feeling angry, humiliated or sad.

Writing about China's national literature, Rey Chow argues that since it was born in the throes of imperialism, it has been characterised by a desire for justice.[23] This desire results in modern Chinese intellectuals investing in the trope of suffering, an investment, which according to Chow, aims to expose social injustice. These tropes of shame and suffering continued to be potent in the history-writing of Mao's era which drew on the rich repository of 'remembered grievances' and 'cultivated glories'. Along with shame and suffering, another mobilising trope in the Chinese history-writing is the fear of the death and disintegration of the nation, as Fitzgerald points out: 'Fear of the death of the state has played a critical part in China's identity as an historical community this century, informing political intention and behaviour much as personal memory informs individual action'.[24]

Contrary to the contemporary official non-cathartic approach identified with the Chinese official representation of Japan's war crimes, the narratives on the Nanjing Massacre website have a definite effect of playing up, rather than playing down, anti-Japanese feelings. The most attention-grabbing, if not gut-wrenching, parts of the site are the 'museum', 'gallery', memorial hall', and 'archive' which contain the most compelling photos of the Massacre - a baby on the tip of Japanese soldiers' bayonets, a close-up of the naked lower part of a female body with a dagger stuck into her vagina, civilians being forced to dig the graves they will be buried in. Visitors to the site are ushered to these virtual spaces, where they are free to linger, go back and forth or make any of the pictures as big as their computer screen. In this sense, cyberspace, with its own dimensions of space and time, allow a particular Chinese diasporic community to challenge the PRC's official narratives by facilitating a discursive shift from verbal to visual, mind to body, rational to cathartic. In other words, the capacity of the cyber-technology to be virtual, allows the narration of the Chinese nation to bypass the Chinese Communist Party's current politics of recourse to shame and suffering - the more primordial, though still culturally constructed elements of nationalism.

Take, for example, the site on the 'Japanese Imperialism and the Massacre in Nanjing'.[25] Even without accessing every page to read the gruesome details, it is possible to fathom the degree of humiliation and outrage expressed:

23. Rey Chow, *Writing Diaspora: tactics of intervention incContemporary cultural studies*, Indiana University Press, Bloomington and Indianapolis 1993.

24. John Fitzgerald, "'Reports of my death have been greatly exaggerated": the history of the death of China', *China Deconstructs*, D. S. G. Goodman and G. Segal (eds), Routledge, London 1994.

25. See: http://www.cnd.org:8023/njmassacre/index.html

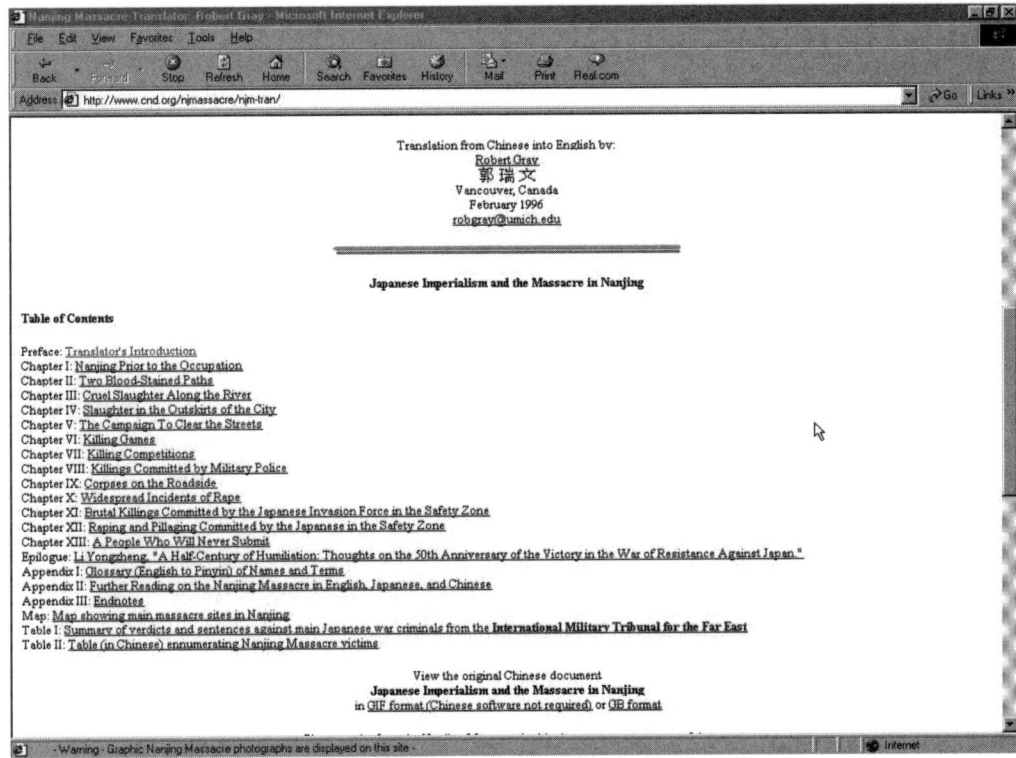

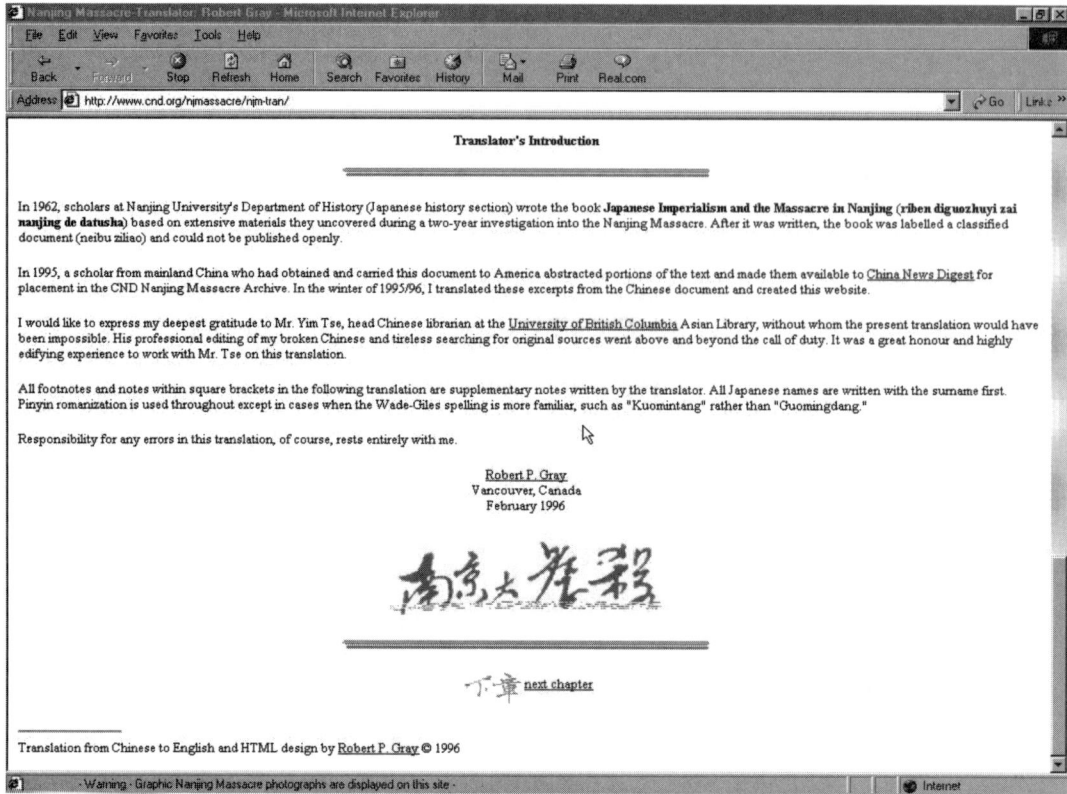

A common sentiment expressed in these narratives is that the PRC government has failed to act firmly in response to Japan's unwillingness to apologise for its war crimes. The English version of the site is prefaced by an introduction by the translator, who reveals that scholars at Nanjing University's Department of History (Japanese history section) wrote the book 'Japanese Imperialism and the Massacre in Nanjing', based on extensive materials they uncovered during a two-year investigation into the Nanjing Massacre. After it was written, the book was labelled a classified document and could not be published openly in China. In 1995, a scholar from mainland China, who had obtained and carried this document to America, abstracted portions of the text and made them available to China News Digest for placement in the CND Nanjing Massacre Archive.

Another popular sentiment expressed in these narratives is the anger at the Japanese government's frequent relapses into the unrepentant rhetoric about the War. This is evidenced in Guo Peiyu's virtual gallery. Guo Peiyu is an art student from Shanghai now residing in Japan. In the introduction to his virtual gallery, Guo recounts a series of failures and frustrations he had met with in his attempts to exhibit his work detailing the Japanese war crimes. As a last resort, Guo turned to cyberspace, where he displays 3000 faces in clay, which, according to Guo, represents 300,000 Chinese massacred:

There are 3000 faces clay works exhibited in the museum. They express the souls of the 300,000 victims who still do not rest peacefully. For the remaining 277,000 faces, I would like to make them agents to co-operate in reforming the Japanese conscience. Please come to my museum, and let's make a society where such tragedies never happen again.[26]

26. *Ibid.*

Guo's frustration at being an artist in Japan points to an important dimension of the nature of cultural memory. Although memory is about things past, their enactments are engendered by the conditions and constraints of the present. Guo's artwork in cyberspace is premised on his material experience of marginalisation as a Chinese. For this reason, remembering the past is not only important in the name of 'truth', but is also useful as an intellectual exercise, because it allows him to assert his identity both in racial and professional terms. In other words, Guo's own otherness in Japan may have contributed to the hardening of the self/Other boundary which marks his work. In this sense, internet technology enables him to articulate a culturally different position - a crucial exercise in effectively negotiating a diasporic identity.

AWKWARD HISTORY AND POSTNATIONAL IMAGINARY

Guo and his cyber-colleagues' strategic use of on-line space points to some structural contradictions in post-national identity-formation on the internet. On the one hand, the hypertextuality of web technology makes the permanence and centrality of any given texts impossible. The possibility of linking to other pages makes the direction and intensity of the visitors movements totally unpredictable. 'Wandering' from the museum to the gallery, 'browsing', reading in the virtual library, the visitors may be glued to the computer screen for hours only to find that they cannot find their way back. The internet has produced a group of self-appointed 'cyber-historians' - artists, writers and academics who consider photos and images to be much more accurate and authoritative evidence of historical truth. In other words, in spite of cyber-technology's textual capacity to destabilise, fragment and intervene, the ontology of the writing subject, the narrative presented in this space seems to be grounded in an equally linear and totalising understanding of history. Lavish use of photographs, which are usually associated with historical/journalistic credibility, seems to be premised by an empiricist notion of 'seeing is believing' and 'one picture is worth a thousand words'.

I am not suggesting that the Massacre never happened, and that these photos were simulacra - the uneasiness which comes from the fear of giving such impression has always haunted me. Rather I want to argue that in an attempt to provide an 'authentic', spectacular version of the historical event, many important questions are elided. The use of photographic images as 'evidence-and-witness' is, as Rey Chow argues, often problematic.[27] This is

27. Rey Chow, *op. cit.*

even more so when images are transferred from a 'hard copy' onto a virtual space, given that computer technology makes the reproduction of images not only easier but also more ephemeral. In this context the questions of photographic authorship, narrative context, and narratorial intention are even more problematic.

The ease with which computer technology produces cyber-historians alongside images of suffering has also resulted in a proliferation of images of Chinese women's bodies. Pictured while they are, or in the process of, being violated by Japanese perpetrators during the Massacre, cyber-technology consolidates a long-established complicity between an anti-imperialist discourse and a masculinist point of view. The visitors to the virtual galleries - most of the people who run and visit the Nanjing Massacre's sites are bilingual, professional and male - can, at their will, download, print or enlarge the images on the screen.

This is a concern when images of violated female bodies may also be used either as a metonym in representing the traumatised nation in anti-imperialist discourses or as a metaphor for the oppressed in the class struggle narratives.[28] Any analysis of the recruitment of images of suffering and shame needs to start with interrogating, not eliding, questions of the materiality of the producers of these images. Even though these cyber-historians consider that it is their Chinese *tongbao* (compatriots) who were victimised, their status as 'invisible writing subjects' is unclear. Internet technology, in spite of its capacity for hypertextuality and fusion of the authorial and the reader's position, normalises rather than highlights the absence of a critical consciousness - a position much needed in the constructions of anti-imperialist critiques. Chow's point about the Third-World male historians and writers' visualisation of the female in anti-imperialistic discourses becomes even more relevant in the age of internet: 'What results is neither a dismantling of the pornographic apparatus of imperialist domination nor a restoration of the native to her 'authentic' history but a perfect symmetry between the imperialist and anti-imperialist gazes, which cross over the images of native women as silent object'.[29] There also seems to be an incongruity between a continuous use of familiar narrative style and an absence of the ritual of collective participation which sustains such traditional pathos. Many visitors to the sites are people who grew up in mainland China in the 1960s and 1970s when 'class struggle' was the privileged political discourse, and should remember the ritualised act of 'speaking bitterness' (*su ku*). Model workers or peasants spoke to organised crowds about life hardships under the oppression of *Guomindang* (the Nationalist Party) and feudal landlords before the CCP liberated China. These mass rituals were conducted in a spirit of 'lest we forget'. The speakers usually showed their audience some material objects as evidence of hardships and oppressions, and their talk was regularly and ritualistically interrupted with emotional, tearful audiences shouting 'the past bitterness must never be forgotten' (*bu wang jie ji ku*). Although 'speaking bitterness'

28. For the female body and the Chinese nation, see Lydia Liu, 'The female body and nationalist discourse: Manchuria in Xiao Hong's field of life and death', in A. Zito and Tani. Barlow(eds), *Body, Subject, and Power in China*, The University of Chicago Press, Chicago 1994, pp57-180; for the female violated body as metaphor in class struggle narratives, see Meng Yue, 'Nüxing biaoxiang yu minzu shenhua' (Representations of the female and national myths), in *Ershiyishi ji* (The 21st Century), April, 1991, pp103-112.

29. Rey Chow, *op. cit*, p41.

rituals stopped with the disappearance of the discourse of 'class struggle' their rhetorical techniques of achieving emotional engagement and maximising audience participation seem to be still at work in these virtual memorials.

This is especially evident in the style and content of the accounts of the Nanjing Massacre, by individual survivors and witnesses of the event, which once publicised, acquired a collective significance. The combination of the close-up visual presentations of traumatised bodies in virtual-photo archives and emotionally charged personal accounts detailing atrocities, culminate in a surge of anti-Japanese feelings for the website visitors. However, although they may have physical and emotional responses to these images, in the absence of a corporeal ritualised collective catharsis they can only resort to the virtual by entering their names in the guest book of the website or by 'posting' their responses in the message board as a way of voicing their moral support. Similarly, the cyber-historians have no access to the physical experience of addressing an empathetic audience, as one used to do in the *su ku* setting. In other words, cultural signs are still deployed, but are at once disabled by a lack of signifying context. CND, like other diasporic websites, is a mediated space: a territorial nation, which *is* China, is substituted by a deterritorialised site *about* China. Instead of going back to the PRC or to donating money to the people in the homeland, these displaced Chinese maintain their connection not just with China, but increasingly with things Chinese, by offering their volunteer work and donations to CND. As the CND editorial says:

> Many of them (CND volunteers) ... work co-operatively through the computer network. As the years pass by, groups of CND members have held joyful mini-gatherings whenever they have the chance. Still many of them have never met their colleagues in person.[30]

30. See: http://www. cnd. org

It is clear that it is partly through the embodiments of cyber-technology that this communality is maintained. Here we see a highly complex and ambiguous scenario: cyber-technology is embraced by a group of dispersed Chinese wanting to maintain some kind of collective sense of belonging, and the internet, as a deterritorialised space, makes it possible by overcoming space and time. However, the mode of address on the net, which is marked by a body/text split, also seems to heighten rather than overcome the sense of displacement experienced by the diasporic Chinese in their regular imaginings of a Chinese community.

These sites also highlight a contradiction between a tendency towards an increasingly displaced and fractured post-national identity and an essentialist discourse of national Self and Other. Because of its deterritorialised nature, cyber-technology makes such contradiction not only possible but also normal. Many of the Chinese scholars and professionals now living in the West are self-exiles who left China before and around the

1989's June 4 Incident, and although some of them succeed in their professional or academic pursuits, they may have lived a peripheral existence in their adopted countries. In the meantime, the culture of the natal country continues to change, transforming and developing in ways that the migrants may not be able to anticipate or even understand. The double marginalisation they experience has caused them to develop a complex array of divided loyalties, hierarchies and systems of reference. Many members of these diasporic communities would agree that experience of being a migrant can be a disorientating, alienating and lonely one. The constant traversing between the inclusion and exclusion, the familiar and the strange, here and there, us and them, results in a somewhat liminal existence; the unbearable lightness of being in-between.

CYBERSPACE AND CHINESE DIASPORA

The very existence of the Nanjing Massacre pages, as well as those on the Cultural Revolution and June 4 Incident, suggest that in the enterprise of using history as sources of appropriation, partial forgetting and selective remembering, cyber-technology is not fundamentally dissimilar from other forms of representation. Estranged from their 'homeland', members of the diasporic communities tend to hold on to a sense of history, as collective memory is one of the few things which they have in common with their increasingly imaginary homeland. Given this, cyber-technology, with its capacity to transcend distance, will continue to be regarded as empowering to those whose desire for cultural affinity with China comes from the material reality of not being 'there'. This geographic lack will continue to be compensated for with temporal excess, manifested in the growing importance of memories - memories of the past which are portable, potent and available for constant and repetitious retrieval.

The 'radical process of Othering' - indispensable in the history of the Chinese nation - is clearly continuing in the identity politics of cyberspace. The softening and hardening of the self/Other boundary is determined not only by images of collective identities circulated in mainstream mass media, but more importantly by their individual experiences of being 'Othered' - either in terms of race, gender, or class - in their adopted countries. In this sense, cyberspace may become a new forum for a re-organised hierarchy of ignorance, prejudice and political agenda.

Reading the '(post)nation' and its Other in the Nanjing Massacre sites as well as in their many related pages seems to suggest that nationalism is becoming less an ideology of the nation-state and more a personal project motivated and sustained by the desires of post-national diasporic individuals. In the constant articulation of one's position, the self/Other boundary is subject to constant shifting. A related change is that Chineseness becomes less an unproblematic and privileged marker of identity for those living in the mainland, and more a free-floating signifier whose ownership is up for grabs among those who have left China. Furthermore, though history is still written and rewritten to 'make the past serve the present, the foreign Chinese', the totality and singularity of the official history of modern China is open to challenge, with its repressed memories mobilised elsewhere in the formation of new Chinese communities. Cyber-technology, with its capacity to transform spatiality, temporality and embodiment, provides an enabling matrix - for those who have access to it - under which conflicting narratives of the national past contest one another. This is particularly powerful in the case of the representations of the Nanjing Massacre, whereby the virtual museums, galleries and archives are available as web pages in the absence of, rather than alongside with, the real ones.

Writing about the experience of migrants, Madan Sarup observes that for migrants identity is about becoming, not 'being', and expressing nostalgia and loss is part of that becoming.[31] This process of becoming, according to Trinh Min-ha, is a process of ongoing articulation.[32] This constant articulation of what one has become or what one is becoming in post-national contexts, also constitutes an important part of Bhabha's 'narration of the nation'. In the case of the Chinese scholars now living in North America and other Western countries, in order to remain Chinese, one has to keep telling stories of being Chinese. Collective memories of China are kept alive by these self-exiled Chinese not only by the constant retelling of familiar national stories, but also by the repetitive deployment of familiar forms and strategies of story-telling. Cyberspace in this sense becomes a vitally significant space for the telling of national stories. In the same way that remembering the past is more motivated by the politics of the present, condemnation of the historical Other says more about the fear and desire of the self than about the Other. For the *hai wai you zi* (Chinese descendants wandering overseas), the internet technology will continue to activate Chinese memories, a history of 'remembered grievances and cultivated glories' .

What is uncanny is the fact that in spite of, or because of, the tension between new technology, which is without memory or territory, and identity, which is bound by a specific notion of time and place, the internet and its attendant cyberspace prove to be hugely enabling in articulating a strategically 'pure' collective identity. Here we see an interesting reversal of the argument concerning identity and internet. As Turkle argues, role playing in MUDs (Multi-User Dungeons) allows individuals to take on an identity which is more different, multiple, heterogeneous and fragmented than in real life.[33] Meanwhile, on a collective level, the internet can be used by trans-local members of a particular community to negotiate an essentialist identity position as a way of coming to terms with an identity which, in material life, is marked by difference, multiplicity, and fragmentation.

However, post-national identities, characterised by 'translocal solidarities' and 'cross-border mobilisations'[34] are still stuck in a discourse of the nation rooted in the nation-state. Post-national discourses continue to deploy both a sublime and a mundane sense of nationalism. These discourses not only

31. M. Sarup, 'Home and Identity', pp93-104, in *Travellers' Tales: narratives of home and displacement*, George Robertson, Melinda Mash, Lisa Tickner, Jon Bird, Barry Curtis and Tim Putnam (eds), Routledge, London and NY 1994, p98.

32. Trinh Minh-ha, 'Other than myself/ my other self' pp.9-26, in Travellers' *Tales: Narratives of Home and Displacement, op. cit.*, p14.

33. S. Turkle, *op. cit.*

34. A. Appadurai, *op.cit.*

inherit a notion of place based on territoriality, they are also trapped in a nation-state's memory of the past. Internet technologies seem to highlight, rather than resolve the predicaments of dispersal and displacement. It is this lack of a political language that explains the contradictions, tensions and ambiguities that I identify here. Whilst internet technology can overcome traditional notions of time and place, it nevertheless also highlights, rather than compensates for, the limitation and inadequacy of the existing discursive resources in diasporic identity politics. As we head towards a post-national diasporic public sphere in the next century, we see that the uncertainties of its constitution suggest that a 'diasporic public sphere' will not be truly possible unless and until diasporic collectivities find themselves a political 'voice' which best serves the interests of the post-national identity. Internet and computer-mediated technology may 'amplify' that voice once it is found, but should never be expected to substitute or produce that voice *per se*.

I wish to acknowledge the funding support of a 1998 Internal Research Grant of Southern Cross University. I would also like to thank the editors for their helpful comments, and Mabel Lee for providing useful materials.

GOING SOUTH

Audrey Yue and Gay Hawkins

I begin my first and last interview at the same place, on the same street in the same house. In the home of what is now considered retrospectively as our 'main' Taiwanese household, abstracted in our research data map as 'Unit TW1'. Not far from Box Hill in the upper middle class suburb of Toorak in South Eastern Melbourne, a family comprising four post-adolescent daughters and two adults, arrived from Taiwan in November 1989 to a newly purchased house.

Surrounding this free-standing, double storey, brick veneer is a lovingly kept garden. On its front porch two pots of chrysanthemums form and maintain the spatial fengshui co-ordinates of its ornately carved French doors. Inside the house I am ushered into the prayer room on my right. A rosewood Buddhist ancestral altar inlaid with mother-of-pearl lines the walls, alongside are several side tables of similar description, a desk and a phone. TW1 came to Australia with about two cargo loads of furniture that did not arrive in time, so they spent the first month or so in a foreign country in an empty house. A fax machine sits conspicuously in the corner.

Sydney, another stage of the research; this time we are doing the interviews together and the interviewees are pay-TV programmers in the new Chinese languages narrowcast-channels springing up everywhere in the deregulated Australian media landscape. We are trying to track the sources of various satellite news services on New World TV, a subscription service in Mandarin and Cantonese. Things are getting complicated: uplinks, downlinks, feed time in Hong Kong, reception time in Australia. Finally, after a complicated explanation, Audrey exclaims: 'So your subscribers are actually watching yesterday's news!', 'Yes, that's right'.

Stories about moving, about the Chinese diaspora in Australia, about researching and being researched. All of them a product of a nationally funded project investigating 'Audiovisual Media Use for Cultural Maintenance and Negotiation by Asian Diasporic Communities in Australia'. That's the official title, the one devised for funding bodies and CVs. Beyond this are fifty Chinese households in Melbourne and an array of Chinese and Anglo media workers with whom 'we', mainly Audrey, have developed complicated and various relations. The first stage of the Chinese module (as opposed to the Vietnamese, Thai and Indian modules that were also part of the project) involved informal interviews based on a questionnaire that was given to households, documenting viewing habits and preferences, particularly of Chinese-related material. Film, video, radio, karaoke and computer use were all investigated. At the same time various axes of identity were tracked: birthplace, citizenship, education, occupation. Out of this, ten households in each of the five major Chinese-origin groups: Mainland China, Southeast Asia, Taiwan, Indochina and Hong Kong, were selected for more extensive interviews. The next stage focused on industry dynamics, on the circulation flows and distribution patterns of broadcast and non-broadcast (film and video) media. The aim was to track the circuits that connect the countries of origin of such media with diasporic markets in Australia. Many of these circuits were informal, outside of industry and institution; friends bringing back tapes and exchanging them through the deployment of *guanxi* relations. Tracking these informal circuits of circulation and consumption from the responses of households and mapping them alongside institutional logics was a major challenge. What's available in the Chinese audio visual space often had little correlation with what people watched. Finally more extended interviews were conducted with selected households. These were open-ended and unstructured and often involved comparative discussions of experiences of migration and settlement. We asked households to audit their technological hardware and to chart diagrams of the local, interstate and international routes of their telecommunications. Lots of tea was drunk, sample tapes viewed and discussed.

If research is about anything it is about relations, those complex and shifting movements, exchanges, investments between those who ask the questions and those who answer. Knowledge isn't found. It is created in the negotiations and spaces between speaking and listening. Subjects and objects are inadequate terms to describe the poles of this relation, for we 'the researchers' were often the focus of interrogation: 'Why do you want to know this?', 'When did you come to Australia?', 'Who else are you talking to?', 'Surely you've seen the Chinese channel on Optus!'. But there was more to the research than chronic ambiguity around the meanings of expertise and experience; there was also the vast difference in *our* relations to the project, the little borderland created by the fact of a multilingual Senior Research Assistant from Singapore and a monolingual Chief Investigator from Australia. Same gender but vastly different racial, geographic and cultural backgrounds and all of this overlaid with the classic industrial relations hierarchy of 'assistant' and 'chief'. The interface between us generated its own complex 'ethics of encounter' even before we left the office.[1]

First there was the issue of speaking and not speaking Chinese. For Gay access to much information was absolutely dependent on Audrey's occupation of that curiously objectified subject-position of native informant and its shifting locations: observer, observed, translator, transcriber. Audrey has written about the ambiguities of this role elsewhere; what needs to be said here is that she brought to the project the privileges and partialities of her different subject-positions as a diasporic Chinese person in Australia.[2] She shared with most of the interlocutees experiences of

1. Ien Ang, 'Doing Cultural Studies at the Crossroads: Local/Global Negotiations', *European Journal of Cultural Studies*, vol. 1, no. 1, Winter 1998, p20.

2. Tony Wilson and Audrey Yue, 'Australian Television: Chinese Audiences: A Postcolonial Dialectic', *Asian Journal of Communication*, vol. 6, no. 1, 1996, pp18-42.

migration and the syncretic multilingual fluidity of the English language, infused with various accented forms of Mandarin, Taiwanese hybrid *minnanhua*, and the different Chinese dialects such as Hokkienese, Teochew and Cantonese. And she shared with Gay an esoteric theoretical language known as media and cultural studies.

During the 1990s, the favoured representation of our particular borderland would have been 'Asian/Australian relations'. These relations, predicated on a supposedly new geopolitical orientation, were promoted by Labour Prime Minster Paul Keating as the source of a more modern, maybe even post-modern, Australia. In the shift from Europe towards Asia, Keating argued that Australia would find not only new markets but also a new national and regional identity. In many senses the research project we were part of was symptomatic of this 'Asian turn'. But reading our relationship and the sorts of interview and institutional material we encountered through the governmental discourse of 'Asia/Australia' seriously limited the production of meaning. For this turn to Asia was nothing more than an updated orientalism in which the binary divide of us and them was simply recast.[3] We wanted to theorise the situatedness of the Chinese diaspora in Australia and that meant much more than documenting the 'Asian experience' in and of Australia. We needed to take into account the long history of 'Asia' in Australia and the heterogeneous tempo-spatialities engendered by 'Australia' and 'Asia'. These were a product, more often than not, of contradictory and overlapping modernities. Yet the discursive function of 'Asia' as the Other to Australia's western identity continually denies the ways in which 'Asia' and 'Australia' are both products of European colonial expansion.

3. Ien Ang and Jon Stratton, 'The Asian Turn', *Art and Text*, no. 50, January 1995.

GOING SOUTH

In our analysis, 'going south' was the paradigm we developed to disrupt the fixity of the Asia/Australia binary, to foreground relationality and flow, to examine the landscape of encounters that were produced at the intersections of these places. Going south, then, functions as a critical trajectory as well as a geographical distinction. For the transnational Chinese diaspora in Australia, the status of 'going south' is a metaphor inflected with shifting meanings. Inscribed in a migratory movement of literal displacement and reoriented in the racialised landscape of a postcolonial settler Australia, it aligns itself with south of Asia, south of China and south of the East and the West. This trajectory locates the emerging identity of a transnational Chinese-Australia in a spatial-temporal mobility. It also articulates itself as a place of cultural negotiation, a very distinctive borderland. And nowhere is this more evident than in the example of Chinese narrow-casting in Australia, our focus in this paper.

For Ross Gibson, Australia is 'south of the west', a place that is 'both a long way from the world (as it always has been) and ... nowhere in particular,

4. Ross Gibson, *South of the West: Postcolonialism and the Narrative Construction of Australia*, Indiana University Press, Bloomington and Indianapolis 1992, pxi.

in the swirl of electronic information and entertainment'.[4] In Gibson's account, south of the west is much more than an evocative spatial description. It is also a way of thinking about the nature of Australia's postcolonial condition. While south of the west acknowledges formations of nation produced through various spatial distinctions: down under, south land, antipodes, terra nullius, such an identity is also a product of time. Implicit in Gibson's spatial analysis is a temporal distinction that accords Australia's time of the 'post' to the moment 'where the national simultaneously exists and disintegrates in a volatile space-time of transnational media and economic systems'.[5] For Gibson south of the west refers to the complex discursive processes that have produced new representations of Australia as contemporary and post-modern. However, at the heart of such a spatial and temporal re-inscription remains an Anglo-Celtic Australian nationalist project which attempts to, on one level, inscribe a discourse of Aboriginal indigeneity as the sign of an essentialised and exotic otherness and, on another level, discount a discourse of NESB immigrancy.[6] Gibson's account of Australia, then, is both productive and problematic. Productive because it foregrounds how new relations of space and time de-centre colonial formations of nation. And problematic because it conflates the placelessness of the global post-modern with the postcolonial condition. These are not the same and in conflating them Gibson reproduces the invisibility of migration and diaspora in representations of Australia. While difference may be everywhere in post-modern Australia, its specificities and politics are persistently denied.

5. *Ibid.*, px-xi.

6. 'NESB' is an Australian census category which refers to people from non-English Speaking Background.

A crucial starting point, then, in rethinking the politics of the encounter between the south of the west and the south of Asia, involves a shift to the particularity of diaspora. This particularity recognises what Paul Gilroy describes as the double consciousness of diaspora; the constant movement between where one is at, and where one is from.[7] Notwithstanding rhetorics of globalisation and their hype about social and spatial mobility, everyone in settler Australia is a migrant, or a descendent of a migrant. Yet the specificity of immigrancy is not highlighted in the idea of south of the west. The effect of this is an inability to recognise the force of desires produced in the ambiguities of migration and diaspora. Implicit in the modern condition of migration is a dialectic of desire signifying the contradictions of belonging and longing. Belonging is an affect of departure tied to the desire of uprootedness to rootedness. Longing is a yearning for change and transformation connected to the nostalgia of arrival. Belonging and longing, past and present, home and away, these oppositions highlight the politics of diasporic space and time. Yet what Gibson's argument fails to acknowledge is that the diaspora of marginalised others consolidates a sense of belonging for the postcolonially dominant and established.

7. Paul Gilroy, *The Black Atlantic: Modernity and Double Consciousness*, Verso, London 1993.

8. Poo-kong Kee, 'The New Nanyang: Contemporary Chinese Populations in Australia', in J.H. Ong, K.B. Bun and S.B. Chew (eds), *Cross Borders: Asian Transmigration*, Prentice Hall, Singapore 1995, pp290-315.

So it is necessary to consider going south as a literal and critical movement. Chinese migration to Australia comprises periodic phases which reflect shifting policies governing differences. Migrants from the Sze Yap

(Four Districts) in the Pearl River Delta in the Guangdong Province, first arrived during the Gold Rush in the latter half of the nineteenth century. During the 1950s when the enforcement of the White Australia Policy favoured European immigrants, the number of Chinese immigrants was drastically reduced. It was not until the implementation of multicultural social policies in the 1970s that Chinese migration increased again. During this time the main settlement groups came from Chinese diasporic countries such as Malaysia, Hong Kong, Singapore, Vietnam, Taiwan, East Timor, Indonesia, Cambodia and Papua New Guinea.[8] In the late 1980s when education policies permitted the admission of full-fee paying overseas students into Australian universities, the flow of Chinese students from the PRC increased. When the Hawke Labour Government granted residence to PRC students who were here before and during the June 1989 Massacre, more than 30,000 PRC students remained.[9] This marked a prominent increase in the Mandarin-language speaking community. While the newest Chinese immigrants are from Beijing, Shanghai and Guangzhou, what is inflected in the linguistic turn is an unsettling in the traditions of diasporic Chinese hierarchy. Although Cantonese predominates as the spoken language of the Chinese diaspora in Australia, the emergence of Mandarin highlights the disjunctures surrounding what Ang calls the differential politics of Chineseness.[10]

The Chinese experience of going south often embodies more than one set of dislocations. For many immigrants, their journey to Australia has already been preceded by previous displacements. Elizabeth Sinn writes that in the years prior to 1939, Hong Kong, as the south of the South of China, was negotiated as a transit point by over six million Chinese who had left to settle elsewhere.[11] She documents that from the 1850s, the bulk of the traffic was concentrated in emigration to the United States and Australia.[12] Pointing out that it was only in the 1870s that Chinese left China to settle in the areas surrounding the South Seas, Sinn's account of emigration from Hong Kong recalls not only the Gold Rush history of Chinese arrival in Australia, but also the southward dispersion of the Chinese into the regional Nanyang enclaves of South-East Asia. For Chinese-Australian immigrants in particular, this trope of going south is a crucial referential paradigm for articulating the grammar of diasporic consciousness.

Literalised as a geographical displacement, going south highlights an emerging cultural circuit inflected by the Chinese spatial politics of south (*nan*). Here, a peripheral south is displaced when a diasporic south is produced. Reflecting on the exodus of refugees from communist China to Hong Kong in 1949, Ng Ho notes that for many left leaning commentators or communist sympathisers at that time, this exodus was defined as 'going south'.[13] 'Going south' became syntagmatic for what Ng calls the 'Age of Literature of Exile in Hong Kong', a term that he has invoked to incorporate all the writings and novels which describe the pain of intellectuals who became refugees.[14]

9. Poo-kong Kee, 'The Growth and Diversification of Australia's Chinese Community', in J.H. Chang, P. Kee and J. Chang (eds), *Chinese Cultures in the Diaspora: Emerging Global Perspectives on the Centre and Periphery*, National Endowment for Culture and the Arts, Taipei 1997, pp139-153.

10. Ien Ang, 'On Not Speaking Chinese: Postmodern Ethnicity and the Politics of Diaspora', *new formations* no. 24, Lawrence and Wishart, Winter 1994, pp1-18.

11. Elizabeth Sinn, 'Emigration from Hong Kong before 1941: General Trends', in Ronald Skeldon (ed), *Emigration from Hong Kong*, The Chinese University Press, Hong Kong 1995, pp11-34.

12. *Ibid.*, p12.

13. Ng Ho, 'The Cinema of Turbulence: The Emotional State of Shanghai Film Talents Working in Hong Kong in the Period 1946-1950', in *The 18th Hong Kong International Film Festival Retrospective: Cinema of Two Cities: Hong Kong-Shanghai*, Urban Council, Hong Kong 1994, pp30-34.

14. *Ibid.*, p30.

Notwithstanding the modern politics of exile, such a condition of the longing for belonging is spatially historicised. The status of the south in China, which has always been accorded with an inferiority, resonates as a referent pertinent to the history of the Chinese diaspora as predominantly comprising people from the southern regions of Fujian and Guangdong. The North-South divide, characterised by the Northern and Southern dynasties (*Nanbeichao* 317-587 BC), is reflected in the contemporary terminology for Chinese ethnicity. The term Han Chinese (*hanzu*), derived from the Han dynasty (206 BC- AD 221), inflects a nationalist attempt at homogeneity and unity. Referring to around 94 per cent of the population while designating the rest as National Minorities, what is noteworthy here is that the Han Chinese from the southern provinces prefer to call themselves Tang people (*tangren*), after the Tang dynasty (618-906). The use of Han as an official discourse delegates Tang as a southern vernacular and supports the homogenising claims that the North uses to establish itself as the centre of China. Such a claim bears a historicity connected to the Song dynasty (960-1279). When North China was lost to the Jurchen invasion in 1125-7, the south of the Southern Song dynasty (1125-1270) was delineated. While the Northern Song dynasty refers to the period where the two halves were reunited, the Southern Song dynasty chronologises the period after division; semiotically inferring a superior/complete North and an inferior/incomplete South. This disparity is displaced when going south is reposed as a cultural site of re-imagining. Dispersing from the place consigned as the peripheral south of China, the diasporic trajectory of southern marginality is re-framed through the linguistic hierarchy of Cantonese. Although Cantonese is the dialect of only about 5 per cent of the population, its dominance as the spoken language of the Chinese diaspora in Australia marks itself out as a particular moment when going south emerges as a tactic of diasporic re-imagination, reflected in the use of Cantonese as the official language of New World Television.

Taking the immigrancy of Australia into account is to make the transition from south of the west to going south. As a critical trajectory this entails a recognition that the particular history of the place of departure must come into play when it negotiates itself at the place of arrival. It also entails an analysis attentive to the ways in which place is mediated by various logics of time and space. In our research we wanted to understand how narrow-cast television services were used by Chinese audiences; how the specificity of transnational programming realigned experiences of space and time for these audiences in ways that produced a very distinctive sense of going and being south.

THE CASE OF NARROW-CASTING

In turning now to a very particular example of Chinese media in Australia we want to investigate the relationship between narrow-casting, news and diaspora. Going south in this example means a recognition of the specific media landscapes in Australia and their various relations with diasporic audiences. It also means an analysis attentive to the ways in which the reception of Chinese audio-visual products is mediated by different experiences of diaspora and the different institutional, economic and policy dynamics that structure news programming in Cantonese and Mandarin.

Within the diverse media complex used by Chinese viewers in Australia, narrow-cast television services have a special place. While broadcasting is driven by the logic of maximising audiences across difference, by the production of an abstracted 'mass', narrow-casting fragments the audience using specialist media targeted at minority or niche publics. While broadcasting converts difference into demographics, narrow-casting often fetishises it, privileging notions of singular or 'special' identities determined by a fundamental essence: ethnicity, race, sexuality or whatever. There are, of course, other forms of narrow-casting servicing various taste markets or restricted localities, but for diasporic Chinese viewers in Australia it is those televisions that speak directly to their Chineseness, that invite various forms of diasporic identification that are the most significant. As the marketing slogan for New World TV declares: 'Intimacy is to speak your language'.

For Naficy, narrow-casting remains an under-appreciated discourse.[15] He argues that the processes at work in the specialisation and fragmentation of television demand more thorough attention. Not simply because these developments are important evidence that the media imperialists and global homogenisation theorists are wrong, but also because ethnic narrow-casting is evidence of the emergence of new media sites that speak to the disruptive spaces of postcolonialism that address the experience of hybridity, migration and diaspora. Narrow-cast media then, are one example of a growing third or multiple cultural space where various othered populations are creating sites for representation, where all kinds of 'resistive hybridities, syncretism, and mongrelisations are possible, valued'.[16] Implicit in this valuation is a fundamental opposition between broadcasting as the heartland of nation and family and narrow-casting as the space of the migrant, the exile, the refugee. But the space of narrow-casting is not simply a space of representation, it is also a space of consumption, a space where otherness circulates as a commodity. How then to understand the distinctive cultural economies and topographies of desire shaping narrow-cast television services for Chinese viewers in Australia?

The crucial point, Naficy argues, is to recognise the various ways of being narrow, to understand the specific dynamics of inclusion and exclusion ordering minority media. This is the reason why we investigated two Chinese languages narrow-cast services available in Australia, in order to track patterns of similarity and difference in their institutional and cultural logics. By looking closely at the Chinese programming of the Special Broadcasting Service (SBS), Australia's free to air multicultural public service broadcaster, and at New World TV, it is possible to see the complexities and variety of narrow-cast televisions.

15. Hamid Naficy, *The Making of Exile Cultures*, University of Minnesota Press, Minneapolis 1993.

16. Hamid Naficy and Teshome Gabriel (eds), *Otherness and the Media*, Harwood Academic Publishers, Pennsylvania 1993, px.

The other reason for focusing on these two services is because they provide the main source of audio-visual news for Chinese audiences in Australia. As many studies of migration have shown news from or about 'home' has special status and value. It is a privileged form, watched and read avidly and intently and often in a state of what Naficy terms epistephilic desire.[17] News generates strong demand; all services programming Chinese news in Australia report intense viewer requests for more. So, in the maze of diverse textual forms available to Chinese audiences, news is distinctive not just in terms of the way that it is watched but also in the symbolic value it holds as a source of supposed direct access to information about homelands. News generates very specific relations between here and there because of the way it mediates the play of separation and connection, then and now. Fictional texts obviously function quite differently.

17. Naficy, *op.cit.*, p107.

In focusing on these two services, SBS and New World TV, the intention is to examine the nature and meanings of their narrow-cast organisation through the specific example of news. This makes it possible not only to understand how news is implicated in particular forms of diasporic identification but also how two narrow-casters differently use news to establish distinctive relations with Chinese viewers.

SBS television was established in 1980 with the mandate to be both multicultural and multipurpose. The channel has to service various special communities (ethnic, indigenous, minority), reflect multiculturalism to all Australians, and increase diversity in the broadcasting system. As a public service broadcaster SBS is unique in the world. It is charged with the dual tasks of representing and maintaining different identities and adding quality and innovation to the Australian television landscape. The complexity of SBS's mixture of objectives adds up to a bizarre and pleasurable heterogeneity. To scan its programme guide in any week is to encounter a strange collection: last night's news bulletin from Beijing in Mandarin without subtitles, the OUT show, a studio debate about cultural diversity in Australia, an avant-garde animation, a movie from Turkey. This heterogeneity means that SBS has several different logics of narrow-casting at work within the one service, unlike exilic TV or other single purpose specialist TV services.

At the simplest level SBS is a narrow-caster because it imagines the nation as a series of fragments, as a multiplicity of constituencies produced through various axes of difference, often those very differences that broadcasters are unable to see in their obsession with maximising audiences. And in fragmenting the nation SBS also recognises its member's connections with other places, it acknowledges identities constituted through relations of movement and longing across national boundaries. Programmes in languages other than English, programmes imported from outside the dominant Anglo-American nexus, implicitly disrupt narratives of national cohesion. Most significant here is the example of *WorldWatch*, SBS's morning news services which broadcasts satellite-delivered national news bulletins from around the world. *WorldWatch* began on SBS in 1993 with screenings from 6.30am of daily news services from *CCTV Beijing* in Mandarin, *France 2 Paris* in French, *Deustche Welle* Berlin in German, the Russian News, *Vreyma*, and two current affairs programmes from public broadcasting stations in the United States. Access rights are free and since its inception *WorldWatch* has steadily increased its representation of nightly news services. *WorldWatch* is evidence of SBS's capacity to establish a particularist or minority stance within a broader multicultural framework. While most non-English shows are subtitled in the interests of national access, in *not* subtitling these news services (a decision predicated on cost and time pressures), SBS addresses migrant and diasporic audiences without assimilating them into the nation. However, the absence of subtitles also means these bulletins are subtly marginalised within the overall institutional politics of SBS. Prime time is the privilege of accessible multicultural rather than minority or narrow-cast programming.

SBS's CCTV news in Mandarin has generated a significant number of letters and phone calls protesting that the service is nothing more than a propaganda exercise. CCTV is China's national broadcaster; Channel 4, its international service, is aimed at diasporic audiences and reaches almost every part of the globe. It is compiled from the evening domestic service with few changes except for additional stories with a slightly more international focus. SBS's access to this service is free after official authorisation which is never completely assured. When SBS considered developing a Taiwanese service there were concerns that Beijing would revoke its license to CCTV4.

Screening directly before CCTV4 is *Hong Kong News* from Asia Television Limited aimed at balancing the Mandarin service with one in Cantonese coming from outside the mainland. *Hong Kong News* was picked up as a direct result of community demand and helps SBS avoid accusations of privileging one section of the Chinese audience over another. These sorts of delicate and ongoing negotiations reveal the impossibility of assuming any sort of coherence within a category like 'Chinese viewers' or the 'Chinese community'. They also reveal the capacity of narrow-cast services to fragment the audience into ever more specific niches.

The significance of the Chinese news services on *WorldWatch* is that they represent a very unique and innovative form of public service narrow-casting within the overall context of a multicultural free-to-air channel. While SBS is without question a niche service, its political rationality has historically favoured rhetorics of access and tolerance in the name of servicing 'the whole nation'. This is most evident in the symbolic economy of English subtitling which has functioned to make all shows in whatever language accessible in the interests of national cohesion. Yet, in switching on *WorldWatch* in the morning, the monolingual English speaker can have the interesting experience of exclusion, of confronting what Anderson aptly describes as the vast privacy of language.[18] Non-subtitled Chinese and other news services disrupt the hegemony of the singular national language and

18. Benedict Anderson, *Imagined Communities*, Verso, London 1983.

narrative; they manifest a form of narrow-casting that is militantly particularist, that implicitly contests multicultural rhetorics of unity across difference. The absence of subtitles on *WorldWatch* could mean forms of identification unmediated by the obligations of multiculturalism: diversity without access, difference without nation. Perhaps this form of news even prefigures a post-national public service television?

The example of SBS is extraordinary because of its singularity. Here is a free-to-air public service channel offering a diverse array of narrow-cast programming from avant-garde video aimed at a yuppie market to un-subtitled news bulletins for diasporic, migrant and refugee communities. In contrast, pay-TV operates within a quite different set of cultural and economic dynamics. It is fundamentally demand-driven in its relationship with its subscriber base. This means that it is not necessarily committed to increasing media diversity, more channels do not mean more variety in programme types or sources. Pay services are still driven by competition for big audiences and therefore favour mass appeal shows. The genuinely narrow-cast-pay channels exist on the margins and there is a fear that too much targeting of niche audiences could undermine the search for a big and therefore broad subscriber base.

In Australia narrow-cast-pay channels generally exist as add-ons to the basic service. This is the case with *New World TV* (NWTV) and all other non-English language channels. NWTV transmits 24 hours per day using a mixture of MDS and satellite. Nearly 100 per cent of programming is imported from three main sources: *Television Broadcasts International* (TVBI), which offers satellite news, variety, movies and special programmes in Cantonese; *Chinese Television Network* (CTN), which offers two channels in Mandarin; one on news and finance updates (the Chinese version of CNN) the other focusing on lifestyle and entertainment; and *Television Broadcasts Superchannel-Newsnet* (TVBS-N), a popular cable channel from Taiwan in Mandarin. A small minority of drama and documentary programmes come from *Radio Television Hong Kong* (RTHK). On NWTV, only around ten minutes per week are allocated to Australian productions. These sources of programming reveal NWTV's strong links with Hong Kong, the centre of Chinese languages audio-visual production and export. They also reveal the way in which NWTV could be classified as a form of diasporic narrow-casting. This almost complete reliance on imported content is a product of economic and media policy dynamics. Australian pay-TV regulations do not demand local content on narrow-cast or non-drama channels. In contrast Canada has foreign content rulings on pay-TV which means that forty per cent of programming on Chinese channels has to be locally produced. NWTV has no such obligations and this has significant implications for the overall feel of the service. On New World viewers are rarely addressed as members of an imagined community known as 'Australian Chinese', linked by their common location in Australia and their common pleasure in NWTV; instead they are internally fragmented by programmes that speak to diverse forms of Chineseness and diverse senses of homeland. This audience fragmentation is linked to wider hierarchies in overseas Chinese identities, to the complex politics of inclusion and exclusion within the diaspora. Within this hierarchy Hong Kong Chinese have higher status than mainland or Vietnamese Chinese.

News services are a major component of NWTV's schedule. Audience surveys conducted by the channel consistently reveal strong demand for news, and this is always rated as the most desired content. But this desire is qualified by demands for very particular types of news. CTN's global orientation, its address to the 'global Chinese' is not valued nearly as much as news bulletins relating closely from homelands.

WATCHING YESTERDAY'S NEWS

This account of Chinese narrow-cast news confirms Naficy's argument that there are many different ways to be narrow. It also reveals that in the process of going south via satellite these news programmes are mediated by the distinctive institutional logics ordering their transmission in Australia. However, what this account doesn't do is examine the uses of these services and their meaning in the everyday semiotic landscapes of audiences. How do audience practices around narrow-cast news reflect the spatial-temporal paradigm of going south?

James Hay makes an argument for mobilising the concept of landscape in audience studies. He defines audience spatially, emphasising that listening, reading and viewing occur in and around particular sites and through a social world organised geographically.[19] Because landscape concerns 'the reservoir of innumerable "minor" practices or ones that do not seem to matter because they lack the structural coherence imparted through a discursive formation to some of these practices', Hay argues that landscape marks 'the margin of any audience formulation, identity, or site, and it is also the margin of audience study'.[20] Landscape is useful for extending the spatial-temporal meanings of going south. It enables a deployment of movement which foregrounds the domesticity of home as the site that reproduces a field of social relations to a field of spatial references beyond domestic space. These spatial references call attention to Arjun Appadurai's argument about global cultural flows; they imply a shift in theorising domesticity as a field of fixity to a field of fluidity.[21]

For Hay, 'audience' is primarily a social and spatial landscape, yet what our studies of narrow-cast news watchers revealed was the centrality of time in many viewing relations. For transnational Chinese audiences the domestic is a place of not only spatial but also temporal fluidity. This is partially a product of the specificity of news as a text and the ways in which time is commodified. It is also a product of the phenomenologies of viewing. Chinese audiences of narrow-cast media in Australia begin the day with yesterday's news. TVBI's international news service, which is compiled from

19. James Hay, 'Afterword: The Place of the Audience: Beyond Audience Studies', in J. Hay, L. Grossberg and E. Wartella (eds), *The Audience and Its Landscape*, Westview Press, Boulder, Colorado 1997, pp359-379.

20. *Ibid*., pp361, 354.

21. Arjun Appadurai, 'Disjuncture and Difference in the Global Cultural Economy,' *Public Culture*, vol. 2, no. 2, Spring 1990, pp.1-24.

their Hong Kong evening domestic service is uplinked to PanAmSat2 at 8pm Hong Kong time, received by New World TV (NWTV) at 11pm Australian time, recorded and then screened at 11.30pm and again at 7am the next morning when most subscribers watch it. Chinese Television Network's (CTN) *Zhong Tian News* channel is broadcast via live satellite feed but this means it is screened for the first time at 1.30am Australian time. The update (repeat is more accurate) at 7.30am is, like TVBI, far more popular. So yesterday's news is the norm at NWTV and so too at SBS, where a similar story can be told about their Chinese news services which are picked up late at night, recorded and then screened on *WorldWatch* during the morning of the next day. Here then are minority audiences beginning their day with yesterday's news.

The significance of this experience is in the evidence of other and diverse temporalities. For Homi Bhabha these different cultures of time contest the dominance of historicism in national narratives. He argues that historicism, with its 'linear equivalence of event and idea' has problematic epistemological and political effects.[22] First, it reduces time to a singularity and second it imposes an essential unity on 'the people' who function as historical objects of a nationalist pedagogy, a pre-given homogenous consensual community. Thinking the nation as a temporal process rather than an historical narrative makes trouble for this conceptual field. For not only does it foreground the fact of multiple and unequal times but it also makes it possible to see that the location of culture is a question of temporality rather than historicity; that the temporal is a crucial part of the symbolic and affective processes of the landscape of audience identification.

There is nothing startling in Bhabha's claim that time is fundamentally implicated in senses of location, dislocation and identity. It echoes Berger's beautiful analysis of the multiple temporalities of Turkish guest workers in *A Seventh Man*, where memory (the past) and anticipation (the future) become so overdeveloped they categorically deny the present.[23] What is valuable and important about Bhabha's argument is, rather, his exploration of the specific temporality of ambivalence. For Bhabha, the nation is marked by an 'archaic ambivalence that informs the time of modernity'.[24] This ambivalence is produced in the tension, the split, between rhetorics of progress with their ordered sequentiality, their 'continuist, accumulative temporality of the pedagogic' where a unified homogenous people move from the past to the future and the margins of the nation, specifically the discourse of minorities, where the non-sequential energy of lived historical memory and subjectivity foreground the nation's enunciatory present.[25]

In the example of Chinese languages narrow-cast news services, these issues of temporality are clearly manifest. For a start this form of narrow-casting explicitly addresses minorities' desire for immediate, simultaneous access to homeland news, a form of longing structured not by a return to the past, rather by a desire to inhabit two presents, two nows. This distinctive form of longing is specific to news; it is directly related to the textual and

22. Homi Bhabha, *The Location of Culture*, Routledge, London 1994, p140.

23. John Berger and Jean Mohr, *A Seventh Man*, Granta, Cambridge 1989.

24. Bhabha, *op. cit.*, p142.

25. *Ibid.*, p145.

temporal logics of news. For news, more so than virtually every other genre on television, is deeply implicated in mediating everyday senses of time, in ordering the lived experience of time. While media theory has long established that the structuring principle of broadcasting is time, it is news that marks out particularity, that generates what Paddy Scannell has described in phenomenological terms as the sense of dailiness.[26] While the commodity form of television may give us a sense of the return and the return of ever the same news has a very distinctive function within this logic of sameness, it is news that marks out difference, it is news that labels each day as *this* day.

26. Paddy Scannell, *Radio, Television and Modern Life*, Blackwell, London 1996.

Scannell's argument about the day to day or 'dailiness' is richly suggestive. It opens up an alternative approach for thinking about the television/temporality relation beyond the usual poststructualist accounts which focus on the textual effects of liveness. While these accounts recognise television's effect of immediacy, simultaneity, being in the now, this form of presentness is not the same as dailiness. Dailiness is a quite different temporal category based not so much on the internal textual logics of programmes rather on the relation between the institutional logics driving the schedule and the ways in which these are imbricated with audiences' everyday ordering of their lives. For Scannell, experiential or qualitative senses of time are fundamentally caught up in broadcasting time. And while broadcasting may take its structure from commodified time - the fifty minute slot, the two minute commercial - it is also always intimate time, part of the temporality of the viewer, part of their sense of everydayness. What is so useful about this phenomenological approach is its sensitivity to the relational, to the movements and negotiations between broadcasting structures, where time is most definitely money, and the ways these are made meaningful, the way audiences apprehend and inhabit them; the ontological characteristics of the medium.

What then of the qualitative meanings of time for those diasporic audiences watching narrow-cast news? Is Scannell's concept of dailiness only relevant to broadcasting news and its narratives of nation as homogenous chronological time? Or can it be usefully mobilised to analyses of narrow-casting which rebroadcast both national news services in other times and spaces and 24 hour globalised services driven by the logic of the never-ending update? In our research, uses of news services by Chinese diasporic audiences were various. Most of those interviewed watched both local broadcast news services on commercial and public service channels as well as narrow-cast news bulletins from homelands. This negotiation across different national news discourses exposes differential time-space continuums underpinning the disjunctive present of diasporic consciousness. In this cultural circuit, different modernities collide to evoke an ambiguity constituted in the desire to simultaneously belong to several temporal presents.

TW1, one Taiwanese family in our research, provides an exemplary model for this transnational practice. TW1 subscribed to NWTV precisely because of their, particularly the mother's, desire for news from Taiwan. The mother watches the TVBS-N service on NWTV every day. TVBS-N is one of the most popular channels in Taiwan; its midday news bulletin is immediately up-linked to satellite and received and screened in Australia at 4.30pm. A significant pleasure in this news service is that it is screened relatively close to real time in Taiwan. This is a service that the parents watched over lunch every day in Taiwan and now watch in Melbourne over afternoon tea. For the mother, especially, it has intense epistephilic value; it makes her feel, as she said, 'very close to home', it generates a strong sense of temporal-spatial connection. This is definitely not yesterday's news, unlike all the other services available on NWTV. The ritualised use of this news service and the ways in which it is incorporated into the specific domestic culture of this Taiwanese family allows them to maintain a dual sense of dailiness, a doubling of time that produces not so much a desire for return, for the past, rather, a fluid ontology of being in two everydays.

For other viewers of narrow-cast services spatiality and questions of home mediate viewing far more than time. This was highlighted in the linguistic mobility of the Indo-Chinese. Here, the many meanings surrounding a differential 'narrow' call attention to the contingency of 'home'. One of the Indo-Chinese interviewees (VC2) said: 'While I am in Germany, I watch CNN because it's in English and I can't speak German'; VC2 tells of his desire for news while visiting his father, his two brothers and their families in Germany. At home, he listens to the Chinese radio on SBS because his English is not good enough to follow the English-language news. For VC2, Germany, his place of kinship and blood connections, becomes an 'other' when positioned alongside his home, Australia. Here, from the diasporic Indo-Chinese-Australian response, the English language American-centric CNN reaffirms its place as a global specificity, mediating the discursive distance between the localities of Australia and Germany. In Australia however, the visuality of the English-language news services take on a marginal status when placed alongside the ethno-specific Chinese-language radio service. From the narrow-cast narrative of a Chinese-language radio service in Australia, the 'place' of 'home' is constructed as ambiguous and contingent; like identity, home is 'mobile'. This is especially manifest in the response of another interviewee, VC11, who says she enjoys listening to the music, story-telling and local events on Chinese-Australian radio because 'it's entertaining and it takes me back home'. Clearly, the fetishised 'home' that is inflected in Chinese music and Chinese-language story-telling differs from the contemporaneity of 'home' that is referred to in the now of 'local events'. In the space of one sentence, the 'place' of 'home' surfaces as a virtual, mobile and disjunctive present that connects 'here' and 'there', then and now, mediated in this instance through the local ethno-linguistic service of a narrow-caster. Such a construction is made explicit in the response of yet another interviewee, VC6, who watches the Mandarin CCTV *WorldWatch*

News on SBS. He says, 'Speaking as an Australian-Chinese though I come from Cambodia, I like it but they broadcast news mainly from the People's Republic, not Hong Kong, Taiwan or other places ... News and new developments from SEA should be introduced'. At the same time, he laments that Chinese films screened in the cinemas are from Hong Kong, and therefore 'very commercialised, very Americanised. I would like to see something that's more of a real Chinese movie.'

His response succinctly highlights the multiple and contradictory imaginations framed by the discursivities of Orientalism and Occidentalism, as well as displaying the heterogeneities of diasporic Chineseness. For example, Hong Kong films are 'not real' because they are commercial and America-centric. At the same time, the hypocrisy of his desire for a 'real Chinese movie' is exposed to be as fake as his desire for 'authenticity' in his speaking position as a diasporic Chinese from Cambodia living in Australia. From his criticisms about the People's Republic centredness of the CCTV news service, and his call for content to reflect the diversity of what actually constitutes 'Chinese' news, (for example, from places like Hong Kong, Taiwan and South East Asia), his expression of Chineseness can be argued as simultaneously heterogeneous, liminal and conflicting. Clearly, within the epistemics of a transnational Chinese modernity, 'China is not the ontological privilege of epistemological positioning as it is one of the many sites within and across which Chinese transnational practices are played out'.[27]

Narrow-casting enables a diasporic Chinese imaginary to emerge through access to homeland news but this access is always mediated by particular audience landscapes. These landscapes produce different viewing experiences according to the desires of watchers and in this way going south refers to the processes whereby cultural flows are situated, not only by the institutional logics ordering reception in Australia but also by the heterogeneous temporal and spatial relations that shape uses of transnational media flows. For some Chinese viewers in Australia the uses of narrow-cast news services are intricately connected to questions of time, to the relation between the distinctive temporalities of televisual news, which privilege presentness and the live, and the ritualised, phenomenological experience of dailiness. For others, diasporic identity emerges in linguistic and visual invocations of 'home'. These various practices and meanings are a product of flows of people and programming and their particular intersections in postcolonial Australia. If narrow-casting is a site where other news becomes available, it is also a site where other temporal-spatial relations de-centre the identity of nation as narration, making going south a space where Chinese identities foreground Australia's multiple enunciatory presents.

27. Aihwa Ong and Donald Nonini, *Ungrounded Empires: The Cultural Politics of Modern Chinese Transantionalism*, Routledge, London 1997, p12.

Xiao Ye: Food, Alterity and the Pleasure of Chineseness in Malaysia

Souchou Yao

A REPORT FROM THE FRONT

Jalan Alor, a narrow street running next to the busy Jalan Bukit Bintang, has always enjoyed a certain reputation among residents of the Malaysian capital Kuala Lumpur. By day it is a parking space for shoppers, but by night it becomes a site of pleasure. Jalan Alor is one of the city's red light districts, and here, not surprisingly, are also found some of its best food stalls. Every evening at eight, as if by clockwork, they magically spring to life on the shop verandas and parking spaces in the street. In the cool evening air, families, courting couples, drug addicts, sex workers and their 'guests' rub shoulders with each other, consuming fresh seafood, turtle soup, python, fruit bat and other wild meat stewed in Chinese herbs, and the speciality of the area: Hokkien fried noodles in dark soya sauce garnished with pork crackling and raw garlic. For many, it is Jalan Alor's delicious and diverse foods that have taken them there, but as they eat, they cannot help being reminded of the other offerings of the place. As they look up from their tables, there are a myriad of neon signs advertising services of massage parlours, karaoke lounges, beauty clinics (offering face whitening and 'surgery-free breast enhancement'), and Chinese physicians promising delivery from 'weaknesses of the kidney' and relief from 'exhaustion of the *yang qi* (masculine rigour)'.

At this place of secret carnality and culinary pleasure arrives Diana, a nineteen year-old Chinese hostess from the Sakura Karaoke Lounge, and her lover Ah Keong. They are in deep conversation, and she is in tears. They sit down, and with his arm around her shoulder, Ah Keong tries to comfort her. The anthropologist who accompanies them for supper already knows the story. Diana has just returned from an assignment with a client at the Federal Hotel just down the road. Having been in the trade for barely two months, it is the first night out with a client arranged for her by Ah Keong. What rubs salt into the wound is that, as she only found out at the hotel room, the client was an old Malay man, a politician and businessman from Sarawak, and he had demanded - with insistence, as she tells Ah Keong: '*kou jiao*' (fellatio). Apparently Ah Keong had arranged Diana's visit on instructions from two Chinese merchants, who paid handsomely for his services. The Malay man is a backbencher in the Sarawak state parliament who has promised the merchants an introduction to the 'right people' in Kuching who can deliver a lucrative timber concession. Diana has been a part of the 'gift' to the Malay man, who has specifically requested the company of a Chinese girl during his stay in Kuala Lumpur.

The anthropologist silently recalls the 'ethnographic background' as he shares the meal with the lovers, and the quiet drama slowly unfolds before him at three o'clock in the morning. Interrupting his whispers of comfort and endearment to Diana, Ah Keong signals to the waiter that he is ready to order.

We are having *bah ku teh*, the only item on the menu. Literally meaning meat-bone-tea in Hokkien dialect, the dish is a thick stew of pork knuckles and ribs, simmered for hours in a stock flavoured with Chinese herbs, garlic cloves and soya sauce. With its full-bodied flavour, dense with medicinal goodness and nutritional value, there is perhaps no food more appropriate for restoring the tired and defiled bodies of those in the sex trade. As the waiter takes the order, Ah Keong retrieves two small packets from his breast pocket, and asks him to put some of the contents in the dish. These are ginseng and deer horn powder - the most expensive Chinese tonics available. As Ah Keong hurries the waiter to be quick with the dish, he smiles, kisses Diana's cheeks, and says in Cantonese: 'See, how much I care for you'.

HISTORY, MEMORY, ENJOYMENT

To partake of the pork dish, spiced with medicinal goodness and flavoured with personal solicitude, is to nestle in a private sanctuary away from the glaring light of public judgement and conventional culinary taboo. This is perhaps the lesson of the 'deep play' I have just described. Following the anthropologist Clifford Geertz, what takes place this particular evening in the foodstall connects the personal with the public, linking immediate social concerns with wider structural realities.[1] Located in this dialectic, the ethnographic episode is a portent of the foundational elements of national life in Malaysia. All the real and imaginary peculiarities are there: the pain and social estrangement of ethnic relations, Malay hegemony and Chinese complicity, the pecuniary rewards of political office, the arrogation of private pleasure as a 'sanctified' place of personal meaning, and of course, the gender disparity in these transactions. These features give *bah ku teh* a certain allegorical quality which is at the heart of Chinese self-recognition in Malaysia. Not only the dish, but the site of culinary enjoyment too, is imbued with significance, 'imprinted with our tenacious, inescapable obsession', to borrow a phrase from Simon Schama's masterly *Landscape and Memory*.[2] In this site, what we have to reckon with is precisely the immediacy of our own 'topofilia' which couples sentiment with place, cultural memory with locality, where 'imagination augments the values of reality'.[3]

For the Chinese diners in Jalan Alor, the culinary enjoyment of *bah ku teh* is never purely that; it is also about something else, incited by something beyond the senses. That pleasure can be located in history and in the political is, of course, the tradition of the Frankurt School. For Adorno, Horkheimer

1. Clifford Geertz, 'Deep Play: notes on the Balinese cockfight', in *The Interpretation of Culture*, selected essays by Clifford Geertz, Basic Books, New York 1973.

2. Simon Schama, *Landscape and Memory*, Harper Collins, London 1995, p18.

3. Gaston Bachelard, *The Poetics of Space*, Maria Jolas (trans), Beacon Press, Boston 1964, p2.

and Marcuse, the enjoyment of cultural products in capitalism is a sign of the degradation of the European culture, and a major force in the mystification of the individual mind.[4] In spite of its elitist - and humanist - assumptions, it is nonetheless the crucial insight of the Frankfurt School that highlights the secret and insidious presence of the political/ideological in pleasure. In this sense, pleasure may be said to have a material base. And the task of discursive intervention, as Frederic Jameson suggests, must involve writing history back to pleasure:

> (A)s far as pleasure is concerned, it may readily be admitted that it is materialist; whether or not 'unconsciousness', the psychological subject is always and in all moments of history and modes of production constitutionally and irrecuperably idealistic, the generalization is probably safe for us ... Pleasure is finally the consent of life in the body, the reconciliation - momentary as it may be - with the necessity of physical existence in a physical world.[5]

If the senses indeed have a history, then we can fruitfully use the phrase 'social formation of pleasure' and we may speak of its origin which charts its social arrival as the embodiment of the 'consent of life'. All things visceral are located in a sensual geography of individual sensation and collective historical experience. In this dialectical realm, pleasure mystifies by its endless return to the preserve of private experience, and by offering a powerful affirmation of selfhood through the senses. And the task of deconstructing the social formation of pleasure may well begin here, by retracing the history of its social judgement and cultural consensus in the first place.

EATING BITTERNESS (*CHI KU*) FOR THE BODY

Among the Chinese of Southeast Asia, *bah ku teh* is normally eaten as a stew, either by itself, with a bowl of rice or with pieces of fried-rice-dough bread called *you zha gui* (literally 'oil fried devil'). In a culture which believes that food provides not only nutrition but also therapeutic values, this pork dish has a distinct 'culinary identity'. Rich in protein, heavily spiced with garlic and Chinese herbs, the stew sits in that hybrid category between a *tang* or soup and a *bu* or tonic. Without a restrictive culinary tradition, *bah ku teh* has proved to be a highly versatile dish subject to creative innovations in restaurants and domestic kitchens. At home, it is a common practice to add fried tofu (bean curd) and Chinese white radish (*Raphanus sativus*) cut into cubes, as a way of improving the 'texture' of the dish, and to absorb and 'disguise' the medicinal taste of the herbs. For the discriminating cook, the herbs and spices – these are the main ingredients of the dish and are hand-packed in a muslin satchel by a Chinese medicine shop rather than bought from the supermarket shelf - are chosen according to the taste and medicinal

4. See Adorno's classic, *The Culture Industry : selected essays on mass culture*, edited and introduced by J.M. Bernstein, Routledge, London 1991.

5. Fredric Jameson 'Pleasure: a political issue', *Formations of Pleasure*, Routledge, London and Boston 1983, p10.

effects one wishes to achieve. At the foodstall in Jalan Alor, the herbs that go in to the pot include: *tang kui (angelica sinesis)*, *yu zhu (polygonatum odoratun)*, *yu gui (Fructus lycii)*, *ji zi (Radix codomopsitis)*, *dang shen (Rhizoma linguistici)*. These herbs give the stew a slightly tangy, bitter taste, a sign that this is more than simply a flavoursome food. Indeed the medicinal flavour of the dish, rather than something to be disguised, becomes the significant 'trademark' for a tasty *bu* stew which 'patches up'the weak body and restores the spirit.[6]

For Diana, who has spent five years in a Chinese primary school and has therefore acquired a rich repertoire of useful proverbs, the sharp medicinal taste of the dish must seem like a culinary reflection of her favourite expression *chi ku* or 'eating bitterness', which she often uses to describe the fate she shares with her 'sisters' in the trade. In this instance, partaking of the dish becomes the literal enactment of a linguistic metaphor. Eating and speaking, the bitterness of food and the bitterness of life's experiences: their connections may not be too far fetched after all. If nothing else, as Derrida has pointed out in his critique of Western logocentrism, speech and eating are bodily functions which deploy the same organ - the tongue.[7] Derrida might well have turned to the Chinese proverb, for *chi ku* shames the logocentric privilege of speech by the crucial reminder that words too - their concepts and associations - have 'taste'. If *chi ku* bridges the literal and the metaphoric, then what Diana 'spits out' as she consumes the dish with a quiet melancholy are not only grit and bone, but text itself.[8] *Chi ku*, the 'swallowing' of the excruciating 'bitterness' of ones life and work, signifies an experience of endurance and suffering. However, just as partaking of a dish like *bah kuh teh* has a 'surplus of operations'[9] flooding into the realm of medical therapy, *chi ku* too promises redemption by validating the virtue of silent endurance and fortitude. Diana and Ah Keong may well remember the ancient tale of Qu Yuan who, having lost the kingdom of his emperor, tastes each night the bitterness of gall bladder hung above his bed to remind himself of his humiliation and the urgent task of revenge and the restoration of the kingdom. If there is a point to the pork dish, it perhaps lies in its 'bitter taste' which echoes the bitterness of the social deprivation of the world of Sakura Karaoke Lounge. In food as in life it is the 'bitter taste' which endorses the wisdom of patient forbearance as a strategy of recovery, just as it nurtures the longing for life's redemptive possibilities.

What the food-stall in Jalan Alor offers is indeed a food of the place. As a metaphor of moral hope, a tonic stew of humoral balance would not do. The stew must carry an 'excess' in its ingredients in order to do battle with all that conspires to wear down the body and spirit. Indeed, the dish - because of the heavy protein stock and the addition of *dang gui (Angelica sinensis)* - is geared towards producing an appropriate 'heat' in order to compensate for the loss of *yang* - the positive *qi* of rigour and strength in the Chinese humoral system – in both the sex workers and their male clients. Mildly 'warming'

6. See Emily M Ahern, 'Sacred and Secular Medicine in a Taiwan Village: a study of cosmological disorders,' in Arthur Kleinmen et al., *Medicine in Chinese Cultures*, U.S. National Institute of Health, Washington D.C. 1975, pp91-114.

7. Jacques Derrida, *Glas*, John P. Leavey, Jr., and Richard Rand (transl), University of Nebraska Press, Lincoln 1986, p161.

8. Derrida, 1986, *op.cit.*, p161.

9. Gregory L. Ulmer, *Applied Grammatology*, John Hopkins University Press, Baltimore 1985, p55.

rather than aggressively 'heating', the dish improves the pallor, cures anaemia, and rebuilds the body drained of vitality by cigarettes, alcohol and late nights. As though united by a common destiny of loss, men and women devour the herbal stew, not with grimaces on their faces, but with relish and the knowledge that suffering its bitter 'taste' is a precursor to the reaping of therapeutic benefits.

If it is moral hope as much as medicinal goodness which makes *bah ku teh* such a tasty dish, then Ah Keong's solicitude for Diana is charged with a similar significance. What Ah Keong offers is indeed a culinary epitome of himself. The tonic dish gives bodily strength and social comfort to the frailty of the young woman's body crushed by the circumstances of her trade, just as he does as her lover. The addition of expensive ginseng root and deer horn powder to the dish may be a self-conscious gesture of male bravado, nevertheless it is a genuine expression of care and affection in a world of flagrant transactions of the flesh.

However there is a catch: the bitterness of the pork stew promises bodily cure and social redemption, but its final purpose is to prepare one to re-enter a world without atonement. For all its culinary enjoyment and social comfort, the pleasure of the tonic dish merely blunts the brutal reality of the karaoke-lounge world. It is a pleasure that, inevitably, mystifies as it paves the way for further transactions of sin and hopelessness. This is surely the gloomy understanding of the lovers that evening at the food-stall. It may be suggested that the private realm they have so anxiously carved out for themselves is futile: a province of personal emotions cannot prevent the intrusion of the wider social forces, in this instance to the world in which the trading of Diana's body is a stark reality. This knowledge must have cut deeply into Diana's feelings of hurt and disappointment, and these feelings take us at once to that world, and further still, to the terrain of state power and the violent politics of ethnic relations.

XIAO YE AND BODY TRADING

For Diana and Ah Keong, therefore, social regrets, the misfortunes of gender and the power of the state cannot but intrude upon and reshape their very enjoyment. Instead of pleasure being a haven from the woes of the world, it reproduces and intensifies them. In the early hours of the morning, the enjoyment of *bah ku teh* seems remarkably close to that fetishistic, dreamy quality of the 'calamitous state' before breakfast which Benjamin describes:

A popular tradition warns against recounting dreams on an empty stomach. In this state, though awake, one remains under the sway of the dream. For washing brings only the surface of the body and the visible motor functions into the light, while in the deeper strata, even during the morning ablution, the grey penumbra of dream persists, and, indeed, in the solitude of the first waking hour, consolidates itself. He who shuns contact with the day, whether for fear of his fellow men or for the sake of inner composure, is unwilling to eat and disdains his breakfast. He thus avoids a rupture between the nocturnal and the daytime worlds ... [10]

10. Walter Benjamin, *One Way Street and Other Writings*, New Left Books, London 1979, pp45-46.

Against the pull of sleep, to break out from the 'protection of dreaming naivete',[11] one has to muster all the strength and clear-headedness which a nutritious breakfast brings:

11. *Ibid.*, p46.

> The narration of dreams brings calamity, because a person still in league with the dream world betrays it in his words and must incur its revenge. Expressed in more modern terms, he betrays himself ... For only from the far bank, from broad daylight, may dreams be recalled with impunity. This further side of dream is only attainable through a cleansing analogous to washing yet totally different. By way of the stomach.[12]

12. *Ibid.*

It is not inappropriate to read Benjamin here, as Terry Eagleton does, in terms of his virulent injunction against the fetishistic power of ideology as he outlines a tactics of its subversion. History and its narrative, like dreams, reside in a terrain beclouded by the seduction of memory, by the siren song of ideology and by the mystified unconscious. To recall such a history, Eagleton suggests, both the past and the unconscious must be subject to the violent rupture of rude awakening:

> Dream may fructify history, but only if it is first subjected to a certain violence - ruptured, distanced, purged, and only thus refracted into the vigilance of conscious life ... It is only through the radical discontinuity of past and present, through the space hollowed by their mutual eccentricity, that the former may be brought to bear explosively upon the latter.[13]

13. Terry Eagleton, *Walter Benjamin or Towards a Revolutionary Criticism*, Verso, London 1990, pp43-44.

Therefore the 'taste' of a dish like *bah ku teh* is never innocent. With this in mind, we can look at another aspect of *bah ku teh*. For all its health-fostering qualities, it is simply the favourite dish for karaoke-lounge hostesses when they go for *xiao ye* or 'late night supper' after work. In tropical Malaysia, to sit in a food-stall near midnight and order a bowl of noodles, sticks of satay or spicy soup of mutton (*sup gambing*) is as much about meeting the body's call for food, as trying to prolong the evening cool before bedtime. In the world of karaoke lounges this pleasant ritual - of 'eating the air' (*makan enging*, in common Malaysian parlance - is given a subtle semantic twist).

Xiao ye is in fact the trade jargon for the practice of a hostess spending a night out with a male client. For the six hostesses in the Sakura Karaoke Lounge - a number occasionally supplemented by young women from Thailand and China on tourist visas - to be invited out for late-night supper is both a privilege and a burden. In the first place, such an invitation is a clear sign of their desirability and professional attainment. For it is only the more popular - and thus physically more attractive and financially more viable - hostesses who can entice men to 'buy ticket' (*mai piao*) from the manager in order to take them out for supper after closing time. For the 'star' of the place, this popularity complements her flirtatious charm and social skills, most evident as she strains her voice, while applauding the similar effort of the clients, in following the lyrics on the television monitor of songs by Neil Diamond, Air Supply, Andy Lau, and Anita Mui. All the time, she urges the men to order drinks from the bar to smooth the throat, coyly asking for herself the in-house special 'brandy' - (Chinese tea) in a large cognac balloon glass.

DUPLICITY AND THE PLEASURE OF CHINESENESS

For the women in the karaoke lounge, *xiao ye* represents several things: the partaking of delicious food, a pleasant respite from the tropical heat, a sign of their desirability among men, an euphemism for commodified sex, and above all, a comforting and an ironic ritual which smoothes the path for the trading of (their) bodies. If *xiao ye* embodies a grammar of pleasure which redeems the 'damaged' body, then Diana's anguish clearly has further meanings: *xiao ye* is not a matter of choice, and Diana's evening out with an old Malay man elicits universal sympathy among her 'sisters'. Why, in a world where trading of the body is the norm, does the ethnic origin of the client matter so much, and cause so much grief?

In Malaysia, procuring a young Chinese female body for a Malay politician all too eager to exploit the opportunities of his office, has all the flavour of a 'social myth'. Indeed, tales abound in Sakura among Chinese men about their busy wheeling and dealing in bidding for government tenders by working with a Malay *bumiputra* (literally, 'son of the soil') partner. Partly reality and, no doubt, partly masculine boasting, these tales are frequently garnished with one spicy detail: the supply of a young Chinese woman as a part of the 'deal'. As some stories go, in more substantial transactions involving senior politicians, the 'gift' is no less than a film starlet from Hong Kong or Taiwan..

To summarise an informant's convoluted explanation, the demand for Chinese 'flesh' by Malay politicians is a privilege of office which allows them to indulge their 'special attraction to the white skin'. In the absence of *Mat Salleh* (European) women, Chinese women with their fairer skin, are objects of carnal interest among Malay men. Blind to their own complicity and almost proud of their moral misadventures, Chinese informants spin out enticing tales which draw from, and fuel the myth of the erotic fantasy of whiteness among Malay men. In the El Dorado of new economic riches of East Malaysia, the timber trade offers another elaboration of the myth. Kuala Lumpur is the place where 'State Assemblymen' come: some are genuine, some are carpetbaggers, out to make a quick *ringgit* from equally duplicitous Chinese *towkays* (merchants) who promise government contacts and useful connections leading to highly lucrative logging concessions. Perhaps aware of the frailty of their pledges, the 'State Assemblymen' do not demand exotic imports, but are content with the more modest choice of a local Chinese girl during their stay in the capital.

As though to give these tales of new riches and transactions a more solid and believable foundation, Chinese men, in Sakura, talk about their own enjoyment in the language of the timber trade. When timber merchants gather, they drink Remy Martin or Johnny Walker Black Label and shout, in appreciative approval, 'Ah, this is worth a log or two'. And, since there is no higher value that can be put on things than the price of a log of stripped timber extracted by hardy men from deep in the Sarawak jungle, they call out to a young hostess in what they think as a flirtatious compliment: 'Now you are worth two logs, but don't forget an old love like me'. The crudity of such jokes mark the hostess' routine, but it is only the more seasoned ones who can deflect the phallic reference with a reply suggestive of a comparable insult: 'Well, we have to see how much your log is worth (for me to love you again)'.

What all this adds up to is, in fact, a set of collective clichés which one comes to identify with political life in Malaysia.

Returning to ethnography and Diana, we might say that the medicinal properties of *bak ku teh* have to work against, on the one hand the health-draining lifestyle of a karaoke hostess, and on the other the wider state processes which impose their impeccable, violent logic on her body. The pleasure of the body is at once traceable to the desires and social impulses constitutive of the order of political life. Moving beyond their physiological self-obsession,[14] the 'realms of the senses' in the pork dish, as in Diana's body, are opened up to their public lives and social significance. The taking of Diana's body is at the same time the sad fate of her gender and profession, an exercise of epistemic violence, and the logical destiny of a state discourse anxiously affirming the need to possess and manage the enjoyment of the Other: to this complex field of power and desire we shall now turn.

14. Frederic Jameson, 'Pleasure: a political issue', in *Formations* Editorial collective, *op. cit.*, p1.

STATE HEGEMONY, ETHNICITY AND ALTERITY

To contemplate the nature of state power, and ethnic identity in Malaysia - what it means to us and the way it gives significance to others - is to place the conventional narrative of the state under a new critical light. All narratives, Hayden White reminds us, carry 'an illusionary coherence', and the process of their telling invariably 'charges them with the kind of meanings more characteristic of oneiric than of waking thought'.[15] There is nothing more illustrative of this than the measured normalcy of the 'story' of modern Malaysia. Bathed in the radiance of national progress and the wise political leadership which has helped to achieve it, the story tells of Malaysia's struggle from British colonialism to nationhood, of the success of the anti-communist campaign during the Emergency of 1948-1960, of the installation of Malay

15. Hayden White, *The Content of the Form: narrative discourse and historical representation*, John Hopkins University Press, Baltimore 1987, p124.

political, cultural and economic hegemony as a necessary condition of ethnic peace and, of course, of the rapid industrial modernisation under the Prime Minister Dr Mahathir bin Mohamad, whose tough political skills and pragmatic economic management will steer the country out of the current financial crisis.

16. See, for example, Fernando Coronil, *The Magical State: nature, money, and modernity in Venezuela*, University of Chicago Press, Chicago 1997.

Like all state narratives, this one too is imbued with a seductive magic.[16] It is a magic which is derived from the narrative's endless retelling of one heroic enterprise after another undertaken by the various regimes of wise and capable political leadership. However, as one would expect, the narrative cannot achieve its astonishing power without a quick sleight of hand and a rapid shuffling of cards. And what is rehearsed in the theatre of legerdemain is that which has become the foundational premise of the modern Malaysian state: Malay hegemony as a necessary condition for managing the tension and contradictions of a ' multi-ethnic society'. In this staging, the watershed of the May 1969 race riots is customarily brought in and invested with contemporary relevance. If the bloody event - which took place twelve years after national independence from the British - deeply traumatised the nation, it is no less true that the communal killing has provided crucial ideological resources to 'naturalise' the current state formation based on pro-Malay 'affirmative action' policies and power sharing in the coalition government. After all, Malaysia had been wont to describe itself as the exemplar of ethnic harmony in Southeast Asia - 'the Switzerland of Southeast Asia' as school text- books describe it. Offering its explanation on the 1969 riot, the official discourse tells a passionate 'story' of Malays being denied a rightful place in a country to which they, as *bumiputra*, should have the first claim; of other ' immigrant communities' - mainly the Chinese and lesser extent Indians - which dominate the economy and middle class professions; and, above all, of the impotence of the *bumiputra* to define 'in their own country' national identity and cultural agendas according to their social and religious aspirations. Infused with all the features of a rehabilitative project, the *bumiputra*'s policy is about 'restoring' the right of ownership and control, (only) to those who can trace their primordial connection 'by blood and the soil' with the country.

The outcome, somewhat inevitably, is a form of multiculturalism firmly rooted in a zero-sum game of power-sharing and cultural legitimacy. From the installation of the pro-*bumiputra* New Economic Policy (NEP) to the promotion of Malay as the sole national language, the state is able to insist on a real continuum between the 'backwardness' of Malay community and the effrontery of 'immigrants' enjoying fruits they do not deserve, in a place to which they do not belong. Therefore in the imaginary the Other's enjoyment is the reason for the Malay subject's deprivation. The Othering of non-Malays has remained a persistent theme of the state narrative. It has become a kind of political common-sense even among the Chinese and the Indian communities and the opposition parties, among whom acceptance is always motivated by a mixture of ideological agreement and political pragmatism. The forging of this consensus, further enshrined in the constitution, says much about the successful ideological enterprise of the state over the last decades since independence; and it remained fundamentally unchanged in the volatile conditions of the late 1990s.

To trace the intricate relief of the state narrative, it is useful to turn to what is regarded as the master text which has provided the ideological rationale of the current state policy: *The Malay Dilemma* by the Malaysian Prime Minister Dr Mahathir bin Mohamad.[17] First published in 1970, its continuing relevance for understanding the configuration of power in Malaysia says as much about the cogency of the text as about the sad fate of national political life. At the time Dr Mahathir was still in the wilderness of UMNO - United Malay National Organisation, the major Malay political organisation and dominant partner in the ruling coalition government - and the book is remarkable for its mixture of social, environmental and genetic explanations of what he sees as the 'problems affecting the Malays'.[18] As a medical doctor, he draws on laws of hereditary science and applies them to Malay social practices. What emerges is a fusion of crude biology and bad sociology, both confining Malays in a *cul-de-sac* of social disadvantage and stunted biological development *in relation to other immigrant communities*.

The basic origin of the problem, Dr Mahathir argues, lies in the natural fecundity of the tropics in which Malays had traditionally founded their settlements. Living with the rich blessing of nature:

> (n)o great exertion or ingenuity was required to obtain food. There was plenty for everyone throughout the year. Hunger and starvation, *a common feature in countries like China*, were unknown in Malaya. Under these conditions everyone survived. Even the weakest and the least diligent were able to live in comparative comfort, to marry and to procreate. The observation that only the fittest would survive did not apply (to Malays), for the abundance of food supported the existence of even the weakest.[19]

Natural abundance, in other words, has ironically become an evolutionary trap by protecting Malays from the strenuous logic of natural selection. Here, in the richness of the tropics, even the weakest and most feeble minded survive and propagate themselves. However in a multi-ethnic society, the 'survival of the weak' would not have been as serious if the 'immigrant communities' were not already toughened by the hardy environment in their home countries. As Dr Mahathir outlines the woes of Malays - from genetic fault-lines and poor social discipline to an inward-looking Islamic world view - the subtext is clear. Malay's frailty has to be seen against the strength of the Chinese who came from a tough environment which truly tested the fit and stout-hearted, weeding out the weak and turning them into 'hardened and resourceful' people.[20] The intellectual genius of *The Malay Dilemma* lies in its construction of the tragic vision of a Malay

17. Mahathir bin Mohamad, *The Malay Dilemma*, Donald Moore for Asia Pacific Press, Singapore 1970.

18. *Ibid.*, p1.

19. *Ibid.*, p21, emphasis added.

20. *Ibid.*, p25.

communal fate - the Faustian dilemma of a nature that with the same stroke rewards and undoes the good work of Darwinian evolution. In this vision, not only Malays, but the figure of the Chinese Other too carries a tragic mendacity: the hardworking, cross-breeding, biologically tough and socially outward-looking 'Chinese' has been constructed to fulfil a singular purpose - to mirror the 'relative disadvantage' of Malays, and excavate the analytical depth of the 'Malay dilemma' .

Not surprisingly, both the notions of Chinese endowments and Malays' lack of them have the ghostly quality of a dream, immortal in their endless rebirth in the state discourse, socially gripping for their haunting realism. For it is within the ambivalent geography of desire that we can evaluate Dr Mahathir's project. Speaking of the preferential allocation of government scholarships to Malay students, he writes:

> To answer (the criticism of racial favouritism), one has to go back to the basic reason for the preferential treatment of the Malays. The motive behind preferential treatment is not to put Malays in a superior position, but to *bring them up to the level of non-Malays* ... The scholarships are not a manifestation of racial inequality. They are a means of breaking down the superior position of the non-Malays in the field of education ... The Malays are not proud of the 'privilege' of being protected by law like cripples. They would like to get rid of these privileges if they can, but they have to let pride take second place to the *facts of life*.[21]

21. *Ibid.*, p75, emphasis added.

Here the destinies of the Malay's subject and its (Chinese) Other are fatefully intertwined. Not only is the Other's endowment a gauge of one's lack, but the Malay subject's socio-economic ambitions and the question of their attainability are ultimately measured by the level of achievement of the Other. This process of Othering, based on the twin convent of promoting Malay's cultural and economic interest and suppressing the enjoyment of the Other, has all the ruling principle of the psychic economy described by Zizek:

> Nationalism ... presents a privileged domain of the eruption of enjoyment into the social field. The national Cause is ultimately nothing but the way subjects of a given ethnic community organise their enjoyment through national myth. What is therefore at stake in ethnic tension is always the possession of the national thing. We always impute to the 'other' an excessive enjoyment: he wants to steal our enjoyment (by ruining our way of life) and/or he has access to some secret, perverse enjoyment ... The basic paradox is that our Thing is conceived as something inaccessible to the other and at the same time threatened by him.[22]

22. Slavoj Zizek, *Tarrying with the Negative*, Duke University Press, Durham 1993, pp202-3.

Returning to Dr Mahathir's text, what explains the 'ground of incompatibility between different ethnic subject positions' is precisely the mathematics of national enjoyment as a limited good, the principle of 'the more of it for the Other can only lead to less for me'.[23] But why is the Other so remarkably capable of enjoyment, of always extracting something from his relationship with 'the national thing', in a way which fatally threatens my effort to do so? The genetic biology of *The Malay Dilemma* tries to provide the answer, but doesn't quite succeed. For if Malay subject positionality is constructed out of desire's longing, then neither the 'Malay Problem' nor the project of 'bringing Malays up to the level of the Other communities' can ever find a satisfactory ending and resolution. Like chasing the whistling presence of a phantom, the 'level of achievement of the Other' cannot ever be caught up with simply because the desire which produces the Real in the Malay subject position cannot be pinned down. The Chinese Other in Dr Mahathir's (Orientalist) discourse - genetically endowed, hardened by the good work of evolution - is a screen upon which authorial desire can be displaced or deferred.

23. *Ibid.*, p203.

This is the most ironic moment in the tortuous discourse: the Other is both the thief of my pleasure and the measure of my achievement. In the context of this contradiction, the Chinese Other becomes at the same time a target of Malay resentment and an object of cultural adoration. After all, the cultural and biological endowments of the Other are identified as those very qualities which the Malay's subject desperately needs in order to bring itself to the same or at least a comparable level of achievement.

The New Economic Policy (NEP) thus has a more significant cause than the greed of a Malay elite conspiring to prolong - in collaboration with local Chinese and Indian capital - its rich harvest. In spite of the dramatic redefinition of Malay identity by wealth redistribution, and particularly through a modernising secular Islam, the ethnicisation of state policy has meant the enduring need to construct and vitalise the discourse of the tragic and 'natural' disadvantages of Malays (relative to the Other). Seen under this light, the 'Malay dilemma' so evocatively laid out by Dr Mahathir may indeed point to another problematic: how to manage and repossess that which rightly belongs to us.

THE DEFERRED PLEASURE OF THE CHINESE BODY

There is something in Dr Mahathir's narrative of the 'knotting' quality which Barbara Johnson refers to as charting any representation of the Real in the transference and counter-transference of desire. For all the biological and social determinism in Dr Mahathir's text, the discriminatory differences in the relative cultural and economic endowments of the Malay subject and the Chinese Other cannot be projected 'out there' into the social Real. Denied of its realist authority, the Malay subject has to discover its completion in the Chinese Other, which is itself a construction of desire. Returning to our ethnography, is it this double fantasy which incites the Malay politician's urgent call for Diana's young body? The taking of Diana's body is a classic

24. Ann Laura
Stoler, *Race and the
Education of Desire :
Foucault's history of
sexuality and the
colonial order of things*,
Duke University
Press, Durham 1995.

25. Patricia T
Clough,
'Poststructuralism
and Postmodernism:
the desire for
criticism', *Theory and
Society*, 21/4, 1992,
p547.

26. Maurice
Blanchot, 'Everyday
Speech', *Yale French
Studies*, 73, 1987,
p13.

27. *Ibid.*, p14.

28. *Ibid.*, p16.

move of desire in the displacement of its longing for the Chinese Other. What the enjoyment rehearses is the 'education of desire', to use a phrase by Ann Laura Stoler,[24] which circulates in an endless relay between the narrative of the state and the Malay subject's fantasy. It is a fantasy which draws succour from the powerful *bumiputra* discourse of the state, just as it fuels the subject's imaginary mastery of selfhood through the triumphant taking of pleasure in/from the Other. The process is one of double inscription. At the level of official discourse, the need for - and the erasure of - the Chinese Other is traceable to the social, environmental conditions and genetic consequences which Dr Mahathir has painstakingly described. Yet the Real in all these articulations is always already infected with the work of fantasy precisely because it has been 'formally composed to establish itself as "truly" real, as an element of discourse, the discourse of truth'.[25] For the Malay subject, the pleasure of the Chinese body is thus never 'sufficient' nor 'complete' in itself. If such pleasure is one of sensual enjoyment, then there is pleasure too, ironically, in its delay and when it falls short of total fulfilment. For the ecstasy offered by the Chinese body is always deferred to 'something else', as it draws its constructed significations in 'some other place', located in the mobile terrain between the sites of fact and fantasy, truth and fiction, narrative and discourse.

In the world of the Sakura Karaoke Lounge, if the nutritious *bah ku teh* repairs the body and restores the spirit, for Diana it is also the painful experience of the night excursion with the Malay man from which such rehabilitation is sought. The sighing acceptance of a woman's fate, the deprecating solicitude of a lover who sells her body, and the harvesting of redemption from 'eating bitterness' - what lies in the midst of all these is the deep humiliation of having *xiao ye* with a Malay man. Even in a world in which the transaction of the female body is a normal affair, Diana's insistence on the 'ethnic import' of her pain is highly suggestive. However, if such a transaction is an everyday occurrence in Sakura, then it is precisely in the routine banality of the women's leisure and work which we find 'the hidden present, or the discoverable future'[26]of their lives. It is not only that Diana's humiliation signifies the burden of 'ethnic differences' in a repressive state politics and discourse; rather the everyday of her world is always merged with the fragmentary processes of social life, constituting 'the very moment of society'.[27] And the crucial issue of gender and power is surely this: Diana's suffering signals her (personal) embodiment of the meanings and consequences of the tortuous discourse of ethnicity as they imperceptibly become a part of her life and understanding, as they distribute through her body, as Foucault would say.

The quality of 'unserious seriousness' - the term is Blanchot's[28]- of the everyday is also crucial when we turn to look at yet another modality of the enjoyment of *xiao ye* and a dish like *bah ku teh*. For the 'privatisation' we have witnessed in the subterranean world of Jalan Alor way past midnight is not only discernible in the cosy intimacy and gentle whispers of lovers. More potently, it is also authorised, literally, in the street. For the social comfort of the food-stall's offering, as I have said, lies in their carving a sanctuary out of the tedium and discomfort of daily life. But ironically, this social comfort is only feasible because the banal, quotidian quality of the street renders open what is obscure, what is hidden by forces which conspire to achieve its concealment. In Blanchot's rendering of Lefebvre's political reading of the street, 'The street tears from obscurity what is hidden, publishes what happens elsewhere, in secret; it deforms it, but inserts it in the social text'.[29] The culinary pleasure offered by the food-stalls in Jalan Alor takes on a similar quality, of linking the enjoyment of the moment to the grim silences and discriminations of the state.

29. *Ibid.*, p17.

Here the busy and violent interference of the state seems far away, discernible only in the light of day. In the dead of night no police constables are in sight. Shrouded by the secret transparency of night, what is partaken of at the food-stall suddenly appears to assume a special significance. Isn't *bah ku the*, with pork knuckles and ribs, a *haram* (polluting) food in Islamic belief? Have not we all heard that in the PAS (Party Islam Malaysia)-dominated state of Kelantan such a dish can only be consumed in the inner section of a Chinese restaurant, away from the street? And, by the same token, have not the Chinese businessmen who come to Sakura complained of the increasing difficulty of obtaining restaurant licences from the state authorities when the proposed establishment is to include pork dishes on the menu? In the face of these realities, the pleasure of *bah ku teh* seems to take on an insidious quality perhaps because, one might suggest, such a culinary choice is forbidden by the state and its official religion; it is only consumed by non-Muslims. For Diana at least, it is as if the enjoyment of the *haram* dish helps to regain a sense of herself, if she would put it so, lost in a transaction in which her body has been a key commodity. 'The everyday escapes' as it slips through the net of significance constructed by the anthropologist, just as it seems to break through the pervasive gaze of the state. There is undoubtedly pleasure too in these ventures of 'disappearance' as one sinks one's teeth into the thick pork chunks, dripping with dark sauce and medicinal goodness.

***

Looking back at that late evening at the food-stall with Diana and Ah Keong, it seems easy to recall, with a tingle of the tongue, the bitter-sweetness of the dish and to give shape to its taste from memory. However, there is always a danger in narration from memory, as Benjamin has warned. When taste comes to be remembered as an experience of incorrigible innocence affirmed by the senses, then the magic of the fetish begins to assert itself. Taste always 'disappears' into itself. If I have evoked Benjamin to drive home the point about the potent, dreamy quality of the fetish, my analysis is even more primarily orchestrated by Marx's insight into the relationship between history and the senses: 'Man is affirmed in the objective world not only in the act of

30. Karl Marx, *The Economic and Philosophic Manuscript of 1844*, D. J. Struik (ed), International Publishers, New York 1972, pp140-1.

31. Terry Eagleton, *The Ideology of the Aesthetic*, Basil Blackwell, Oxford 1990.

thinking but with all his senses. The formation of the senses is a labour of the entire history of the world down to the present'.[30] Just as aesthetics, even that witnessed in the display of food in restaurants and supermarkets, tends to escape into the ideological realm,[31] we can only 'taste' through history. We cannot enjoy a meal without the intrusion of social memory, any more than we can create for the poor in these times of post-Thatcherite economic rationalism, the vulgar optimism of social hope by the display of the temporary abundance of a soup kitchen.

My attempt to retrace the enjoyment of *bah ku teh*, has been to tell another history, other genealogies of pleasure, in the political landscape of Malaysia. In this enterprise, I return to the fundamental feature of Malaysian political life: state power based on Malay hegemony, and its effect in the formation of Malay subjective positioning. To be foundational in this sense is not, I submit, to commit the theoretical mistake of foundationalism. In a condition where complex and uneven forces work to create collective silence if not social amnesia, the unsettling of the bedrock of state formation is intended as a conscious political gesture. These forces of silence range from state enforcement, complicity of Malays and non-Malays (middle class and capitalists alike), to the (vulgar) Marxist fantasy of the progressive circle for whom 'ethnic issues' are but false consciousness to be put right by the unifying project of class struggle. Against these forces, what I have been at pains to bring to light is the very endurance of the tearing ethnic divide in Malaysian life. To witness such divide and its more subtle articulations, one has to move away from places where the instrumentalities of the state are immediately visible, and turn to the sites of the everyday and ordinary pleasures.

Instead of communal peace, a 'fact' invariably brought up by the state to justify its racist policies, intense passion and anguish are witnessed in these sites. And this is precisely the remarkable insight of Benjamin and Blanchot which underpins my analysis: in Malaysia, it is not that ethnic violence has somehow disappeared from daily life, with the dying traces hidden in the quotidian; rather it has always been self-evidently and pervasively ' there' in the shadow. For those who have eyes to see, and those who live and work there, these banal and marginal places are never what they are commonly perceived to be, but are charged with profound significance. As in taste, what nestles in these places is another history, another narrative of life's ambitions and disappointments. And like taste, history too has to be perceived, not as a factual 'thing' - like a supermarket shelving into which we slot all our understandings and passions, as Michael Taussig has sardonically described it[32]- but as a narrative subject to the vagrancy of its telling. It says much about the ideological tenor of the *Reformasi* movement organised around the former Deputy Prime Minister and Finance Minister Anwar Ibrahim following his arrest that ethnic-based policies are to be upheld as a part of its political platform, because they are 'in the constitution and put there by the forefathers (of the nation)'.[33] For all its anti-Mahathir

32. Michael Taussig, 'History as commodity in some recent American (Anthropological) literature', *Food and Foodways*, 2, 1987, pp151-169.

33. Email interview

radicalism and appeal to democratic reform, *Parti Keadilan Nasional* (National Justice Party) under the leadership of Anwar's wife, Dr Wan Azizah Wan Ismail, fails to attract wide support across the ethnic groups. The ambivalence many Malaysians feel about the *reformasi* movement may well lie in this ideological blind spot, in its inability to resolve a historical burden at the centre of political life. If the past indeed repeats itself, then the *reformasi* project too, like the taste of *bah ku teh*, is spellbound by the intimate merging of state narrative and collective amnesia, cultural enjoyment and ethnic aspirations.

Allegorical figures
Placing the work of Pamela Leung

Katie Hill

Pamela Leung is a London-based ceramic sculptor from Hong Kong. She creates a world of not-quite-human-size animal figures which might, at first sight, be seen as the sculptural manifestation of illustrations in children's stories. Her work reflects and redirects imagery absorbed by the artist during her childhood and adolescence in Hong Kong, including Shakespearean stock characters and mythological figures from kung fu films.[1] The diversity of her sources raises questions about identity, memory, history, place and the impossibility of allegory across cultures.

The initial development of her work stems from the time when she was a 'foreigner' in London. The moment of her self-discovery as an artist came exactly as a loss of identity was experienced. This phenomenon is echoed in the life of Paris-based artist Huang Yongping who admits that he first actively engaged with Chinese culture on moving away from China. 'I was more interested in Western culture when I was in China. Today, since living in the West, I try more to introduce Chinese culture into the Western art and cultural context'.[2] Although Leung does not deal with overtly Orientalist or even Oriental imagery, she alludes to Chinese tradition decoratively. There are powerful references to Shang dynasty vessels in the size and solidity of her work, and her motifs resonate with pre-historic key fret patterns.

Living in London becomes an image of rural labour in one piece of work. Leung places herself in the position of the ox whose burden is to carry the city on his back. It is a deliberate travesty of the city and the rural idyll. Not only are the figures transferred, translated and domesticated by Leung, they are subject to her vision of herself. They become her or she becomes them. They are 'real-ised' versions of Leung's loss of identity in a different British city. Leung's sculpture is anchored in her childhood and in the shapes of childhood. It acts as a link not only to the artist's past however but also to a broader historical past. Which past is that (?) is a question familiar within the gamut of cultural forms with any relation to Hong Kong.

Craig Owens argues that allegory has the 'capacity to rescue from oblivion that which threatens to disappear'.[3] The symbols of Chinese culture which appear in Leung's work retrieve fragments of her past into the present. Her conscious engagement with this material means produces a double allegory: an allegory of allegory itself. The myth of an essential China is held more strongly than the images conjured up by a rapidly expanding Hong Kong, a city of high-rise and economic boom. The aesthetic purity of a mythologised pre-history becomes part of the detail of the hybrid reality which the work evokes.

The hybridity of her work links the strange with the suggestion of the urban.

1. Interview with the artist at her Kennington studio, London 10 October, 1998.

2. Hou Hanru and Gao Minglu, 'Strategies of Survival in the Third Space: A Conversation on the Situation of Overseas Chinese Artists in the 1990s', in Gao Minglu (ed), *Inside Out: New Chinese Art*, exhibition catalogue, San Francisco Museum of Modern Art and Asia Society Galleries, University of California Press, Berkeley/Los Angeles/London 1998, p186.

3. C. Owens, 'The Allegorical Impulse: Toward a Theory of Postmodernism', in Scott Bryson, Barbara Kruger, Lynne Tillman and Jane Weinstock (eds), *Beyond Recognition. Representation, Power and Culture*, University of California Press, Berkeley/Los Angeles/London, 1992, pp52-53.

There is an almost surreal juxtaposition of images which characterise Hong Kong here and elsewhere in the imagery of the almost diasporic community. Leung's turn to the hybrid also serves to neutralise the gap between past and present in its evocation of the space of childish imagination. This does create problems in the world of adult art consumption. Is childish art necessarily read as illustrative? Does representational form borrowed from the naivetés of pre-history and popular mythology promise narrative and explanation? If so, we are deliberately disappointed. The characters are left open to interpretation with the viewer forced into the position of a child, left to 'make up' the story. Both Chinese and British readings are denied clarity: the fox is wearing a Chinese robe, the Shang dynasty vessel is decorated in blue-and-white, usually associated with the Ming (late seventeenth century). This work denies the purity of 'tradition' on both sides. Myths are mixed, styles are bastardised.

British colonialism and Chinese imperialism collided most in the applied arts - and there is direct reference to the dialogic history of ceramics in Leung's choice of material. There are also less direct links to Chinese tradition. In Imperial China large-scale ceramic lions or Fu dogs would be placed at the doors of temples as guardians of the spirits. Likewise, Leung's figures appear universally benevolent, acting as spirit-like presences whatever the setting.

Setting and place is at the centre of Leung's work. Her figures demand beauty as a backdrop. Yet despite their size, the appropriate place for them is domestic, a room or a garden. If the notion of diaspora is linked to the imagined 'homeland', then these travelling creatures of an unspecified past-time find their home in imaginary homes. Their domesticity is localised to the room or garden of occupation, whether in Hong Kong, London or Vancouver (where most of Pamela Leung's family have emigrated).

Many artists of the Chinese diaspora move between places around the world exhibiting their work globally. But this does not make them homeless. In talking about the 'multiple resonances' of displacement, Angelika Bammer states her intention as 'to put the 'place' back into 'displacement'.[4] In contesting Harvey's conceptualisation of space as interaction and place as enclosure, Doreen Massey puts the view that 'place is thought of, not as an inward-looking enclosure but as simply a subset of the interactions which constitute space, a local articulation within the wider whole'.[5]

Leung's sculptural figures enable the space between the personal, geographical and the cultural/historical to merge through the universal domestic space of home and garden. The solid physicality of the work belies the multiple myths which it embodies.

'Allegorical figures' all courtesy Pamela Leung

4. Angelika Bammer, *Displacements: Cultural Identities in Question*, Indiana University Press, Bloomington 1994, ppxiii/xiv.

5. Doreen Massey, 'Double Articulation. A Place in the World', in Angelika Bammer, *op.cit.*, pp110-121.

Figure 1

Figure 2 below
Figure 3 facing
Figures 4 & 5
overleaf

GLOBALISATION AND MINORITISATION: ANG LEE AND THE POLITICS OF FLEXIBILITY

Shu-mei Shih

1. David Harvey, *The Condition of Postmodernity*, Blackwell, Cambridge 1990.

2. Aihwa Ong, 'On the Edges of Empires: flexible citizenship among Chinese in diaspora,' *positions: east asian cultures critique*, 1:3, 1993, pp745-778.

3. Aihwa Ong and Donald Nonini, 'Introduction: Chinese transnationalism as an alternative modernity,' in *Ungrounded Empires: the cultural politics of modern chinese transnationalism*, Ong and Nonini (eds), Routledge, London and New York 1997, pp3-33.

4. Arjun Appadurai, *Modernity at Large: cultural dimensions of globalization*, University of Minnesota Press, Minneapolis 1997, Chapter 1.

5. Mike Featherstone, 'Global Culture: an introduction,' in, *Global Culture: nationalism, globalization and modernity*, Mike Featherstone (ed), Sage, London 1990, pp1-14.

6. Frederick Buell, *National Culture and the New Global System*, John Hopkins University Press, Baltimore and London 1994, pp122, 137, 205, 247.

Much has been said recently by scholars in the social sciences and humanities regarding the emergence of flexible subject positions in our late capitalist world governed by what David Harvey calls the 'flexible regime of accumulation'.[1] We have seen the repetition of the word flexibility in such notions as 'flexible citizenship' that tries to yoke the production of contemporary subjectivities to late capitalist processes.[2] Frequently connected to the notion of flexibility is the widely used metaphor of flow. The mass migration of people, the hyper-compression of space-time brought about by advancements in communications and electronic technologies, the hyperreal, disembodied movement of money and commodities, have all taken on the characteristics of flow, all appearing to move freely and fluidly through space and across boundaries. Affirmative readings of flow have emphasised its liberating and resistant potential against disciplines of the nation-state,[3] charted the emergence of transnational and diasporic public spheres,[4] and identified the potential for new transcultural cosmopolitanisms, of which the notion of a 'third culture' is a good example.[5]

Extending the utopic readings of the consequences of flow to the peripheral communities, or to put it more precisely, out of a competitive motivation to claim deterritorialised subjectivities for the margin, scholars have also rushed to identify Third World postcolonial hybridities as the quintessentially transnational, and some claim, postmodern. Frederick Buell argues that the Third World is 'au courant' today, much further along as a contemporary hybrid cultural formation than the metropolitan centre, since its colonial hybridisation is a precedent for the hybridity engendered by globalisation in the metropolitan centre. The Third World, for Buell, thus constitutes the source of new cosmopolitans.[6] According to this line of argument, due to colonialism and imperialism, which disrupted native systems and forcibly imposed metropolitan cultures, third world cultures can now readily flaunt hybridity, and can serve as examples and models for the centre. In a similar vein, Anthony King maintains that third world colonial cities with their multiracial, multicultural, and multi-continental urban cultures were precursors of today's world cities.[7] Colonialism seems to have accidentally and ironically become a historical benefit that enabled the production of exemplary transnational, de-territorialised, and therefore contemporary and postmodern subjectivities and cultures in third world postcolonial nation-states.

Conversely, the migration of postcolonial people to the metropolitan centres as immigrants has also hybridised metropolitan cultures and turned these centres into world cities. Particularly with the post-1965 immigration of Asians to the United States, older paradigms of assimilation into the US nation-state are said to have become increasingly obsolete, resulting in a de-centring of the core by the periphery.[8] Encompassing all Americans of Asian descent, Lisa Lowe similarly argues that since Asian immigrants and Asian Americans have always been prevented from becoming authentic, assimilated citizens, their unassimilatability actually helped them carve out a space of critical resistance to the US nation-state.[9] Due to the racialised policing of the US nation-state, unassimilatability could be actively imagined and deterritorialised subject positions could be effected against the nation-state. In sum, in the articulations of postcolonial and immigrant agency, the erstwhile sources of oppression - colonialism, imperialism, and state racism - seemed to have now become the basis of constructive and resistant dis-identification with the nation-state, which, in the context of globalism, becomes a marker of some kind of power. In our era of transnationalism, allegiance to the nation-state can no longer be taken for granted, and its absence actually allows for agency and subjectivity for both the immigrant and the minority.

But the potential of transnationalism is both utopic and dystopic. With the exception of Buell, the various scholars mentioned above also evoked its dystopic potential, even though a celebratory tone remains dominant in their works. Ong and Nonini note how transnationalism can work in complicity with oppressive nation-states to further the exploitation of labour;[10] Lowe emphasises the oppression of sweatshop labourers as a symptom of the new international division of labour and flexible production;[11] Appadurai warns how migration exacerbates difference and deterritorialised fundamentalisms can heighten ethnic violence.[12] The fact that none of these dystopic possibilities and actualities received in-depth and detailed analyses in these texts betray to me not so much the limits of their arguments as their felt need to effect a theoretical coup d'état. This coup involves the overthrow of the oppressive view of immigrants and minorities as the always already victimised, and the institution of the non-reactive view of them as transnationally-constituted subjects who need not be dictated by their oppressive nation-states, whether native or adopted. It involves also the enlargement of the frame of reference and discourse from the national to the transnational terrain, in which there are more possibilities of empowerment for the immigrant and the minority.

This coup d'état is, I suspect, also motivated by the desire for theoretical coevalness. The conferring of deterritorialised citizenship, in its proximity to postmodern subjectivity, acquires for the immigrant and the minority the status of being a contemporary with the metropolitan subject, not the embodiment of the perennial 'past' of Western modernity as was the case in older modernisation paradigms. The rhetoric of transnationalism applied to the third world subjects allows them to be coeval with the West in the

7. Anthony King, *Urbanism, Colonialism, and the World-Economy: cultural and spatial foundations of the world urban system*, Routledge, New York 1990, pp39-45.

8. Buell, *op. cit.*, pp196-205.

9. Lisa Lowe, *Immigrant Acts: on Asian American cultural politics*, Duke University Press, Durham 1996, Chapter 1.

10. Aihwa Ong and Donald Nonini, 'Afterword: Toward a Cultural Politics of Diaspora and Transnationalism', in Ong and Nonini, 1997, *op. cit.*, p324.

11. Lowe, *op. cit.*, chapter 7.

12. Appadurai, *op. cit.*, chapter 7.

temporal scheme. But the potential risk in the quest for theoretical coevalness is the flattening of historical and power differences, which may paradoxically repeat the kind of universalism that underpinned modernisation theories. How to avoid falling into the trap of another universalism, maintain historical and geopolitical specificity, and yet argue for coevalness is indeed a profound challenge. We may begin by defining coevalness not as a 'peaceful co-existence' of cultures, but as the 'co-temporality of power structures'.[13] Contemporaneity, then, is marked at every turn and at every moment by the operation of power.

From my vantage point as a multiply displaced immigrant scholar working within both the disciplines of area studies and ethnic studies, I worry about the seeming contiguity constructed among the transnational subject (Asian cosmopolitans), the minority subject (Asian immigrants and Asian Americans), and resistance against the nation-state. I understand the necessity of identifying agency in postcolonial and minority subjects as I have mentioned above, but I wonder whether this necessity should always bear the burden of reactively employing vocabulary and terminologies that are current and therefore appear to confer power. What I worry about is that agencies have not been so much examined through their production and embodied practices as they have been identified or discovered via available terminologies in a theoretical turn towards coevalness. It may be fruitful for us to ask, for instance, what are the material consequences of flexibility? In David Harvey's conception of the flexible regime of accumulation, flexibility empowers the holders of capital not the workers and producers of commodities - it is an extremely uneven practice. In the way late capitalism has moved the Fordist structure of production to the global arena to form an international division of labour, and in the way it sanctions flexible labor processes that deepen the exploitation of labour, flexibility is not only the prerogative of the few but also one that hurts many.[14] Stuart Hall's penetrating statement that 'the global is the self-representation of the dominant particular'captures aptly the extreme unevenness governing the production and circulation of cultures across the globe.[15] Pushing Hall's statement further, I would argue that the so-called postcolonial hybrid cultures that we celebrate today are usually seen by the centre as but corrupted versions or poor cousins of metropolitan cultures and seldom, if ever, seen as precursors. The proliferation of *McDonalds* in Taiwan is a confirmation of metropolitan culture's inevitability, not the occasion to study cultural hybridity as model for American *McDonalds*. Seldom does postcolonial hybridity provide enough of a threat or inspiration so that the metropolitan centre feels the need to emulate. Neither has postcolonial cosmopolitanism ever shared the same exalted place on the pedestal with metropolitan cosmopolitanism. Postcolonial and metropolitan hybridities embody two different histories, are derived from two very different experiences, and can never be equal.[16] When these postcolonial cosmopolitan cultures do travel to the metropole through migration, they are met with

13. Rey Chow, *Primitive Passions: visuality, sexuality, ethnography, and contemporary Chinese cinema*, Columbia University Press, New York 1995, p196.

14. David Harvey, *op. cit.*, chapter 9.

15. Stuart Hall, 'Old and New Identities, Old and New Ethnicities,' in *Culture, Globalization and the World-System: contemporary conditions for the representation of identity*, Anthony King (ed), University of Minnesota Press, Minneapolis 1997, p67.

16. R. Radhakrishnan, *Diasporic Mediations: between home and location*, University of Minnesota Press, Minneapolis 1996, pp159-160; Shu-mei Shih, 'Nationalism and Korean American Women's Writing: Theresa Hak-kyung Cha's Dictee', in, *Speaking the Other Self: American women writers*, Jeanne Campbell Reesman (ed), The University of Georgia Press, Athens and London 1997, pp144-162.

profound ambivalence and efficient policies of containment, which include either naked racism or a multiculturalism that suppresses difference in the name of authenticity or utilises difference for the purpose of commercial gain or absolution of liberal guilt.

It is also imperative to re-examine the metaphor of flow so frequently evoked in studies of globalisation and transnationalism. Flow is always affected by topography - it must follow specific contours, layouts, and routes, which affect its speed, direction, and density. The directions of flow are also always historically marked. The flow of postcolonial people to the West in our historical moment mainly appears as economic migration, while the flow bound for the postcolonial sites appears chiefly in the form of tourism. Furthermore, for the production of meaning, flow is always arrested at a specific conjuncture of time and space, that is, it has its own chronotope, albeit a continuously shifting one depending on context and therefore avoiding fixity and determinism. Like the way narratives achieve meaning through the application of closure as in classical theories of narrative[17] or in Hayden White's useful discussion of how 'proper history' acquires narrativity through closure,[18] flow acquires meaning only at a moment of temporal and spatial arrest within one or more contexts. Like 'reality effects' that are produced by the artful arrangement of everyday objects and the provision of descriptive details in realist narratives,[19] larger meaning-effects that are of crucial social consequence are usually constructed and manipulated by dominant institutions with their governing laws and discourses, and are always permeated by power. Using a different metaphor, Ernest Laclau and Chantal Mouffe call these privileged mechanisms of closure or fixity 'nodal points':

> The impossibility of an ultimate fixity of meaning implies that there have to be partial fixations - otherwise, the very flow of differences would be impossible. Even in order to differ, to subvert meaning, there has to be a meaning. Any discourse is constituted as an attempt to dominate the field of discursivity, to arrest the flow of differences, to construct a centre. We will call the privileged discursive points of this *partial fixation*, nodal points. (Lacan has insisted on these partial fixations through his concept of *points de capiton*, that is, of privileged signifiers that fix the meaning of a signifying chain. This limitation of the productivity of the signifying chain establishes the positions that make predication possible - a discourse incapable of generating any fixity of meaning is the discourse of the psychotic).[20] (emphasis in the original)

For signification to be possible then, meaning has to be temporally and provisionally fixed at nodal points, and the agents who have the privileged access to nodal points are institutions, organisations, and individuals whose wills to power and domination are forcefully expressed through discourses that repress differences, or in our new historical moment, re-contain

17. Frank Kermode, *The Sense of an Ending*, Oxford University Press, New York and Oxford 1967; Marianna Torgovnick, *Closure in the Novel*, Princeton NJ, Princeton University Press 1981, pp3-8.

18. Hayden White, 'The Value of Narrativity in the Representation of Reality,' in *On Narrative*, W.J. T. Mitchell (ed), Chicago University Press, Chicago 1980, p22.

19. Roland Barthes, 'The Reality Effect', in *French Literary Theory Today*, T. Todorov (ed), Cambridge University Press, Cambridge 1982, pp11-17.

20. Ernesto Laclau and Chantal Mouffe, *Hegemony and Socialist Strategy: towards a radical democratic politics*, Verso, London 1985, p112.

differences through channelling them to unthreatening venues. Examples are numerous. The discourse of multiculturalism that so easily slips into a re-containment of differences is a ready example. Another example: the flow of postcolonial migration to the US is governed by the nodal points articulated by the Immigration and Naturalisation Services in terms of priority and desirability clearly favouring immigrant investors over economic and political refugees. Likewise, the virtual flow of images and money, theoretically always in transit and deferred of their consumption - as in Mitsuhiro Yoshimoto's intriguing formula of M-I-M (money-image-money) and I-M-I (image-money-image) in which capital 'accumulates not only through the circulation of money but also through the circulation of images without end', that is, 'without being consumed'[21] - nevertheless accumulates meaning-effects, or in Laclau and Mouffe's language, confront nodal points. The endlessly circulatable image is Stuart Hall's 'dominant particular,' to which the challenge from the margin is deferred and whose vitality is renewed through circulation and re-circulation, whereas money, even in its virtual form, lines the pockets of some and not others.

21. Mitsuhiro Yoshimoto, 'Real Virtuality,' in *Global/Local: cultural production and the transnational imaginary*, Rob Wilson and Wimal Dissanayake (eds), Duke University Press, Durham 1996, p116.

The necessary tension and contradiction between fluidity and fixity can be examined in detail through an analysis of flexible subject positions in the transnational context. In the following analysis of Ang Lee's films as well as their reception in Taiwan and the United States, I will illustrate how the nodal points of meaning assert themselves across the global divide in and through flexible articulations of culture. My reading of the operation of these nodal points in Ang Lee's work will suggest the persistence of meaning-production privileging the nation-state, albeit more than one nation-state. In the juxtaposition and interaction between the two nation-states, Taiwan and the US, we will see how two nodal points - nationalist patriarchy and gendered minoritisation - prevalently discussed in Asian Studies and Asian American Studies respectively, operate within and with flexibility. I briefly explain the ways in which these two nodal points are utilised below.

In postcolonial historiography as well as studies of colonialism in general, native nationalism has been an important discursive construct as the predominant form in which resistance was articulated. Being a gendered discourse, nationalism was also most often seen in its complicity with patriarchy and masculinity, which either repressed internal feminist causes or competed with colonial masculinities. The works of Partha Chatterjee, *Nationalist Thought and the Colonial World* and *The Nation and Its Fragments*,[22] have for the most part defined the terms of the discussion, alongside various works on the relationship between gender and nationalism nicely summarised in Nira Yuval-Davis' *Gender & Nation*.[23] On the one hand, nationalism in the Third World is construed as a reactive cultural and political discourse that has ambivalent implications for third world agency; on the other hand, this nationalism delimits the coherence of its power through the repression of internal dissent and differences, in particular, its female

22. *Nationalist Thought in the Colonial World*, University of Minnesota Press, Minneapolis 1986; *The Nation and Its Fragments*, Princeton University Press, Princeton 1993.

23. *Gender and Nation*, Sage, London 1997.

constituencies.

Gendered minoritisation, on the other hand, is a familiar topic in Chinese American Studies. By 'gendered minoritisation,' I mean that the process of minoritisation - to turn an immigrant who was a national subject into the minority subject in the United States - is often structurally revealed to be different for men and women. Sau-ling Wong, for instance, has argued convincingly that gender becomes ethnicised for Chinese immigrants in the American context, and thereby men and women acquire differential access to acculturation and assimilation: female immigrants seem to acquire 'whiteness' more readily than male immigrants, in that they assimilate more effortlessly and they are more easily accepted by white society.[24] In mainstream representations, Chinese American men are more readily associated with their race than their sex (hence they are racialised and desexed or feminised in stereotypes), and Chinese American women more with their sex than their race (hence they are sexually considered enticing and perceived as less threatening). The gendered minoritisation of Chinese Americans and Chinese immigrants has been a condition noted by many scholars who bemoan the fact that Chinese American women writers have always received much more favorable reception by the mainstream audience and media, while male writers have suffered from neglect and prejudice. Hence the perceived necessity to construct hyper-masculinity by Chinese American male writers such as Frank Chin in order to fight emasculation.[25] In sum, in the operation of these two nodal points - nationalist patriarchy and gendered minoritisation- 'nation-ness' dictates the discourses involved, and the category of the 'national' remains the most important determinant of meaning.

24. Sau-ling Wong, 'Ethnicizing Gender: an exploration of sexuality as sign in chinese immigrant literature,' in *Reading the Literatures of Asian America*, Shirley G. Lim and Amy Ling (eds), Temple University Press, Philadelphia 1992, pp111-129.

25. Frank Chin, 'Come All Ye Asian American Writers of the Real and the Fake,' in *The Big Aiiieeeee*, Frank Chin et al. (eds), Meridian, New York 1991, pp1-92.

FLEXIBILITY AND NODAL POINTS

If the realm of legitimacy for nationalist patriarchy is the third world nation-state, and that for gendered minoritisation is the metropolitan centre, how does someone simultaneously situated in both places operate in terms of these two nodal points? The case of film director Ang Lee offers an interesting example of how someone who is both Taiwanese and Taiwanese American - what I would designate as Taiwanese/American - effects a flexible subject position with seemingly flexible gender and race politics. The crucial question for me in the following is this: what does it mean for someone to be a national subject and a minority subject simultaneously? To a large extent, the emergence of Ang Lee as a flexible subject has much to do with the US's cultural hegemony in Taiwan through decades of propagation of Americanism. Knowledge of American culture became a given for the educated Taiwanese to the extent that a national subject from Taiwan can be readily transformed into a minority subject in the US.

Ang Lee's success as a director began with his small-budget *Father Knows Best* trilogy: *Pushing Hands* (1992), *The Wedding Banquet* (1993) and *Eat, Drink,*

Man, and Woman (1994), all produced by the Central Motion Pictures Corporation in Taiwan. The films were major box office successes in Taiwan, especially *The Wedding Banquet*, which was the most successful film in Taiwan film history. Except for the last one in the trilogy, the films were set in the United States, and all deal with issues of cultural, generational conflict and resolution. There have been many movies with immigrant themes prior to and after Ang Lee, for example Clara Law's *Farewell China* and Sylvia Chang's *Siao Yu*, but none has garnered such widespread appeal and box office success. Lee's success begs the broad question of ideology, cultural, political, and sexual rather then the usual query about style and technique. My ideology critique that follows will reveal the reconstitution of patriarchy and patriarchal gender politics, the evasion of pointed political issues, and the subsumption of homosexuality under heterosexual hegemony as prominent features in the films' appeal to Taiwan audiences.

In *Pushing Hands*, we are told that during the Cultural Revolution in China, the patriarch Mr Chu was caught in a situation where he could shield either his wife or his son from the Red Guards. As a good patriarch should, he chose to protect his son instead of his wife, who later died. The diegesis thereby establishes the patriarch's absolute dedication to his son, Alex, and turns any remotely unfilial act of Alex into a moral defect. Alex now lives in New York and is married to a white woman named Martha. When Mr Chu comes to live with his son, his discomfort, due to cultural conflicts with his daughter-in-law, immediately becomes a question of Alex's unfiliality, contributing to Alex's immense sense of pressure from having to mediate between two cultures. The object of sympathy in the logic of the diegesis is therefore always the displaced father, whose patriarchal and patrilineal orientation is sympathetically portrayed. For instance we see him peeking at his grandson Jeremy's penis and calling it his 'root of life' (*ming'genzi*) that will continue the family line (*chuanzhong jiedai*). Throughout the film as well, his conflict with Martha is mainly attributed to her inability to fulfil her traditional role of a daughter-in-law. The unsympathetic representation of the white wife may explain why the film was the only one in the trilogy not publicly released in the US.[26] The patriarch's pathos from being an immigrant in the United States is time and again compensated by his moral righteousness, buttressed by his selfless dedication to his son, his extraordinary mastery of *taichi*, and his attractiveness, confirmed by a graceful widow from Taiwan who falls in love with him. Any potential tension between China (Mr Chu) and Taiwan (the widow) is glossed over by a rhetoric of shared cultural Chinese-ness, and a sense of pan-Chinese sympathy is established. In an earlier version of the film script, there were clear references to the Tiananmen Massacre, which Ang Lee cut out entirely to avoid political connotations.[27] This is the only film in the trilogy that presents a subject position closest to that of the national subject (albeit under the aegis of a politically suspicious 'Greater China').

In *The Wedding Banquet*, a homosexual son must stage a heterosexual

26. The film was released on video only after the success of Ang Lee's later two films.

27. Jiao Xiongping [Chiao Hsiung-ping], 'The Melancholy of Old Age: Ang Lee's immigrant nostalgia,' in *Cinedossier: Ang Lee*, edited by Taipei Golden Horse International Film Festival Executive Committee, Shibao chubanshe, Taipei 1991, pp28-29.

wedding in order to please his Chinese parents. The Caucasian lover of Wai Tung, Simon, occupies the feminine role of the daughter-in-law in a patriarchal household: he buys appropriate gifts for the parents, cooks, and otherwise takes care of them and knows where Wai Tung places all his belongings as a good housewife should. Simon also suggests that in order to win the approval of his parents, Wai Tung should stage a marriage with Wei Wei, an immigrant woman from China who needs a green card. When first meeting Wai Tung's parents, Simon acts nervously, as befitting the role of a new daughter-in-law according to ethnic Chinese customs. So the tale of love configured here is a triangular one, with two women (Wei Wei and Simon) vying for the love of Wai Tung in a heterosexual, hierarchical relationship. Such manipulation of homosexuality into conforming heterosexuality has led the Hong Kong critic Liu Minyi to conclude that *The Wedding Banquet* did not at all subvert heterosexual hegemony.[28] This entire comic drama, of course, leads to the conclusion that the patriarch is the one who always wins: if the patriarch desires heterosexuality, as he always does, then so be it. Although the patriarch knew about the homosexual relationship between Wai Tung and Simon all along, he pretended that he didn't until the marriage between Wai Tung and Wei Wei was consummated. With Wei Wei pregnant, he got what he wanted, and thereupon let Simon know that he would accept the homosexual relationship. Through what Taiwanese audiences would consider benign duplicity, the patriarchal authority of the father is confirmed and shown to be capable of dealing with unexpected and unconventional challenges with flexibility.

In a similar manner, what passes seemingly as a woman-centred narrative in *Eat, Drink, Man, Woman* in the end restores the woman's place in the kitchen, as many critics have pointed out. The old widowed father emerges as the male hero at the end. Unlike his three daughters whose romantic experiences are filled with much bad air, the father has always had a secret lover of his daughters' age. Renewing his romantic life, youthfulness, and virility, the father marries the young woman to everyone's surprise (particularly the young woman's mother who has had a crush on him). One of the last scenes of the movie shows his newly-wed wife heavily pregnant and sitting in a rocking chair in their modern-style apartment. His romanticism and youthfulness are emphasised at the expense of the old lady who is alternately represented as hysteric and nauseating in her overtures to him, and his mature, reproductive sexuality at the expense of his daughters' confused experiences with love and sex. In the end, the most career-minded of all daughters, airline executive Chia-ch'ien, returns to the kitchen, and with her cooking, restores the sense of taste that her father had previously lost. In all three films, the resolutions return the credit to traditional patriarchy which is now seen as even more capable of containing challenge and difference, while renewing its validity through flexible negotiations and 'well-intentioned' duplicity when necessary. These are tales of 'resuscitated patriarchs,' as Cynthia Lew has so succinctly

28. Liu Minyi, 'Heterosexualized Homosexual Love: Ang Lee's "The Wedding Banquet"', *Cultural Criticism (wenhua pinglun)* 2, Hong Kong 1994, pp137-144.

29. Cynthia Lew, 'To Love, Honor, and Dismay': subverting the feminine in Ang Lee's trilogy of resuscitated patriarchs,' in *Hitting Critical Mass: a journal of Asian-American cultural criticism*, Winter 1995, 3: 1, pp1-60.

30. Mark Chiang, 'Nationalism and Sexuality in Global Economy: presentations of the Chinese diaspora in "The Wedding Banquet"', paper given at UCLA's Asian American Studies Center, April 18, 1996.

31. *Chinese Daily News*, 22/1/1996, A1.

characterised them.[29]

There are other reasons why the films were such a success in Taiwan, and why they have invited such lingering appreciation and loyalty from Taiwan audiences. Ang Lee's success has been perceived as Taiwan's national pride, even though Ang Lee refrains from expressing any Taiwan nativist sentiments about Taiwan's independence from China. His fame is considered a reflection of Taiwan's ascendancy in the global cultural arena. The films consistently garnered international attention, with *The Wedding Banquet* and *Eat, Drink, Man, Woman* earning the coveted Golden Bear Awards for two consecutive years at the Berlin Film Festival. Homosexuality, furthermore, is another marker of advanced civilisation in the West: by watching a film about homosexuality, and a largely recontained representation of homosexuality at that, one is qualified to become a global citizen.[30] The films therefore became 'national' representations, exemplars of Taiwan's successful globalisation that would advance the international image of Taiwan. Upon the nomination of *Eat, Drink, Man, Woman* in the best foreign film category competition at the Academy Awards, the Taiwan government launched a much publicised promotional campaign in 1994, including a banquet for thousands of Hollywood personalities replete with the sumptuous dishes so luxuriously festishised in the film. For the occasion the chefs and ingredients were flown in from Taiwan. Ang Lee himself whetted this nationalist appetite by saying in interviews aimed at Taiwan audiences that he would love to receive an Oscar in order to bring glory to Taiwan. When he was not even nominated for the best director category in 1996 for *Sense and Sensibility*, for which occasion the Chinese American film critic Lu Yan and the Reverend Jesse Jackson separately accused the Awards committee of racism, Ang Lee was extremely apologetic to his Taiwan supporters. He thereafter promised that the next Chinese film he made would win the best foreign film award at both the Golden Globe and Academy Awards, saying that he 'must win this honour for Chinese cinema'.[31] He noted that he desperately wanted the recognition from the international community also in order to please his father. A failure in the college entrance examinations by which one's worth was defined by the parents in Taiwan society, and a househusband without a steady job or prospects for five years before he made *Pushing Hands*, Ang Lee wanted his father's approval as much as he coveted national recognition for Taiwan. So even at the personal, psychological level, we can see the collusion between patriarchy and nationalism.

If the trilogy clearly presents the perspective of a national subject, it also displays prominently a representation of culture from the perspective of a minority subject. There is the stereotypical representation of consumable exotica and multiculturalism: the banquet customs, the exotic food, erotic and exotic women, the *taichi* moves and so on. What is at stake in these soft, multicultural filmic representations, however, is not merely the minoritisation of ethnic culture but also what can be called the minoritisation of Taiwan.

Ang Lee himself seemed cognisant of such an implication. In an interview he gave to *China Times Weekly* in 1993, he said that Taiwanese today are Westernised just like Chinese immigrants in the United States, and both groups want to be Westernised yet maintain Chinese familialism and Confucian ethics. He noted that:

> In the process of Westernisation, Taiwanese people have already done many of the kinds of work that immigrants do. Although their bodies are not in the United States, they are immigrants psychologically ... What is the difference between living in Flushing, New York and Taipei? Except that one knows America better and sees more Americans, there is not much difference.[32]

32. *China Times Weekly* 65, March-April 1993, 75.

According to Ang Lee's perceptive comment, Westernisation necessarily turns Taiwanese at home into psychological immigrants, which has the effect of minoritising Taiwan as it must conform to the cultural hegemony of the United States. Increased global traffic of cultural production and consumption has not only subjected national cultural productions to minority status within the United States in the name of multiculturalism, but also has turned the geopolitical Taiwan into the minority 'region-state' of the United States. It is therefore not surprising to hear certain Taiwanese jestingly call Taiwan the 51st state of the United States, since more than 80 per cent of Taiwanese government personnel are graduates of American universities. A serious and organised version is the *Fifty First Club* (*wu yi julebu*) established on 4 July 1994. Its motto is 'Rooted in Taiwan with America in the Heart' (*lizhu Taiwan xinhuai Meiguo*), promoting what they say was China historian John K. Fairbank's original suggestion to turn Taiwan into the 51st state of the United States. The Club intends to call for a plebiscite on Taiwan's union with the US as its main agenda, and if agreed to by a majority of Taiwan citizens, present the proposal to the U.S. congress.[33]

33. *Chinese Daily News*, 4/7/1996, pB2.

Part of the minoritisation process of Chinese culture as ethnic culture in Ang Lee's films also involves the fetishisation of Chinese food. Ang Lee devoted about five minutes of the opening sequence of the film *Eat, Drink, Man, Woman* to the preparation of exquisite Chinese dishes. After the release of this film, there were two consecutive articles in the New York Times by food writer Suzanne Hamlin about the food in the film, complete with a recipe for 'Stir-Fried Taiwanese Clams,' and suggestions on how to find the dishes cooked in the film in local Chinese restaurants in New York:

> To order any of the dishes seen in *Eat Drink Man Woman*, requests must be made in advance. Shun Lee West, 43 West 65th Street, (212) 595-8895, will prepare any of the 14 dishes from the film, given 12 hours' notice.[34]

34. Suzanne Hamlin, 'Chinese Haute Cuisine: re-creating a film's starring dishes', *The New York Times*, 10/8/1994, C3; Suzanne Hamlin, 'Le Grand Excès Spices Love Poems to Food,' *The New York Times*, 31/7/1994, H9, H20.

This passage captures the uncanny transformation of the foreign into the domestic, the national into the ethnic. Ang Lee seemed to have endorsed this transformation wholeheartedly - he himself went to this very Chinese restaurant in New York, and posed in front of a tableful of luxurious dishes in a photo for the food writer.

The Chinese food fetishism here in multicultural America is also appropriately gendered. It is revealing that while the Taiwan poster for *Eat, Drink, Man, Woman* shows the venerable father in a pensive mood in the foreground (since the emphasis is on resuscitating patriarchy), the American poster only shows a sensual set of the three sisters with a beautiful, delectable dish of Chinese food - literalising the Chinese metaphor that women are so beautiful they are edible (*xiu se ke can*). One reviewer notes: 'the people in this movie are almost as great-looking as the food. One dish after another: the women slender, exquisite, volatile; the men, handsome but languorous, waiting to be awakened by the women'.[35] And another reviewer says: 'The meals presented look mouthwatering, and the daughters are an equally tasty trio'.[36] The transference of food metaphors to the women as tasty, delectable, consumable beauties fits neatly the porno-culinary genre into which the film falls. But more importantly, it registers the eroticisation of the exotic female that appeals to the American audience.

The Father Knows Best trilogy, then, embodies the nationalist appeal to a Taiwan audience through resuscitated patriarchy and its craving for international fame, while embracing the exoticist requirements necessary for the approval of the American audience. Vis-à-vis the Taiwan audience, the films are national constructs, even though the 'national' has to remain ambiguous at times due to the confused designation of the relationship between China and Taiwan; vis-à-vis the American audience, they embody the process of minoritisation of national constructs into a global multiculturalism. On the surface, the national subject and the minority subject positions present contradictions. But upon closer examination, the potential contradictions are cleverly suppressed by Ang Lee. In all three films, the patriarchs are situated outside the US context of gender politics. They are old, they are objects of love of other Asian women, and they pose no potential threat whatsoever to the US-centric notions of masculinity. The only attractive Asian male figure, Wai Tung in *The Wedding Banquet*, is also appropriately emasculated as a gay man, hence non-normative. Curiously, therefore, what brings tears and sighs of relief to the Taiwan audience poses no threat to the voyeuristic enjoyment of the American audience. The national subject and the minority subject are successfully integrated. More than that, there is ample proof that the minoritisation of ethnic Chinese culture through exoticism and eroticism has itself become the desirable way of consumption in Taiwan, confirming Edward Said's fear of the 'dangers and temptations' of employing Orientalist structures of cultural domination by the dominated upon themselves.[37]

From the perspective of bilateral political relations between Taiwan and the US, the two constructs of the national and the minority are closely

35. David Denby, 'Someone's in the Kitchen with Ang Lee,' *New York*, August 29/8/1994, p110.

36. Bruce Williamson, 'Movies,' *Playboy*, 41: 9, September 1994, p26.

37. Edward Said, *Orientalism*, Vintage, New York 1979, p25.

intertwined, as Taiwan's national fate is increasingly at the mercy of the United States. In no uncertain terms, Taiwan - a nation without an internationally recognised state, a non-nation-state nation - functions like a US colony or minority state, with the Taiwan government and the entire populace deeply anxious about every minute change in US rhetoric about Taiwan. President Clinton's public affirmation of the Three No's policy towards Taiwan during his 1998 visit to China: 'We don't support independence for Taiwan, or two Chinas, or one Taiwan, one China, and we don't believe that Taiwan should be a member in any organisation for which statehood is a requirement', is an instance of how Taiwan can be expendable for the enhancement of China-US relations. How else should one name the US power to determine Taiwan's fate but as a new kind of colonialism, just as one struggles to name China's containment policy towards Taiwan? For both China and the US, Taiwan functions as a minority to be contained, and a die to be cast at will at each twist and turn in the relationship between the superpowers.

The minority subject position proves to be inescapable for Ang Lee as he begins to deepen his foray into Hollywood after the success of the trilogy. His directorial work in *Sense and Sensibility* (1995) has been quite uniformly applauded as a masterful feat, since somehow a 'director from Taiwan' was able to capture quintessential Victorian England, prompting Prince Charles to say that he did not know England to be so beautiful until he saw the film at its royal premiere at the Queen's palace. Ang Lee employed numerous strategies of flexibility in rationalising his participation in the making of the movie through a prominent evocation of the trope of translation. While facing the Taiwanese audience, he told them that although he made an English film, since he grew up in Taiwan, he directed the film as if it were a Chinese film.[38] To the Western audience, he recuperated, among other things, age-old notions of Zen-like non-action, Confucian morality, *taichi* (he actually taught Kate Winslet *taichi* during the shooting),[39] 'family values,' Confucian notions of *ren* (benevolence) and *li* (ritual).[40] Ang Lee also provided the following rationale:

> I feel very comfortable in the world of Jane Austen. Because as a society we Chinese are still in transition from a feudal culture and filial piety to the modern world. In many ways, I think the Chinese would understand nineteenth-century England better than the English today because we are still there.[41]

> In my films I've been trying to mix social satire and family drama. I realised that all along I had been trying to do Jane Austen without knowing it. Jane Austen was my destiny. I just had to overcome the cultural barrier.[42]

This rationale is unabashedly teleological regarding the West as the more modern and developed in comparison with Chinese communities. In another

38. *Chinese Daily News*, 22/1/1996, A1.

39. Sarah Kerr, 'Sense and Sensitivity,' *New York* 29: 13, 1/4/1996, pp43-47.

40. Donald Lyons, 'Passionate Precision: Sense and Sensibility,' *Film Comment*, January-February 1996, pp36-41.

41. A. Lin Neumann, 'Cultural Revolution: Taiwan director Ang Lee takes on Jane Austen', *Far Eastern Economic Review*, 28/12/1995 and 4/1/1996, pp97-98.

42. Jack Kroll, 'Jane Austen Does Lunch', *Newsweek*, December 18/12/1995, pp66-68.

43. Sarah Kerr,
'Sense and
Sensibility', *op. cit.*

interview he invoked the foot-binding of Chinese women as a cruel Chinese tradition, with the implication of Western teleological modernity as emancipatory at such moments.[43] Likewise, Western film critics and reviewers also had to rationalise why Ang Lee could do such a superb job with the English material - hence various evocations of universalism that are often used in discourses of tokenisation or model minority: Ang Lee is good at depicting generational relationships, family issues, subtlety of human relations, and he also understands 'the strains and stresses of social ritual extremely well',[44] all of which are universal for all cultures. Retrospectively therefore, one reviewer would call *Eat, Drink, Man, Woman* a result of the combination of 'Austen-like acuity with Chinese food'.[45]

44. See for instance,
New York,18/12/1995,
p51.

45. Janet Maslin, 'In
Mannerly Search of
Marriageable Men',
The New York Times,
13/12/1995, C15.

What gender implications can we draw from this fluid marriage between translatable cultures? What is the gendered position of this translatability? To put it differently, what transpired in the process when a director obsessed with resuscitating patriarchy ends up directing a semi-feminist film that criticises patrilineal property inheritance law in England? The minority gender implications of the film for Ang Lee can be discerned both in the production and reception of the film. Firstly, there is the occlusion of Ang Lee's contribution to this film's success. Although *Sense and Sensibility* received three prominent Film Critics Circle awards, swept up best screenplay and best picture awards at the Golden Globe, and was nominated for seven Oscars at the Academy Awards, neither did Ang Lee receive the Best Director award from the Golden Globe, nor did he even get nominated to the Academy Awards, to the dismay of many. I suggest that this is where flexibility ends: racism disregards Ang Lee's strategic flexibility and universal appeal as irrelevant at crucial moments in the production of meaning. The Academy Awards' exercise of gendered and racialised minoritisation is the moment of arrest, a nodal point, in the process of flow. But the absence of the award for Ang Lee is damaging even besides charges of racism: it suggests that Ang Lee, unlike many of his co-workers who have been nominated for the film (best picture, best screenplay, best actress, best supporting actress, best photography, best fashion design, and best music) was merely one of the screws in the making of the machine, his fortune merely being that the producer (who is the designated recipient of the best picture award) did well in hiring him. He was merely a hired hand, not the original artist who made the film possible as one critic noted: 'Ang Lee was no devotee of Jane Austen, having never read any of her books before he was *hired* to direct Thompson's script'.[46] (My emphasis)

46. Graham Fuller,
'Shtick and
Seduction', *Sight and
Sound*, March 1996,
p22.

Therefore it is not surprising to read the same film critic, Graham Fuller, arguing in the influential *Sight and Sound* that the shaping vision behind the film belongs to Emma Thompson, and that the audience is not to believe the credit shown on the screen that says 'A Film by Ang Lee.' After analysing the absence of the father figure in the film, Fuller notes that the older daughter Elinor assumed the 'male position' in the disenfranchised female Dashwood house and the 'heroic role' in the narrative. Extending this argument, he concludes that Emma Thompson is *Sense and Sensibility*'s auteur, its suffragette and heroic 'male' surrogate'.[47] Thompson herself captures her brushes with Ang Lee during the shooting of the film: she and other actors had different opinions on how certain shots should be done, and Ang Lee was supposedly 'deeply hurt and confused'.[48] Unlike shooting in Taiwan, where 'directors are allowed to do exactly what they want', and Ang Lee was accustomed to be 'followed with chairs, ashtrays, wet towels, tea in constant attendance',[49] the actors in England dared to challenge Ang Lee's despotic directorial style. Thompson observes: 'It's easy to feel a terrible bully with Ang'... 'Hugh has taken to calling him "the Brute"'.[50] Ang Lee began as the consummate combination of Oriental despot and 'self-contained calm';[51] one who was authoritarian and yet taught the crew Eastern rituals (including meditation, *taichi*, and the good luck opening ceremony) - all of typical 'Oriental' import with their stereotypical authoritarianism, exoticism, and spirituality. Towards the end of the shooting, there is an ample sense that Lee is no longer a despot, but is tamed into a democratic director who listens to opinions and buys champagne and Chinese food for his crew. Ang Lee's directorial debut in Hollywood, the making of *Sense and Sensibility* and its reception, involves the taming of the shrew, the feminisation of a despot, and the minoritisation of a national subject.

When *Ice Storm* appeared, again to everyone's acclaim, Ang Lee's credibility as an Asian director making a film about 1970s America was again tested. With the success of *Sense and Sensibility*, all manners of rationales for Ang Lee's superb direction compared his sensibility to that of Austen's favorably, as I illustrated above. But *Ice Storm* was not showered with such rationales of compatibility. At the Cannes Film Festival in 1997, *Ice Storm* was branded as a Hollywood commercial film by French judges and considered an inauthentic representation of America by American critics.[52] When Ang Lee tries to translate not the remote Regency England but 1973 New England in the home-front, and very negatively at that, American film reviewers were predictably not as forthcoming with their praise. It was too close for comfort.

FLEXIBILITY AND TRANSLATABILITY

If Ang Lee embodies the Taiwan national subject at moments when he tries to appeal to the Taiwan audience, he at times prefers the anonymity of the US minority position. When Ang Lee was not nominated for best director for *Sense and Sensibility*, he begged Taiwan media reporters not to make it a 'national' issue or one of national shame at the hands of racism, repeatedly saying that he felt less pressure as an individual, as opposed to being the national representative. When short Jackie Chan was paired with the tall Kareem Abdul Jabar at the Academy awards ceremony, it ignited an angry reaction in the Chinese media accusing Hollywood of 'dwarfing the Chinese' (*aihua Zhongguoren*). Jackie Chan told the media just to leave him alone, and Ang Lee mentioned in an interview that he

47. *Ibid.*, pp20-22.

48. Emma Thompson, *The Sense and Sensibility Screenplay and Diaries*, Newmarket Press, New York 1996, p220.

49. *Ibid.*, p226.

50. *Ibid.*, p232, 228.

51. *Ibid.*, p207.

52. *Chinese Daily News*, 20/5/1997, D6.

understood Chan's reaction completely. Chan is honoured with the label 'Hong Kong National Treasure' and Ang Lee, 'Taiwan National Treasure,' hence their sense of pressure.[53]

53. *Chinese Daily News*, 9/4/1996, D1.

The ease and flexibility with which Lee oscillates between and incorporates these two subject positions begs the question of translation, or rather, translatability. The success of his trilogy owes much to the translation of a national culture (of China or Taiwan) to that of an ethnic culture. This translatability ensured easy assimilation, commodification, and consumption of ethnic Chinese culture by an American suburban audience. It is perhaps ironic to evoke here Walter Benjamin's rather positive assessment of a work's translatability as the mark of its capacity for future flowering in the afterlife as a translation.[54] If for Benjamin translatability secured a longer life for a literary work, translatability of Ang Lee's films commandeers a bigger, transnational market and higher profit. If Benjamin's translatability of the original text presumes a linear temporal relationship between itself and the translation, Ang Lee's translatability is built on flexible encodings that can be readily decoded by both American and Taiwan audiences, so that the reception of both Taiwan and American audiences is contemporary, coeval, and simultaneous. But this contemporaneity encoded by easy translatability is more a symptom of the neocolonial cultural relationship between Taiwan and the United States, by which Taiwan is minoritised. Translatability, in this sense, is a necessary mode for the minoritised to acquire access to and acceptance by the centre. Through flexible negotiations between national and ethnic cultural codes, easy consumption and assimilation is guaranteed. This is what I call 'decipherable localism,' the presentation of local national culture with the anticipation of ready decipherability by the non-local audience.

54. Walter Benjamin, *Illuminations*, by Hannah Arendt (ed), Harry Zohn (trans), Schocken Books, New York 1969, p71.

The reception of both *Sense and Sensibility* and *Ice Storm* furthermore, shows how flexibility and translatability can be denied to Ang Lee and he can be squarely placed within the minority position by US racial politics. Translatability, in other words, is only accepted when it is non-threatening. Unassimilatability becomes a ready excuse to circumscribe Lee's success as a foreigner and a racial Other. Hence there have been lingering doubts about the authenticity of Ang Lee's translation of New England cultural codes from 1973. The co-production and dialectical operation of neocolonial minoritisation of Chinese culture from Taiwan and the racialised, gendered minoritisation of the immigrant cultural producer in the United States have circumscribed and will continue to constrict the production of true contemporaneity, even for someone like Ang Lee who seemed to have crossed many boundaries. Although I agree with Rey Chow that there is power in the superficial and the surface in cinema in their ability to reach a wider audience and thus make a difference, it is important to continue to ask on whose terms and on what terms that reaching is made possible.[55]

55. Chow, *op. cit.*, pp173-202.

If translatability and flexibility that draw from the terms of the dominant can easily be contained for assimilation and consumption, they are also limited forms of empowerment when institutional nodal points arbitrate upon the worth of minority and immigrant cultural production by way of conservative and reactionary criteria. The flexible subject's resistance towards the containment of the nation-states by evoking transnational paradigms of subjectivity is itself dictated by what the nation-states involved will allow of him/her. In examining popular culture, such as popular fiction and cinema, this contractual relationship between the flexible subject and the nation-state becomes especially apparent, as marketability has always been a game of marking the right boundaries or of targeting the right consumers. Marketing specialists have always taken heed of cultural differences traced along national borders. In the constellation of forces operating in the creation and reception of Ang Lee's films, the nodal points of meaning, as I have shown above, seem to continue tracing national boundaries by alternately extolling nationalist patriarchy and gendered minoritisation.

Preliminary versions of this paper were read at Rice University, Harvard University, UCLA, UC Berkeley, the annual meeting of the Association of Asian American Studies (1998), and the annual meeting of the International Association of Philosophy and Literature (1998). I am grateful for oral comments on this paper given by Ketu Katrak, Jinqi Ling, Rob Wilson, and Sau-ling Wong, and for written comments by Allen Chun, Arif Dirlik, Stephanie McDonald, and Harriet Evans, and for encouraging words from Efi Hatzimanolis. I am particularly grateful for the research assistance of Curtis Lin.

ALIENATION, AESTHETIC DISTANCE AND ABSORPTION IN TSAI MINGLIANG'S *VIVE L'AMOUR*

Richard Read

I was drawn to Tsai Mingliang's movie, *Vive L'Amour* (1995), by several of its qualities, not just because it is Taiwanese. When I watched it I didn't know much about Taiwan: I knew a little of its trouble with China and that a number of products sold in the country where I teach (Australia) bear the label 'Made in Taiwan'. I was conscious of having taught Taiwanese students, mainly of architecture, but for a long time I perceived them as 'Asian', not discernibly different from Korean, Malaysian, Singaporean, or Indonesian students. Clearly I hadn't talked with them enough.

The film is set in Taipei, of which I really did know nothing, though I looked it up on the map. After I had determined to write about the film odd things came up about the city of Taipei, perhaps the oddest being in a foreword added in 1987 to the first, 1906, edition of E. P. Evans's *The Criminal Prosecution and Capital Punishment of Animals* which I was reading for a different purpose. The book is a quite self-consciously bizarre compendium of ancient European trials in which misbehaving animals or plagues of locusts or even statues toppling onto hapless bystanders, were brought to trial in early European societies to appease their superstitious compulsion to apportion blame for otherwise unaccountable events. The story quoted in the foreword, however, concerned humans rather than animals, and originated not in medieval Europe but in a London *Evening Standard* newspaper article on Taipei of 1986:

> A jilted woman who attempted suicide by leaping from a twelfth-floor window but landed on and killed a street salesman has been charged with manslaughter. Prosecutors in Taipei, Taiwan, said twenty-one-year-old Ho Yu-Mei was responsible for the death of the food salesman because she failed to make sure that there was no one below when she jumped. Ho had argued that she thought the man would have moved away by the time she hit the ground. She also said she had threatened earlier to sue the salesman because 'he interfered' with her freedom to take her own life. If convicted, Ho could be imprisoned for two years.

1. Nicholas Humphrey foreword, E. P. Evans, *The Criminal Prosecution and Capital Punishment of Animals*, Faber and Faber, London and Boston 1987, pxxvii.

'Who says the mediaeval obsession with responsibility has gone away?' retorts the author of the foreword.[1] An event in contemporary Taipei attracts semi-whimsical attention in London as a 'curiosity' signifying the uncertain rule of reason in a foreign place, yet the author of the foreword also sees the event as typical of practices long abandoned in Europe. The details of the trial are hailed as an alien reminder of forgotten European history, as something noteworthy for being outside or 'before' modern Western culture, but also strangely familiar.

Nothing so bizarre befalls the characters of Tsai Mingliang's *Vive L'Amour*. Their behaviour wouldn't make the headlines anywhere, yet it manifests a low level of strangeness throughout on account of something strained or stilted in all their everyday encounters and pursuits. Perhaps even for viewers in Taipei it is self-estranging, like a film of a foreign place. For me cultural alterity is certainly one of the attractions of the film; it gives more access to the lives of three young people than any tourist could hope - perhaps really would want - to find. 'So this is what Taipei is *really* like', it seems to say. But how can I know? What can a film tell me of a culture of which I am almost wholly ignorant? And as a consequence: how may I have misread it? How specific is a film to its culture, how 'universal', how dependent is it for its meaning on the films of other cultures? (Antonioni's films, for example, which John Stratton referred to on introducing the film to viewers of the Australian Special Broadcasting Service, thus drawing it into their likely range of appreciation.) But perhaps what strikes me in the film are actually reminders of past encounters with 'strangeness'. The permeating strangeness it conveys has less to do with foreignness than newness. Though Taiwanese mores are certainly coursing through the inner processes attributed to the characters, the film erects a visual barrier to an older time by portraying ceaseless economic renovation as intrinsic to the Taipei-Taiwanese condition (a brief glimpse of workers in peasant costume is the only exception). Even the monuments in which the dead are (to be) housed are relentlessly and resolutely new. For those like myself dependent on the subtitles, this has the incidental effect of removing obvious fixation points of 'pure' Taiwanese origin, remnants of a golden age before Japanese and American occupation to satisfy an outsider's craving for ethnic authenticity - what Dipesh Chakrabarty in another context called 'the nightmare of "tradition" that "modernity" creates'.[2]

My essay presents a critical response to *Vive L'Amour* in which I do not refrain from employing social and aesthetic theories that are inevitable to me as an English/Australian art historian. The exercise might therefore serve not only to interrogate the adequacy of my own discipline, but to act as a litmus test of what 'got through' from the makers of the film to a non-Taiwanese who will nevertheless be projecting convictions, experiences and fantasies of his own onto the film.

Before I begin, let me mention another possibility of interpretation. With its worldly, cosmopolitan title, resemblance to other slow-moving international 'classics' and (successful) entry for a Cannes Film Festival prize, it is likely that the film is a product of an intellectual culture quite at home with sophisticated 'Western' theory. This would be consistent with an inheritance of a hundred years or more of colonial and postcolonial

2. Dipesh Chakrabarty, 'Postcoloniality and the Artifice of History: who speaks for "Indian" Pasts?', *Representations*, 37, 1992, p23.

existence. It is therefore possible that the focus of the film upon a deracinated Taipei and its replication of dysfunctional human relationships, that can probably be found wherever industrial capitalism is in the ascendant, is adamantly internationalist in ambition, despite its obdurately local setting and thematics. In a sense the vision of practical economic endeavour in which all the characters are engaged coincides with Western prejudice against the 'worker-ant' mentality of Asian populations, or what Rey Chow has called 'the dichotomy between the "real-political" non-West and the "imaginative" West'. Yet the physical materiality and economic materialism of the film leads the main characters to lend indirect expression to volcanic fantasies that leave one in no doubt about the force of 'Westernized Chinese subjectivity' under rampant capitalist conditions. [3]

3. Rey Chow, *Woman and Chinese Modernity: the politics of reading between West and East*, University of Minnesota Press, Minnesota and Oxford 1991, ppxiii, xi.

A sure attraction of the film is its intelligent study of alienation, as John Stratton remarked in his introduction. It *is* about alienation. The film concerns three young, bored and lonely people caught in the grip of meaningless commercialism by their jobs, and connected with each other only by the tangent of a vacant flat, in which each of them manages to transgress legal, sexual or social mores in some way, but without forming anything but the most tenuous relationships with each other. Despite their shared occupancy of the flat, two of the characters - the woman and the gay male - never meet, though it is symptomatic of the tortured intimacy of the film that the latter hears the others having sex while hiding underneath their bed. Alienation also characterises the public sphere. One of the two male characters works in a funeral tower, which consists of multi-storey corridors of tombs, which replicate a corporate model of society by varying in price and size, being variously vacant or occupied according to the presence or absence of red markers. There are special twin tombs to commemorate the eternally inert togetherness of deceased couples; two such tombs adjacent to each other are considered by a pair of couples who laughingly talk of playing Mah Jong together in air-conditioned perpetuity. (There are several ways to take this; touching that they can talk so easily about enjoying each other's company, trite that they can overcome the reality of death with the unlikely euphemism - commercially suggested? - of continuing their game in such a cheerless place.) And then there are the palatial family cabinets whose red dynastic lights are illuminated only when their doors are opened. At one point the character walks in upon a group of fellow workers in the recreation area of the funeral tower, where they are playing a version of 'Oranges and Lemons', and where, instead of 'Here comes the chopper to chop off your head', as in the traditional English playground game, each player is captured to the chant of 'We all move together'. Perhaps this is the workers' semi-conscious parody of, as well as a release from, the impersonal sentiment and regimented work ethic of their workplace. But is all this alienation? Does the film require our attitude towards it (the situation of the characters and of the wider society) to be uniformly negative?

In one sense, I conjecture, yes. There can be little doubt that the film engages with themes of social alienation familiar in most parts of the world from the intellectual traditions of Marx and Hegel. Except for the funeral parlour worker, who turns out to be gay (we later see him engaging in private exhibitionism in a glamorous dress) and who, inexplicably at this stage of the film, is playing at suicide, the other central characters are shown in the grip of commercial ideology emptying their life of meaning without being aware of it or able to envisage any alternative. In one scene the female estate agent character tries to catch a mosquito before leaving the premises she has been trying to sell. She stalks and pounces with total feline concentration. Her eyes light up with sadistic aggression. At this stage, with no one there to witness it, the mosquito games seem to offer direct insight into a latently ferocious disposition - this violent intensity is equalled later on when, attired in drag, the gay man suddenly tries to purge himself of effeminacy by engaging in an interminable series of auto-punitive push-ups. But as the scene wears on an alternative reading may dawn on us: that we are witnessing a sufficient allegory of her job - uninhibited, aggressive play as the residue of labour. Now for a while she can openly bound around like a hunting cat whereas all day long she has been obliged to entrap her clients covertly, through unstinting politeness, corporate conformity ('May we be prosperous' - ends the ritual phone call to her boss, allowing him to monitor her location) and risk-taking, promotional verve (we have often seen her ignore jaywalking signs, cross roads and clamber up trees and lampposts to wire up adverts for properties on sale). To hunt mosquitos is also revenge, for example on the obese client in the undersized leather jacket, who staggered round a premises ape-like with arms akimbo in a megrim of machismo, entirely ignoring both her and her sales patter. (This was probably just misogyny on his part, but her blandishments were certainly insincere and perhaps his arrogance was defensive compensation for insufficient funds to purchase an apartment of this size.) Once she realises he isn't even going to look at her, her posture and confidence collapse. Defeated, she wearily follows him upstairs, presumably with a standard patter in readiness to ensure he inspects the upper rooms, but also in an attitude of unsolicited sexual submission. For someone like me from Britain where two-story houses are the norm, this seems to show her in the attitude of a little girl following Daddy 'up the wooden hills' to bed. It reverses the power she sought to exert over him. By contrast, in the sexual encounter with the third main character of the film (they meet in an up-market cafeteria where they dress and behave like actors in an advert), she lures her willing victim without a word through a cinema foyer, out into the streets, down empty shopping arcades, obliging him to wait outside a phone booth before leading him to seduction in the vacant flat. There she takes control completely. She undresses him whilst he is prevented from undressing her, though she will strip for him. Her behaviour triggers a series of stereotypical masculine postures from him, though the lead-up to the inevitable event is also punctuated by moments of paralysed embarrassment before she accedes to the momentum of their lust. His subsequent revenge for, or perpetuation of, the event is a solitary act of masturbation with a mass-produced girlie magazine on the bed on which they had earlier clinked groins so impersonally. This girlie magazine, which he later forgets, is returned to him by his male admirer (another trespassing recluse whom he has met by accident in the flat), a strictly futile act of communication since by its heterosexual nature the gift conceals the gay passion that inspires it. Fetishised objects in transaction eloquently communicate failures of communication throughout the film.

But is it all about alienation? The film is beautiful. It loves the clean symmetries of soulless new stairwells, freshly painted and plastered walls, constellations of inset ceiling lights and rows of chairs (sometimes disordered if the lights are not) in restaurants, tiled bathrooms, industrial trim and decorative panels (often under cool blue lights). Clean cars and mopeds, colourful product-rows in at least one mini-market, the raised lips of undulating concrete paths in brand new parks still under construction and fresh with joggers, the crisp purity of stapled advertising material, both sides of letter boxes (to this I shall return), the symmetries of funeral lockers, the smooth, electrical closing of car windows, the sheen on the skin of a shop-purchased water melon, the stiff integration of a key within a lock, the fit of a suit, the drag of an embossed handbag across an industrially carpeted floor, the deformation of a hairstyle by the wind generated by a speeding moped. The links between a Marxist critique of commodity fetishism and a Freudian critique of sexual fetishism are clear enough in these sequences of images, but they also amount to an enjoyable style which rubs off on one's memory of the film, so constituting *its* style. The camera stands statically before these scenes, making rhymes between them, turning them into abstract art works, moving only to frame the movement of a character within memorable symmetries. In the early shopping scene the panning camera suddenly locks into focus on a circular security mirror in which the gay character grooms himself in an attitude of private reverie. It is intimate yet opaque because we don't know he's gay and because of the introspection of the performance.

Within this sequence of impersonally beautiful scenes and objects I found the scene involving exteriors and interiors of letterboxes puzzling. Perhaps the sequence would seem unremarkable to a Taiwanese viewer, but it prompted me to rewind the video several times to determine whether it was a glitch or a subliminal device to jog our attention and thereby radiate richly enigmatic symbolic meaning. Ostensibly the boxes fill out a detail in the working life of the gay funeral worker. We already saw him in another of the city's impersonal coffee bars neatly folding up promotional literature for the tombs he is trying to sell in the modern cemetery. It must therefore be his arm we see posting the leaflets into letterboxes from a moped shortly afterwards. Why might these shots be anomalous in sequence? We see the leaflets disappear into the boxes, but we also look *from inside* the letter boxes, towards the daylight they came from. Rewindings also establish that the exterior and interior views don't match - they must belong to different letterboxes. Perhaps the mismatch is a way of generalising and impartialising the delivery and receipt of unsolicited promotional material, thereby creating analogies of social incarceration between letterboxes, houses and those rows of barely differentiated tombs his junk mail advertises - 'boxes, little boxes all the same', in the words of the American song. Perhaps, in keeping with a theme I am about to pursue, we are given the aesthetic *frisson* of experiencing the inside of an unattended letterbox as if it had a Pharaoh-like consciousness of its own. This would be like one of Edward Hopper's de-animated urban views, full of implied, anonymous, existential presence.

Why would such a state appeal to me, who as a peripatetic academic came out to the bare walls of strange flats in Australia, thinking it an act of self-determination, and realising only afterwards that I accompanied several hundred other refugees from Mrs Thatcher's education cuts in Britain? 'What is a nature strip?', I asked on first arrival, 'a strip of nature?'

But long before I left I liked the accidental sound that punctuates a stifling conversation in a Chekhov play. Perhaps then it's the masculine lure of empty spaces that free one from the intimacy of mother or the epistemophilia that education warrants - luxurious critical distance, too, for the colonising eye. But do I really like the poetry of filmic scenes in which characters are pinned for scrutiny like beautiful butterflies, still fluttering?

Now they seem to invite a cruel, oblique, inert, detached kind of knowing, appreciating. Perhaps its makers employed a strategy whose operation they would want us to enjoy without being aware of its workings. In this instance Pierre Bourdieu's theory of aesthetic distance in *On Distinction* may be more helpful than Marx or Hegel, to understand why the spectacle of suffering in the film may be aesthetically pleasurable for those who do not share it. Bourdieu defines the degree of elevation or detachment in aesthetic experience as related to the viewers' distance from the means of production, from work and the damage work inflicts on private lives.[4] This would account for the fact that at two points in the film living human heads become decorative objects. In one instance the female character falls asleep upon the mattress during working hours as she increasingly fails to cope with the regimen of her employment. The camera plays so long upon her motionless head and hair upon the top half of the screen that the image flattens out into the semblance of an inert brooch in ornamental style. In another instance, the gay funeral worker climbs gently from underneath the bed where he has been eavesdropping on the sexual activity between the other male character and the estate agent. The latter leaves for work leaving her partner asleep, the funeral worker takes her place on the canvas of the bed to gaze in breathless adoration at his would-be lover. The symmetry of their heads, both male, one asleep, the other alert in torment of frustrated longing, is joined and divided by a diagonal strip of negative space that becomes

4. Pierre Bourdieu, *On Distinction: a social critique of the judgement of taste*, Richard Nice (trans), Routledge, London 1986.

entirely pictorial before it is dissolved by the waking man delivering a kiss that fails to wake his sleeping prince. There is something Bourdieuesque about such cool abstract distance imposed upon trivial working lives, something elevated about our 'take' on the characters' futile tracts of intimacy, leisure and *ennui*.

Perhaps the camera, which austerely presents all this to us, aestheticises social hierarchies whose unspoken criteria stealthily operate on our evaluative ranking of the characters. The estate agent and the funeral worker seem more prosperous than the bogus 'international importer' who turns out to be only a street-seller of clothes bought at the airport. The next time she picks him up (almost certainly it will be the last) she flexes her consumer muscle by threatening to buy a dress from a competitor before she returns to him. He has little more than his clothes to make an impression of power and status on her. There is something pathetically stereotyped about the delusions of grandeur he indulges in, but our sympathy is limited by his relative inflexibility: it is unlikely that he will ever grow and change inwardly. He has not developed enough 'power-protected inwardness', as Thomas Mann called it, to make his suffering real either to himself or us. He is closer in the social order of things to the anonymous washerwomen to whom the estate agent testily hands her washing than to the estate agent herself. As a vessel of burgeoning bourgeois sensitivity she attracts our sympathy more readily than he does. Having enough emotional lability to break down is her final claim on our attention.

To pursue this negative reading for a little longer, perhaps it is a kind of aesthetic fetishism which the camera proposes and conveys to the spectator rather than critiques of events in the film. Against it the characters exude the pathos of their unfulfilled lives, but it is we, not they, who are invited to understand the chains of unconscious motivation that develop against these inert settings. As they appear against these clear, hard milieux, we are given to understand what is almost wholly denied to them. Arguably such distance takes on an intensely scopophiliac form in a film that (as Stratton pointed out) is probably more silent than any made since the advent of the talkies. In the representation of a localised culture on the international stage that Cannes potentially provides, are not all the characters of *Vive L'Amour*, regardless of their sex, feminised for an external, scopophiliac, masculinised scrutiny? For whom, then, is the privileged understanding of the characters' unconscious motivation exposed? For the sufferers or for those, whatever cultural space they occupy, whose cultural capital permits them to adopt superior attitudes of detached appreciation? Might the film not conform to Said's metaphor of the stage on which the whole East is confined? On this stage will appear figures whose role it is to represent the larger whole from which they emanate. The Orient seems to be, not an unlimited extension beyond the familiar European world, but rather a closed field, a theatrical stage affixed to Europe.[5]

This is to disregard the strong possibility not only that the ordinary kind

5. Edward Said, *Orientalism*, Vintage Books, New York 1978, p63.

of people characterised in the film may have been amongst its first spectators but also that, as I suggested in my own case, few of us will have entirely escaped the conditions represented here, however far from Taiwan they were encountered.

The critique I have pursued seems now too cynical, knowing and defensive. To stand in judgement thus is to dismiss the film too easily, substituting a sociology of distantiation for an aesthetic whose potential for anti-imperialist understanding has not yet been explored; though I now turn to methodologies developed for the interpretation of privileged Western art to do so. Said's stage metaphor does not apply because *Vive L'Amour* promotes compassionate identification with overlooked and alienated characters through an apparatus of aesthetic detachment that is fundamentally *anti*-theatrical in character.

To argue this I mount a consciously anachronistic analogy between the aesthetic techniques of this film and those of eighteenth-century French painting analysed by Michael Fried in *Absorption and Theatricality: Painting and Beholder in the Age of Diderot* (1980). The artificiality I have pointed to in the camera work and compositional devices of *Vive L'Amour* corresponds to the necessity in eighteenth-century painting to remind the viewer that paintings are constructed to be looked at. Like many of the more contrived moments in our film, 'a painting, it was insisted, had to attract the beholder, to stop him [sic] in front of itself, and to hold him [sic] there in a perfect trance of involvement'. Paradoxically, however, in order to convey the prized expressive quality of *absorption* in the painted figures (a man lost in concentrated attention to a book, for example, or a woman caught in rapturous distraction at the thought of her lover), 'it was only by negating the beholder's presence that this could be achieved: only by establishing the fiction of his [sic] absence or non-existence could his actual placement before and enthrallment by the painting be secured'. Capturing the private behaviour of the characters when they are least aware of being observed is the salient quality of *Vive L'Amour*. Such conversation as takes place between the characters is so stilted and inhibited that it serves only to enhance the expressiveness of their solitary behaviour before the consciously absent viewer. We know they are acting, but we seem to observe them through a two-way mirror. As with the paintings of Chardin or Greuze, the aim is 'to *de-theatricalize beholding* and so make it once again a mode of access to truth and conviction … What is called for is at one and the same time the creation of a new sort of object - the fully realised, *tableau* - and the constitution of a new sort of beholder - a new "subject" - whose innermost nature would consist precisely in the conviction of his [sic] absence from the scene of representation'.[6]

In a precisely similar fashion, our intensely artificial awareness of being invisible to the characters in their private moments is the reason why we can empathise with them so fully in this film. The difference, of course, is that film is capable of producing what is impossible in painting: 'a direct

6. Michael Fried, *Absorption and Theatricality: painting and beholder in the age of Diderot*, University of California Press, Berkeley, Los Angeles and London 1980, p104.

7. D. N. Rodowick, quoted in Nina Zimnik, 'What Will This Century Be Known As? Deleuze and Resistance for Theory', *Film-Philosophy: Electronic Salon*, 30 June 1998, film-philosophy-request@mailbase.ac.uk

image of time as the force of change'. In emulating 'the goal of the so called "direct time-image" . . . to awaken the power of becoming-other, of change, of creating new modes of existence in us',[7] Tsai Mingliang might seek comparison with Satayjit Ray or Bill Douglas, but he need not move outside his own immediate peers to emulate slow-moving masterpieces. Hou Hsiao Hsien's *The Puppetmaster* (1993), no less than the French painting discussed by Fried, is *anti-theatrical* in that the significance of prolonged sequences of ordinary domestic activity emerge slowly, obliquely and without beholder in strict counterpoint with the formalised theatricality of the puppet-shows that form a public version for each successive epoch.

Though the modernist locations of *Vive L'Amour* are antiseptically tradition-less by comparison, they are similarly concerned with majestic impressions of causality and chance. Exerting an unwitnessed coldness and solidity from which emotional familiarity grows quite as much as social alienation, locations stay in the memory as vividly as the characters they frame, collecting the stain of their presence by association. They are metaphors through which we get to know the neighbourhood of the flat a little: the street outside, at least, with the sign of fines for jaywalking. Though the vacant flat itself is easily confused with many others managed by the estate agent, it is almost the main player in the film. As a place of clandestine refuge and love-making it begins to take on a life of its own. We get to know its geography and structure a little. All three characters stroke the bare mattress in unrequited longing for one of the other characters. Making repeated appearances above their heads, the golden knot that ties the undulating metal fronds of the bed-head together, gains symbolic value analogous to the epigram of an E. M. Forster novel: 'Only connect' - though it's essential to the style as well as content of the film that characters never really do connect.

So far I have pointed to clean and orderly surfaces against which the public face and private suffering of the characters are posed for clinical scrutiny by the detached and leisurely filmic eye. During the course of the film these lose their precedence to metaphors more expressive of internal human chaos. They are conveyed by 'transitional objects', in R. W. Winnicott's psychoanalytic terms, whose less external character dramatises the characters' inner lives. Cigarettes, perhaps, are more eloquent than actors in this respect. As the addictive cost of machine-like efficiency in the work-place, they carry an obvious social point, but it is through vicarious sensations of inhaled fire that cigarettes betray the inner stress of excessively unhappy and compelled behaviour. Blood dripping on the pen-knife from the hand that dropped it on the bathroom tiles is the obvious *organic* metaphor of distress. Less directly, the frustrated tooting of a blocked car, smoking as a substitute for speech when intimacy is called for, the ringing of a phone which continues to ring after several others have been lifted, the wrangling hubbub of the washerwomen and the rough vein of grout that distinguishes the humbler tiles of the estate agent's bathroom from the luxury tiles in the flat she manages, all contribute to this theme. Bathrooms are places of unsatisfied oceanic yearning where characters fail to return to the womb. For instance, the estate agent first lies smoking in the bath next to the ill-laid cement. Then she tries to 'see' herself in the mirror in a space wiped clear of steam, which soon reforms again. As substitutes for human intimacy and envelopment the funeral worker masturbates but also drinks large quantities of bottled water and immerses himself in the turbulent waters of the flat's jacuzzi - though self-contact of this kind strangely merges with further suicidal fantasies. The watermelon he purchased in the shop (so *that's* what he was doing there) is the most explicit of these transitional objects. What does it mean to kiss the watermelon surface and then, with the knife that was previously used to cut his wrist, gouge into it a trio of holes to first make a face and then, through an act of digital or phallic penetration, a ten-pin bowling ball that in a practised, public style he proceeds to roll along a floor into a wall where it breaks up into pieces that are used to wipe his face in post-coital relaxation? It is the act of someone crazed with loneliness and boredom acting out the sexually 'deviant' and companionable phases of an imaginary date for which he craves normality of recognition.

Metaphors of chaos achieve a civic dimension in the final scene. The estate agent has suddenly abandoned her obsessive work-routine to walk in a central city park that is still under construction. For some considerable time before she enters the frame we look at a yellow helium balloon tethered above rough earthworks in the foreground. Perhaps it has conventional meaning apart from its psychological effects of hovering suspense and potential upheaval. The camera then collects her impassive progress through the park which is deserted apart from occasional joggers and labourers in redundantly fluorescent work clothes. We lose sight of her for a while as the camera pans synoptically with ambient sound across the circulating traffic, sparse trees and distant public buildings. When the camera has swung right round for her to re-enter the frame she does so as a personification of the city - all the more so for remaining lost and frail. We then follow her along an undulating concrete path whose lip dramatically surmounts the crest of an artificially contoured landscape. We cut to a frontal close-up of her walking onwards nowhere, clutching her fur coat to herself against inward and outward cold. Finally she sits, four purple benches behind a retired old man who reads a newspaper in an attitude of impassive uselessness. The dry, public information he absorbs will contrast starkly with the subjective impact she is about to make on us - even as a symbol of the city. She begins to cry, and we cut to a close-up of her face that lasts five full minutes. The sobs break out, culminate, exhaust themselves, then in pensive exhaustion she resumes sad normality with flicks of her hair, a further cigarette and a vacant stare. There is nothing different to return to. No solutions have been found. All this time we might wonder about the old man and her decision to sit behind him. Because we hear her cry we suppose he hears her too, but he shows no sign of doing so. What father might he represent for her? Why was there no likelihood or danger of him turning to console her? What more distant chain of events in childhood beyond those we have witnessed brought her to this pass? Against the coldness of its beautiful objectifications, the film's generosity lies in the time it accords to the slow development of such questions. It is a film which 'opens itself up to "penetration" by [other cultures] ... It "remembers", and encourages the viewer to "remember", what might best be characterized as "other people's memories". In the process, it ... engages the Western viewer in an exemplary self-estrangement' that may turn a mental camera on ourselves.[8] All of the distances I have discussed in the film - technical, cultural, social, psychological - leading up to the extreme emotional confrontation of this close-up are obliterated by it; voyeurism cannot be maintained against the onslaught of feeling. In the numbness that ensues the estate agent's partial return to equanimity, the unbridgeable gap presented by the two-way mirror of the camera lens begins to open again, but something has been exchanged with the audience. She is there as an allegory of her city, rescuing the transcience of things.[9] Under the aegis of this peculiarly public and private image we are given the obscurity of our own lives in the darkness of the auditorium. This darkness behind the faces on both sides of the screen makes us relinquish any sense of viewpoint on the film as if it were, in Said's phrase, a stage affixed to Europe on which the East could be confined. No longer a stage of shallow depth on which things simply appear, her elusiveness incorporates our own.

I am grateful to Stephanie Donald for drawing to my attention Tsai Minglian's Vive L'Amour *and Hou Hsiao Hsien's* The Puppetmaster.

8. Kaja Silverman on Chris Marker's *Sans Soleil* (1982) in *The Threshold of the Visible World*, Routledge, New York 1996, p186. Silverman's point about self-estrangement compares with Michael Fried's observation in *Absorption and Theatricality, op. cit.,* p104n.

9. For an account of allegory in these terms see Walter Benjamin, *The Origin of German Tragic Drama*, John Osborne (trans), Verso, London 1977, p23.

FASHIONING IDENTITIES, CONSUMING PASSIONS: PUBLIC IMAGES OF WOMEN IN CHINA

Harriet Evans

Images of women are probably the most prominent feature of public discourses of gender in contemporary China. They are also the most prominent feature of public visual spaces in China's cities. Displayed on the front covers of women's magazines or in TV ads, in street billboards and shop windows, beautiful, slender, and prosperous young women appeal to the desires and fantasies of their observers. Often removed from significant social contexts - except for those symbolically invoked through their dress and make-up - their spatial domination of the frame gives them extraordinary power to beckon to the observer, to invite attention, to provoke, and even to seduce. Image after image of beautiful young women smiles out languorously at desiring spectators, promising romantic fulfilment. They show off fine jewellery, silks and sunglasses, as they lounge in luxuriously upholstered sofas, basking in wealth and glamour. With enhanced bodily shapes, they float through fields of flowers in soft-flowing dresses and pastel colours. They also proudly show off their modern domestic appliances. The beautiful woman appears as the flirtatious coquette, the satisfied sexual partner and the contented home-maker. Feminine beauty, romance and consumer capacity become visually enmeshed in a discourse of desire.

The public image of the 'mainland' woman does not, of course, lend itself to unitary meanings. As various writers have argued, including Shih Shu-mei and Louisa Schein, the image of the 'mainland sister' may signify very different things across local and global audiences.[1] Between Taiwanese and Hong Kong, Han and Miao spectators, the meanings ascribed to the face and body of the young, urban, mainland beauty are multiple, and replete with political significance. Whiteness, whitening creams and their contribution to the fair skin of the contemporary beauty are also susceptible to different meanings. To the Western spectator, they frequently signify an attempt to approximate Western standards of beauty, while to a Chinese audience they signify the smooth skin conventionally associated with elite (because not of the rural/labouring classes) notions of female beauty.[2]

It is a truism to state that public images of women have changed enormously since the Maoist period, that not so long ago these images were completely excluded from public life in China. Yet a brief description of their contrast with dominant images of the Maoist decades is necessary to the argument that follows. With a few exceptions, between the 1950s and the late 1970s the official discourse of gender equality demanded almost complete public eradication of conventional signs of female eroticism. Often

1. Shu-mei Shih, 'Gender and a New Geopolitics of Desire: The Seduction of Mainland Women in Taiwan and Hong Kong', *SIGNS*, Vol. 23, no.2, 1998, pp287-319; Louisa Schein, 'The Consumption of Color and the Politics of White Skin in Post-Mao China', *Social Text*, 41, 1994, pp141-164.

2. Perry Johansson, 'White Skin, Large breasts: Chinese Beauty Product Advertising as Cultural Discourse', *China Information*, Vol. XIII, Nos. 2/3 Autumn/Winter 1998-1999, pp59-84.

positioned in contexts where social production was the dominant theme, women appeared as steelworkers, parachutists and cotton-workers, militant Red Guards, as well as mothers, teachers and nurses. With shining eyes gazing into the distance, strong hands and robust bodies, they symbolised energy, hard work and passionate commitment to a revolutionary ideal. 'External beauty' became a metaphor for sexual licentiousness and ideological impurity. 'Internal beauty' illuminated the simple appearance of the true revolutionary. That clothing should be gender-neutral - the drab greys, greens and blues of the Mao suit - became an automatic corollary of the rhetoric of gender equality.

Between the early 1950s and the late 1990s, images of women have thus moved between what appear to be two poles of gender meaning, roughly corresponding with the differential discursive positioning of women indicated by the different terms for 'woman': *funü* - the 'woman' of the Maoist state - and *nüxing* or *nüren* - the 'woman' of the post-Maoist era.[3] It is less often noted, however, that between these poles have been many variations. Indeed, a detailed semiotic analysis of visual images of women since the early 1950s would give fascinating insights into the changing discursive meanings of womanhood and femininity in the People's Republic. For a brief moment during the mid-1950s, images of women displayed flowered dresses and curled hair. In the violent Red Guard period of the Cultural Revolution (1966-69), women were portrayed as strong, determined revolutionary successors to their great leader, depicted in firm, aggressive lines, with little apparent attention to gender difference in bodily shape. Appearance in these images was banished as a standard of women's social value; sexuality and eroticism were not part of the vocabulary of revolutionary gender relations. By the early 1970s, the use of more intense and diverse colours produced women who despite the so-called 'socialist androgyny'' of the period, were not infrequently quite conventionally feminine in appearance: red or pink jackets and shirts, flowered collars peeping out from under the worker's 'uniform' were clear visual clues giving the lie to rhetoric of gender sameness.[4]

Recent years have seen increasing numbers of publications in English and Chinese concerning the cultural representations of gender identities in Chinese societies. A particular focus of this interest has been on representations of femininity in print culture and the mass media. Set within the dual contexts of China's enmeshment in global capitalism, and the attention cultural studies gives to local receptions of the global spread of images and cultural practices, constructions of the female body and sexuality, of fashion and clothing as markers of gendered, social and national meaning are prominent themes of discussion in the popular and academic writings.[5] Much of the discussion has been framed with reference to perceived influences of 'Westernisation' in shaping public images produced by a market economy. Indeed, official and public discourse often conflates modern consumer culture, as manifested in China's cities, with Western values and

3. Tani Barlow, 'Theorizing Women: Funü, Guojia, Jiating', Angela Zito & Tani Barlow (eds), *Body, Subject and Power in China,*, University of Chicago Press, Chicago 1994, pp253-289.

4. Harriet Evans, '"Comrade Sisters": Gendered Bodies and Spaces', in Harriet Evans & Stephanie Donald (eds), *Picturing Power in the People's Republic of China; Posters of the Cultural Revolution*, Rowman and Littlefield, Lanham, Maryland 1999, pp63-78.

5. For example, see the recent special issue of *China Information* on 'The Body in Contemporary China', Vol. XIII, nos 2/3, Autumn/ Winter 1998-1999.

lifestyles. Popular commentators commonly equate consumerism and advertising with Western, individualistic and sometimes hedonistic lifestyles. Much also has been shaped with reference to women's liberatory desires for diverse possibilities of self-expression and self-identification in response to the bodily and sartorial constraints of the Maoist decades. Yet other aspects of this interest have examined the contribution of consumer oriented cultural representations of femininity to the emergence of a new 'public sphere' outside or removed from the direct intervention of 'state' influences, and crossing boundaries between different Chinese societies.[6]

The work of a number of feminist scholars in this field has been of central significance - indeed I would argue for modern and contemporary Chinese studies as a whole - in examining the discursive practices through which representations of womanhood and femininity have been appropriated in the service of a national and masculinist agenda.[7] In insisting on the mediations of historical moment, region and locality, ethnicity, generation and politics in shaping women's lives and experiences, and the ways in which we approach and analyse them, they have sealed the fate of the conventional narratives about the victimised and forever oppressed Chinese woman. Whether in analyses of the historical and political mediations of language, the rewritings of key moments in China's modern history, or in examining the inscription of gender into ethnic boundaries, they have made the concept of difference - now long embedded in feminist theory - indispensable to our understanding of gender hierarchies in China, between and within genders.

However, many discussions in English and Chinese about contemporary representations of femininity continue to draw on assumptions which undercut the attention to difference. In particular, two key assumptions stand out. The first is that the radical changes in public discourses about women and femininity since the 1980s signify a total rupture with those of the Maoist decades. According to this argument, the marketisation of the economy, the changing ideological priorities of a party-state, and the congruence of state interests with those of global consumer culture have banished former meanings of gender from public discourses. Embedded in this assumption is another; that there is some kind of essential contrast between the constructions of female gender of the Maoist period and those of the reform period. The immense diversity in women's identifications is somehow reduced to a stark contrast between the two generic types of *funü* and *nüxing*.

I want to offer a few reflections on these issues. I do not, of course, want to make an argument for unproblematic continuities between different political and historical moments, any more than I want to deny the impact on China's economy and society of its decision to 'open its door' to global capitalism. However, I want to make some suggestions which problematise the polarised assumptions about gender discourses in China. I want to argue that, to use Nancy Fraser's terms, there is a gender discourse of mis-recognition that runs through the multiple readings of contemporary images

6. Shu-mei Shih, *op. cit.*; see also a forthcoming volume edited by Mayfair Yang, *Spaces of Their Own: Women's Public Sphere in Transnational China*, University of Minnesota Press, Minneapolis 1999.

7. For example, Susan Brownell, 'The Body and the Beautiful in Chinese Nationalism: Sportswomen and Fashion Models in the Reform Era', *China Information*, Vol. XIII, nos 2/3, Autumn/Winter 1998-1999, pp36-58; Yue Meng, 'Female Images and National Myth', in Tani Barlow (ed) *Gender Politics in Modern China*, Duke University Press, Durham 1993, pp118-136; Gail Hershatter, *Dangerous Pleasures: Prostitution and Modernity in Twentieth Century Shanghai*, University of California Press, Berkeley/Los Angeles/London 1997.

8. Nancy Fraser,
'Social Justice in the
Age of Identity
Politics:
Redistribution,
Recognition, and
Participation', in
Grethe B. Peterson
(ed), *The Tanner
Lectures on Human
Values*, Vol.
19, University of
Utah Press, 1998,
pp1-67.

9. Arjun Appadurai,
'Disjuncture and
Difference in the
Global Cultural
Economy', *Public
Culture*, 5, no.3,
1990, pp1-24.

of Chinese femininity.[8] I also want to reflect on the question of whether or not, between local and global contexts, and between different periods, it is possible to identify hegemonic meanings that cut through the contrasts and tensions between different readings of image, through what Appadurai called the 'repatriation' of instruments of cultural globalisation as heterogeneous dialogues between localities.[9] Is there a dominant politics of gender that emerges from the possible multiple readings of the fashionable feminine body? Do the contestations within and between local discourses of gender invalidate claims to hegemonic productions of meaning across them? How might these relate to the politics of gender inscribed in dominant discourses during the pre-reform decades? What kinds of social and gendered exclusions, marginalisations and privileges are constructed through contemporary images? At a time when discussion about globalisation often seems to 'level' images and representations to a relativistic exchange of equal values, does it make any sense to attempt to identify political issues at stake in their dissemination?

My concern with these issues has developed from the attention I have given in recent years to discursive (written and visual) representations of gender and sexuality in China. This work has obliged me, in my self-positioning as a feminist, to analyse the subjective elements at play in the way I make decisions about the gendered meanings of visual images. It has urged on me a demand that I critically revisit my understandings of the texts and images I have been working with. Now is a moment in China's social transformation when ample evidence suggests an unprecedented expansion of spaces and positions for individual and group experimentation with new gender and sexual identities. At the level of public debate and organisation as well as the individual subject, marketisation of the economy has given Chinese women access to exploring notions of self-identity that potentially signify fundamental shifts in social understandings of gender. At the same time, a series of practices and policies, including those designed to protect 'women's rights', seem to consolidate divisions between differently positioned women. Sons are still preferred to daughters and the feminisation of agriculture and exploitation of cheap unskilled female migrant labour mark women as unequal citizens, denied material redistribution and cultural recognition in a way that could classify them as 'equal' to men. Between these poles of empowerment and exclusion multiple meanings of gender are produced and negotiated, within and between local contexts and dominant media discourses. Given the possible, maybe limitless, range of readings, is it possible to ascribe transcendent meanings to any particular set of images, produced within local social and cultural contexts?

FASHION AND CONSUMPTION IN WOMEN'S MAGAZINES

'No beauties were allowed twenty years ago. Today's beautiful women should not thank themselves for their beauty, but the times ... All women want to be beautiful' and 'all women are consumers'.[10] These comments strikingly encapsulate popular narratives about women's natural femininity and desire for beauty. The 'gender neutrality' of the Mao decades precluded overt expressions of femininity and bodily beauty. Maoism is widely presented as a simple signifier of bodily constraint and containment, and of puritan morality. By contrast, the 'times' of 'Western modernisation' appear as the motor-driving release from those constraints. The 'modern woman's choice' (*xiandai nüxing de xuanze*) shares nothing with the uniform and politically correct apparel of their mothers' generation.[11] The historical rupture between the Mao and post-Mao periods in practices of bodily adornment indicated in these comments reinforces a construction of feminine desire and beauty as both natural and as historically specific to the reform period.

Discussions about fashion in contemporary women's magazines in China - as for example in the article noted above about the appropriate apparel for the 'modern woman' of different ages - do not refer only or specifically to the sartorial and cosmetic apparatus of looking fashionable. They prevalently present discussion about fashion and its consumption as an unproblematic aspect of the desire to appear and be beautiful. A recent article expressed this slippage between the two notions very clearly in stating that 'Women all hope to be beautiful, but there are many misconceptions about beauty. Should you wear lots of makeup and adorn yourself with finery? or should you remain simple, and follow nature?' It was also clearly at play in the rhetoric surrounding China's first Supermodel Contest, held in 1991, about which Susan Brownell has recently written. In a context in which the Women's Federation had unequivocally announced its opposition to beauty contests, on the grounds that they degraded women, public commentators took pains to emphasise that the Supermodel contest was not a beauty contest, but was an arena where contestants showed off fashions. However, contestants were judged on their walk, movements, agility, co-ordination, level of ease, aesthetic appeal, and harmony of appearance.[12] While the colour and shape of the contestants' swimsuits and evening gowns might, of course, have contributed to the panels' assessment of these categories, the sartorial details were not the object of the judges' gaze.

Borrowing from Barthes and Baudrillard, fashion refers to an encoding of signs which subject the body to different disciplines of meaning. In the examples I have referred to above, these focus on the shaping, forming or moulding of gender identities in particular ways associated with a particular historical period. The gendered identities that are fashioned, in these articles, have a corporeal form which is specifically identified with the possibilities of a consumer economy. Designer clothes and luxury cosmetics - the material components of fashion - 'fashion' natural gender identities in a specific historical moment. Fashion also connotes the desire to appear and be beautiful. This conflation of desire, fashion and feminine beauty in discussions about fashion is present in a vast range of popular articles, from advice about makeup and how to apply different cosmetic techniques, diets

10. 'Shenmo yang de nüren zui mei?' (What kind of woman is the most beautiful?) *Hunyin yu Jiating* (*Marriage and Family*), 6, 98, pp24-26; 'Nüren de goumai yu' (Women's consumer desires), *Nüxing yuekan* (*Women's Monthly*), 3, 1998, p37.

11. Nüren meirong: cong 20 dao 60' (Makeup for women between 20 and 60), *Nüxing yuekan*, (*Women's Monthly*), 7, 1998.

12. Susan Brownell, *op. cit.*

conducive to maintaining beautiful skin and hair, to women's philosophical concerns about beauty. Fashion, femininity, sensuality and desire are collapsed together in a single composite image of the 'modern woman'.

There are many indications from magazines of the 1950s and the early 1960s (before the only women's journal, *Zhongguo funü*, was shut down in the Cultural Revolution) which demonstrate that the assumption of gendered interests in appearance and beauty has been a recurring theme through dominant discourses of gender in the People's Republic of China (and of course before). Inverse references to feminine interest in clothes was almost routine in framing descriptions of immoral and ideologically unsound young women. Women who 'wasted time' on their appearance, or who spent money on fashionable clothes, were represented as self-seeking temptresses.[13] Erotic beauty and fashionable clothes served as thin disguises for evil intentions and even criminal behaviour. Indeed, female eroticism and feminine beauty were widely used as metaphors for moral and ideological degeneration. Women described as the 'third party' in divorce cases, or as examples of the fate that immoral conduct could visit upon them, often appeared in contexts that drew attention to high-heeled shoes, tight skirts, and sleek hair.[14] Later on, in visual images of the early and mid-1970s, a range of visual cues reinforced the naturalisation of women's interest in 'external appearance', whether these appeared in the form of colourful hair ribbons, patterned jackets, or even shapely bodies.

The conflation of fashion/femininity/desire for beauty and consumption which is so central to the displays of womanhood in contemporary China is also not new in the reform period. It was certainly banished from affirmative representation by the dominant discourse of the Maoist years. The gender discourse of the Maoist period was in some ways one of postcolonial transformation of the former gendered subaltern - the woman subjected to patriarchal and colonial authority (either the subservient wife, married by arrangement, or the prostitute desired for her oriental exoticism) - into full and equal recognition as a person. It made a deliberate and conscious attack on the privileged position and ideologies of the former élite - colonial, bourgeois, and feudal - which sought to exclude women from full public recognition. Its challenge to 'feudal' notions of beauty, and the material apparel and consumer desires that were associated with it, was an important component of its class-based struggle to liberate the subaltern subject. Nevertheless, recurring gender associations and references suggest other meanings to this process. That beauty appeared as a sign of political and moral impurity in women, and not in men, was a means of naturalising such interest as an exclusively female characteristic. (By contrast, descriptions of men's political failings, of the same period, referred to social and financial ambition). The prohibition of feminine beauty was a negative reassertion of a natural trait of femaleness. Without political purity - a quality that had to be acquired - a woman was naturally drawn into the directions established by beauty. The rhetoric of women's liberation included a discursive denial

13. Feng Yu, 'Jintian de funü fuzhuang wenti' (The question of women's dress today), *Zhongguo funü* (*Women of China*), 3, 1955, pp31-32.

14. Harriet Evans, *Women and Sexuality in China: Dominant Discourses since 1949*, Polity Press, Cambridge 1997, pp134-143, 195-202.

of women's ability to function as public citizens - to give them full political and cultural recognition - outside the constraints and the prohibitions of a patriarchal version of socialism.

An abrupt 'reversal' in sartorial politics revealed the depth of this assumption in more affirmative light, when a clothes reform campaign was launched in the mid-1950s, at a time of rising urban unemployment. Aimed at boosting the self-confidence of the urban housewife through encouraging gender distinctions in dress, the barely disguised agenda of the campaign was to encourage women to withdraw from the urban labour force and relieve pressure on the state. Symbolic suggestions of femininity in the form of dress patterns and instructions about how to refashion old clothes started appearing in the printed media while articles in the women's journal, *Zhongguo funü* (*Women of China*) urged women to discard the view that being interested in appearance was 'bourgeois'. Alongside other narratives about women's natural identification with the domestic sphere, this 'refeminisation' of female appearance was premised on the same kind of naturalised equation between femaleness, beauty and the desire for it that is now so prominent in contemporary discourses.

With the end of Maoist politics, and the transition to a market-oriented development strategy in the early 1980s, the supposedly gender-neutral shades and lines to the visual embodiment of the female were replaced initially by soft, wafting pastel shades, and increasingly by images of the young, cosmetically enhanced coquette. Interestingly one of the first 'really' feminine images of a woman I have come across in this period was of Yang Kaihui, Mao Zedong's second wife, whose soft features, gently smiling face, and bodily grace as she stood with Mao Zedong by the banks of the Yangzi River carried political as well as gender meanings (to further dishonour Jiang Qing, Mao Zedong's last and estranged wife who was one of the members of the infamous 'Gang of Four'). The first women's fashion magazine, *Xiandai fuzhuang*, (*Modern Fashion*) started publication in 1980, and articles about feminine beauty, fashions, cosmetics and so on rapidly made their way into women's magazines and TV advertising. By about 1986, images of young urban women, in domestic and occasionally professional contexts, replete with their tailored jackets, snug sportswear, their luxury cosmetics and confident gaze, were *de rigueur* on the covers of the women's press. The innocent romantic was also prominent, with her languorous looks and girlish shyness offset by floral landscapes. The range of women's bodies was also much greater. Though it could be argued that, by contrast with current images in both Chinese and Western magazines, many of these were simplistic and aesthetically unappealing, their departure from previous images was clear. The inscription in the 1980s body of the rewards for conforming to the principle of consumer-oriented reform symbolically echoed the emergence of new structures of economic and social hierarchy in Chinese society.

The affirmative construction of the feminine consumer inscribed in these

15. Baudrillard, *L'Echange symbolique et la Mort*, Gallimard, Paris,1976, pp132-151.

and more recent images reminds us of Baudrillard's argument that fashion sexualises culture.[15] While space does not permit me to debate this argument here, this 'effect' of fashion may - at least in part - explain the amnesia which characterises contemporary reflections on the 'fashions' of the Maoist decades. The 1980s rupture with the Maoist period was made through the affirmative conflation of femininity and consumption, through the emblematic use of the fashioned, feminine body which suddenly, and pervasively sexualised public visual culture.

Fashion, in its modern capitalist guise, has always been linked with femaleness and femininity (though not to the exclusion of fashionable images of masculinity). This, in Jennifer Craik's terms, is in large part the effect of modern capitalism's links between men and production, and between women and consumption.[16] As I have argued above, the links, implicit as well as explicit, between femininity and consumption have been a constant feature of discourses of gender in China since the early 1950s. I would also argue though that the continuities in the naturalisation of female interest in beauty - in its conflation with fashion and consumption- are significant in explaining the rapid saturation of the public media with the erotic female after constraints were lifted in the early 1980s. All these discursive moves around the female body and female gender, through Maoist and post-Maoist periods, could be seen in hindsight as over-determined (in patriarchal terms) responses within the political and media codes available.

16. Jennifer Craik, *The Face of Fashion: Cultural Studies in Fashion*, Routledge, London and New York 1994, p46

DIFFERENCE, PLACE AND TIME IN READING CONTEMPORARY FEMININITY

The publicly displayed woman of the reform period may be read in different ways, depending on moment of production, place, and cultural and gendered self-identification of the 'reader' amongst other factors. But these multiple readings may all be understood as components of a dominant signifier of modernity. 'She' - in her dominant public image - comes together as a composite face, described through all her variations by association with urban culture, education, material success and satisfaction. Through reference to her own achievements, described either visually or in written form, she is invariably denied centre-stage, appearing on the inside pages of women's magazines. The public image of woman is almost never, if ever, rural (unless - rarely in the women's press - it is to boast the achievements of the successful rural entrepreneur, the rural woman in process of acquiring urban-associated skills). The rural woman is not only the feminised 'other' to the masculine creators of market-oriented reform; within the category of her own gender, she is the marginalised, the victimised, the uncultured, unless she approximates urban-centred standards. The multiple possibilities of femininity and femaleness contained within the dominant image are reduced to a more or less unitary representation.

At the risk of stating the obvious, one of the invaluable contributions made by feminist, post-structuralist and post-modernist approaches to cultural representations is their collective insistence on the significance of difference, both in terms of self-identification and in the categories of identification used by others. They reject claims to dominant/'grand' narratives of meaning, and insist on de-centring the subject away from the conventional positions of institutionalised academia. A filmic image, a cultural idiom, or the use of a single linguistic category, may be read in radically divergent ways, depending on place and time, as well as - crucially - on ethnic, gender, religious, generational and other such differences. Some differences may be incommensurable, as Ien Ang has suggested,[17] yet through such attention to difference, to the politics of place and of identity - to which, to extend the title of Henrietta Moore's work,[18] I passionately subscribe - the question of hegemony still remains. Is there a hegemonic politics of gender that cuts through the multiple readings of place and identity in the dominant images of the Chinese woman that reaches us through the print media, TV and film?

Shu-mei Shih, a US based Taiwanese feminist scholar, has analysed the different layers of nationalist and patriarchal meanings inscribed in media representations of the mainland 'sister'.[19] She suggests that the interweaving of political, economic and cultural anxieties in the figure of the mainland woman, as she is represented in the Taiwan and Hong Kong media, consistently undermines the possibility of unitary interpretation and systematically undercuts claims to create a 'transnational' public sphere in gender debated across national and cultural 'Chinese' boundaries. In the Taiwan media, she appears as the criminal, the deviant, the gender representative of the threat from across the Straits, whereas in Hong Kong, she is represented as the prostitute and the mistress, a gendered embodiment of the mainland threat, that can be assimilated by Hong Kong business personified in the figure of the wealthy and successful entrepreneur. Woman neither appears as the 'third term' in the binaric struggle between the coloniser and the colonised, nor as the gendered representation of Chinese identity.

Louisa Schein's work, by contrast, has focused on the shifting meanings of China's national identity inscribed in the juxtaposition between the Chinese woman and the white Western woman, and between the Han and the ethnic minority woman. She argues that the saturation of women's print and advertising media by the beautiful white woman has given way in recent years to a focus on the 'colour' of the ethnic woman. In her analysis, the nationalist sentiments inscribed in the binary between Chinese and Western were particularly prevalent in the late 1980s and early 1990s. But in her essay 'Gender and Internal Orientalism' she argues that 'internal orientalist' representations of minority women have contributed to new postcolonial hierarchies that subordinate minorities, women and peasants in Chinese society. With a somewhat different though related emphasis, Dru Gladney has also argued that popular representations of minority sensuality and

17. Ien Ang, 'Comments on Felski's "The doxa of difference": the uses of incommensurability', *Signs* vol 24, no 1, Autumn 1997, pp57-64.

18. Henrietta Moore, *A Passion for Difference*, Polity Press, Cambridge 1994.

19. Shu-mei Shih, *op. cit.*

20. Schein, *op. cit*, and 'Gender and Internal Orientalism in China', *Modern China* 23 (1), 1997, pp69-98; Dru C. Gladney, 'Representing Nationality in China: Refiguring Majority/Minority Identities', *Journal of Asian Studies* 53(1), 1994, pp92-123.

eroticism have served to delineate internal 'margins' or boundaries, to reshape and consolidate the 'centre' of Han nationalism.[20]

In her earlier essay, 'The Consumption of Color and the Politics of White Skin in Post-Mao China', Louisa Schein also argued that this assertion of Han authority, through reference to the ethnic/minority subaltern, appeared as a shift from an earlier mode of foregrounding national status with reference to representations of the white West. Despite the oppositional force of the Western woman as an object of longing and a symbol of lack - as Rey Chow put it, she represented what China did not have - by the 1990s, the open-door policy had brought MTV into millions of homes, had flooded shops with more or less affordable Western goods, and lifted many former restrictions on travel. The 'West' was accessible as long as you had the money for it. Schein's argument here is that the saturation of public and media spaces with the 'West' had the effect of dissolving the 'self-other binarism between China and the West' and shifting it to the Han/ethnic opposition. In the process the Western woman was desexualised and resexualised. 'She vaporised, disappearing into the commodities she sold or into the bodies she transformed'.[21]

21. Schein, 'The Consumption of Color', *op. cit*.

An analysis of issues of *Nüxing yanjiu* (*Women's Studies*) between the early 1990s, its renaming and 'refashioning' as *Nüxing yuekan* (*Women's Monthly*) in early 1998, indicates a similar shift in the assertion of Chinese identity with reference to Western alterity. As I have argued elsewhere, images of the faces and bodies of the white woman dominated the outside covers of this journal between the early and mid-1990s. The white woman appeared as the voluptuous embodiment of erotic desire, enjoying her own sensuality as well as being enjoyed by the male partner who frequently, though not always, appeared at her side. She signified individual self-realisation, self-liberation, through immersion in her own pleasure. She was also the symbol of consumer capacity and satisfaction, bedecked with jewellery, designer clothing and cosmetics; even in a state of relative undress, her beautiful hair and unblemished skin bespoke the bodily and aesthetic form offered by the consumption of fashion products.

While the white woman of these images appeared in different poses and guises, and within different contexts: in tourist hotels, with domestic appliances, and so on - the variations of her image in their totality created a representation of the West as the 'motif of golden hair' (*jin toufa*), in Schein's words, an emblem of racialised difference, which evoked 'an unequivocal connotation of value'.[22] While suggesting that the white woman's body 'prickled with polysemy', Schein also argued that the dominant motif of this body meant that it would be a mistake to dis-aggregate the different forms and poses of that body into discrete types. This figure rarely appeared with Chinese women. By her total contrast with the Chinese woman, and by her symbolic authority as the goal of consumer desire and the representative of Chinese lack, she literally was appropriated to 'sell' the products on which China's market future depended. At the same time, however, she was upheld

22. *Ibid.*, p144.

as the antithesis of Chinese values, of Chinese national identity. Texts in the same issues of the journal repeatedly privileged values associated with the 'gentle and soft' (wenrou), the unthreatening and servicing characteristics of the 'traditional oriental beauty'. Surveys conducted about the desired characteristics of marriage partner, of the characteristics of feminine beauty, and even descriptions of female sports players, suggested that 'woman's' independent inaccessibility was not a desirable feature of China's self-identity, either in the domestic or the international and global context. In her recent article, 'The Body and the Beautiful in Chinese Nationalism: Sportswomen and Fashion Models in the Reform Era', Susan Brownell points out that public discourse was careful to emphasise that sportswomen who might appear aggressive during competition were 'in fact gentle females'. A judo player, for example, was described as a 'shy, demure-looking girl, but on the training mat she becomes as tough and aggressive as any tomboy'.[23] In the same way, in a series of articles on 'Shenmo shi xiandai nüxing mei', (What is modern feminine beauty?) published in Zhongguo funü (Women of China) many readers suggested that 'strong women' (qiang nüren), those women who had independent careers and positions, were unfeminine and by implication undesirable as wives.[24] By contrast with Western women, as one contributor to the debate suggested, 'Chinese women should preserve their Chinese characteristics and ... should be more reserved and shy'.[25] The counter-positioning of images of the white Western and Chinese woman thus not only signified an affirmative message, in which the Western woman guided the Chinese into the fetishised delights of consumption, but also a racialised, cultural and potentially political dichotomy in which China's claims to national value and authority were paramount.

This value-laden juxtaposition of different images of femininity reminds us of two arguments about the political uses of the appropriation of the female image, that have recently been outlined by feminist scholars in China and abroad. With reference to literature, film and language, these scholars have shown how the trope of female bodily suffering and self-sacrifice has functioned as a signifier of a nationalism which was hurt and humiliated by the West and Japan.[26] The central subject of this nationalism is male; women must suffer because men are too weak to reverse the injustices done to men through women.[27] As part of this process, the privileged position of an entrepreneurial masculinity is asserted through images of Chinese women who not only symbolise China (the oriental beauty), but who also sell on the international market. The Chinese woman of these images, given her prevalent association with service, softness and consumption (no initiative) is not simply an emblem of success, a trophy and a reward for subscribing to the market principles of the open door policy; as a consumer she also reinforces male success in directing that process. The assertion of male dominance in the national reform project through representations of the white western woman is even clearer in Sheldon Lu's analysis of TV soaps, in which male desire is fulfilled through possession of the white woman,

23. Brownell, op. cit., p42.

24. 'Shenmo shi xiandai nüxing mei?' (What is the beauty of the modern woman?), Zhongguo funü (Women of China), 8, 1991, p14.

25. Sun Wanqun, 'Chongsu nüxing mei de kanke zhi lu' (The rough road to remolding female beauty), Zhongguo funü (Women of China), 2, 1992.

26. Meng, op. cit.; Lydia Liu, 'The Female Body and Nationalist Discourse: Manchuria in Xiao Hong's, Field of Life and Death, in Zito & Barlow op. cit., pp118-36. Brownell, op. cit., p13

27. Stephanie Donald, 'Symptoms of Alienation: the Female Body in Recent Chinese Film', Continuum, Vol. 12, no. 1, 1998, pp91-103.

28. Sheldon Lu, 'Chinese Soap Opera: The Transnational Politics of Visuality, Sexuality, and Masculinity', paper presented to the Annual Meeting of the Association for Asian Studies, Washington, D.C. March 26-28, 1998.

29. Schein, 'The Consumption of Color', op. cit., p150.

30. Rae Yang, Spider Eaters, A Memoir, University of California Press, Berkeley/Los Angeles/London 1997.

31. Xiaomei Chen, 'Growing up with Posters in the Mao Era', in Evans and Donald, op. cit., pp101-122.

while his passive, 'traditional' wife is erased as emblematic of 'tradition'.[28]

Recent issues of *Nüxing yuekan* reveal that recent shifts in the imaging of the beautiful Chinese woman show yet another meaning to her bodily appropriation. Coinciding with what a Chinese commentator dubbed the West's 'craze for China' (*Zhongguo re*), seen in recent 'oriental fashions' in western markets, fashionable Chinese women have increasingly appeared in Chinese magazines together with Western women, co-featuring in advertisements and photographic illustrations. Western women have also appeared in Chinese clothes, most notably the *qipao* (Chinese dress) as well as in advertisements of local Chinese fashion products. Schein has suggested that the diminished appearance of the white woman in Chinese commercial culture in the mid-1990s and the use of the minority woman as the emblematic 'other' to the Han, signified 'a turning away from the West in a fervent attempt to cast off the inferior position assigned to China in the dyadic relation with the West'. She called this process 'displacing subalternity'.[29] Here, by contrast, I would suggest that the assimilation of the West into the bodies and fashions of China is another mode of presenting a newly confident nationalism to the world, which simultaneously applauds Chinese and Asian values through clothing Western women in them, at the same time as it asserts China's capacity to contain, if not dominate the West, through the parallel appearance of the two.

For a variety of reasons, writers have made little attempt to read difference into the ways in which the dominant female image of the Mao era was disseminated and interpreted. The romantic appeal of contemporary visual images - an appeal which has been legitimised as a form of public representation since the early days of the reform programme - for many women, re-inscribes notions of self with potentially liberatory attributes and possibilities that were denied by the androgynous discourse of the Cultural Revolution. Yet this view is built on the assumption that multiple readings of womanhood, even of femininity and female sexuality, were denied by the discursive constraints on gender in the previous period.

It is important to mention in this discussion about public images of women two recent works written by Chinese women of, more or less, the Red Guard generation. One, *Spider Eaters*, by Rae Yang, is an autobiographical account of growing up in China, one of the most memorable and moving parts of which narrates her experience, and her agency, as a Red Guard.[30] Yang describes how her dress, in the simple 'uniform' of the Red Guards, far from being a constraint on her gendered sense of self was the symbol of her practice as an equal actor. The other, a recent essay by Chen Xiaomei on memory, subjectivity and the posters of the Cultural Revolution, describes her sense of freedom and delight in experimenting with guises of gendered and sexual identities represented by the fashions of the period.[31] Between her delight in her mother's feminine body and appeal (her mother was a dancer) and her excitement at 'disguising' herself in gendered terms through wearing the gender-neutral clothes of the time, the required dress of the period granted her the possibility of moving between different kinds of identities.

If these two examples show that Maoist representations of women, visual as well as written, were far from holding out a unitary and closed set of positions for women's self-identification, then other - arguably most - autobiographical accounts by Chinese women reveal that dominant narratives, and their corollary in a series of exclusions, are still powerfully at work. While on the one hand, the diversity of contemporary approaches seems to offer multiple possibilities for gendered and even sexual identities, it does so at the cost of almost total exclusion of other, much vaster differences in the day-to-day spaces of women's lives. As I mentioned before, the rural, the older, the disabled, the poor are absent from contemporary discourses, the limited exceptions being on a few inner pages of women's magazines, where occasional articles might focus on a grandmother's growing resentment at being expected to care for their grandchildren, or on migrant women workers' miserable labour conditions. The absence of these women constitutes a marginalisation from the desired image of the modern woman. The accoutrements of fashion currently displayed to appeal to women's consumer passions, by definition express differentiated social relations. As Baudrillard has argued, social differentiation in consumer culture is mediated by the object, and not by the subject. The fashioning of contemporary femininity is conveyed through images of the urban-located female, or the female who has access to the clothes and accoutrements that urban consumption offers. Despite her possible different readings, she relegates the silenced and absent to the borders of the reform project.

HOMOGENISATION AND HEGEMONY

The above discussion shows many ways in which the familiar binary opposition between China and the West is not applicable to describe the changes in meaning accorded the image of the Chinese woman. Prasenjit Duara has argued for an approach to nationalism which is not premised on the awakening of a pristine national subject contesting the claims of the other, but on a relationship between self and other. Louisa Schein's analysis of changes in the imaging of the Chinese, the white Western and the 'ethnic' woman clearly suggests that neither has Chinese nationalism 'stood still' in its appropriation of the female, nor have representations of the female been static.

Appadurai has argued that the process of globalisation of cultural forms and images is not simply one of homogenisation. Repatriation of image and representation in local contexts gives different meanings to images circulating in the global arena.[32] The differences and variations between the meanings given to contemporary images of the Chinese beauty are, of course, significant and have potentially immense political as well as economic impact, as Shu-mei Shih has shown. It is also important to point out that

32. Appadurai, *op. cit*.

even the centralising tendencies to multi-national control of the production of many of these images do not, in themselves close down the potential spaces they represent for contestation of a range of positions and practices associated with non-conformist versions of femininity and female sexuality.[33]

33. Michael Curtin, 'Feminine Desire in the Age of Satellite Television', *Journal of Communication* (forthcoming).

Nevertheless, I would like to argue that despite these divergences and tensions, and their significance for understanding different local receptions in the process of consuming global commodities, key motifs displayed in them consolidate and even reinforce certain gender boundaries. They consolidate many of the ways in which gender is still central in the assumptions governing the economic and cultural aspects of the social division of labour. Susan Brownell has written that 'the transformations in the configuration of gender, body and nation that have occurred over the last two decades are not innocent with respect to power; they moved away from the androgynous ideal, which many women experienced as liberating, and in fact masked the emergence of new forms of patriarchy'.[34] In my view,

34. Brownell, *op. cit.*, p36.

such 'new forms of patriarchy' have been barely masked, despite the rhetoric of emancipation and self-expression that has accompanied their emergence. This, of course, is not to deny or ignore the different ways in which contemporary images may be read. Rather, I want to suggest something else. This paper has looked at a particular area of gendered meanings involved in discussions about images of body and beauty, and fashion. Without engaging in irrelevant debates about the degree of patriarchal constraints between the Maoist and reform period, I want to argue that certain key assumptions, hegemonic assumptions, naturalising women's interest in beauty are not only shared between the different periods. Despite the extraordinary differences, particularly in visual representation through which these are expressed, I suggest that the crucial rupture in gender representations has not occurred in dominant public discourses at the level of expectations of appropriate feminine behaviour - wives are still constructed ideally as servicers of their husbands and children, and daughters-in-law are still expected to maintain family harmony through minimising potential tension with their mother-in-law - but that women's naturalised character as consumers of beauty has been given widespread public and official affirmation. In this, women appear as dominant consumers of a material cultural produced and designed by others. Women are now consumers by design, as well as nature, whereas before that nature was targeted as a negative, 'time-wasting' and politically incorrect aspect of gender. The transformation that has occurred refers not so much to assumptions about gender, though these are changing in many other discourses, but in the political constructions of consumption.

The context within which these images are being produced and disseminated are ones in which women are still, more or less systematically, denied full participation as citizens. They are urban, young and beautiful, whatever their more detailed and specific context. These contemporary images hold out a diverse range of subject positions with which women may identify. Visual images offer women a positive range of positions, from the university educated, to the satisfied housewife, the alluring femme fatale, and the coquettish girlfriend. One might even argue that the recent appearance of white Western women in Chinese fashions - notably the *qipao* - and advertising Chinese commodities, sometimes together with Chinese women, reinforces the interchangeablity of desire between the Chinese and the Western. However, these images are not limitless; they identify woman in a series of fixed relationships with reference to both public and domestic spheres through a series of exclusions of multiple 'categories' of womanhood. In their exclusions, they also contain significant closures against possibilities of experimentation as the 'bad girl', the 'miscreant', the 'other' to the dominant ethos of the consuming urbanite.

Brownell has argued in terms of patriarchy. I would rather use the concept of a hegemony of gender assumptions, according to which the commonalties between all these images continue to marginalise most categories of women from recognition; and exclude all women from agency in the privileged sites of social and economic agency. In perpetuating key divisions of gender, particularly between the female-consumer and male-producer, these images, no longer Chinese or Western but local 'repatriations' of global themes, are central to the social and economic organisation of global capitalism. The discourse of the earlier period only scratched the surface in challenging this order. That it left untouched dominant - hegemonic - assumptions about gender, facilitated their massive and explosive dissemination once they were affirmed with the open-door policy. Through the prohibitions and appropriations of dominant public discourses, women continue to be mis-recognised, despite the differences between them.

Versions of this paper were given to the London China Seminar, SOAS, in March 1999, and to the Anthropology Forum, People's University, Beijing, in April 1999. I would like to thank Stephanie Donald, Kevin Latham, Shen Rui, Stuart Thompson and Wang Mingming for their valuable comments on its different drafts.

OTHER CHINAS/CHINA'S OTHERS: A REPORT ON THE FIRST NATIONAL FORUM ON THE PROTECTION OF THE RIGHTS OF MIGRANT WOMEN WORKERS, JUNE 16-18, 1999, BEIJING

Tamara Jacka

It is mid-June in Beijing - hot, humid and chaotic. This year is the fiftieth anniversary of the founding of the People's Republic, and, in anticipation of the National Day celebration on October 1st, the capital is even more like one giant construction site than usual. The hotel where I am staying, and where the Forum is being held, is in an older part of the inner city, off an avenue that is undergoing major reconstruction. Opposite the hotel's main gateway, a row of boys with dark tanned faces, worn tee-shirts and dust in their hair are squatting with mallets and chisels, chipping laboriously away at the edge of the tarmac. Obviously migrant workers from the countryside, some of them look no more than thirteen or fourteen. Down the road, the old grey walls of traditional courtyard houses have the character for 'demolition' painted on their sides, and in place of those that have already been knocked down, new buildings are going up, surrounded by mud and piles of bricks and makeshift shacks where the workers live. A woman is standing outside a shack, washing clothes with a hose and a basin, her daughter by her side, eyeing the foreigner warily. I go for a walk and buy a pancake and a drink at a stall. The girl who serves me is from a village in Hunan, a long, long way from here. Within the next few months, she tells me, she along with all the other stall workers and all of the construction workers and their families, will be sent back home to the countryside.

These are members of China's 100 million strong 'floating population' (*liudong renkou*); transient migrants who have come from villages all over the country to work in towns and cities in low paid, menial jobs that urbanites shun - as construction labourers, factory workers, stall attendants, waitresses, cobblers and tailors, scrap collectors, beggars, nannies and prostitutes. The burgeoning market economy and wholesale reconstruction of Beijing and other cities could not have been achieved without them, but prejudice against the floating population is strong. Urban residents tend to characterise them as a vast and unkempt horde of ignorant outsiders who pour 'blindly' into the cities, bringing dirt, disorder and crime.[1] In 1949 the revolution was won in the name of the poor peasants, the most virtuous and revolutionary of all classes. In 1999, they will be kicked out of town ahead of the anniversary celebrations, because they are a blot on the shiny new, postmodern, international cityscape.

1. Tamara Jacka, 'Working sisters answer back: The representation and self-representation of women in China's floating population', *China Information*, Vol. xiii, no.1, Summer 1998.

The First National Forum On the Protection of the Rights of Migrant Women Workers
(*Shoujie Quanguo Dagongmei Quanyi Wenti Yantaohui*) was a landmark. Funded
by Oxfam Hong Kong, and organised by members of the editorial office of
Nongjianü Baishitong (*Rural Women Knowing All*), it was the first time that
any of the participants had been involved in a national forum discussing
migrant workers, let alone migrant *women* workers.[2] The 'problem' of the
floating population and its impact on urban society, infrastructure and
environment is a 'hot topic' in contemporary China, and for 'China watchers'
overseas. However, up until now, remarkably little attention has been paid
to the lives of transient migrants or to what migrants themselves have to say
about their experiences. Transient migrants are very much a subaltern group
- they occupy the lowest rungs of the urban society and economy, and they
generally do not have a voice in dominant urban discourses, even those
relating specifically to the floating population. Indeed, those discourses
usually ignore or negate their identity as human beings. So, to be involved
in three days of discussion devoted to listening, understanding and trying
to improve the experiences and lives of migrant women was an extraordinary
experience. Aside from the discussions themselves, this was also an important
occasion for networking and lobbying, and the role of the media was stressed.
Not only were several television stations present to film the opening of the
forum, but journalists were also invited to speak and were lobbied on the
importance of their role in drawing attention to the difficulties and
exploitation that migrants face.

2. *Nongjianü Baishitong* is a monthly journal published under the auspices of *China Women's News* and the All-China Women's Federation, and directed at rural women.

The speakers at the Forum came from all over China, including Hong
Kong and Taiwan, and included lawyers, academics, a trade union
representative, quite a large number of grass-roots Women's Federation
activists, people working in the media, and a number of migrant women.
Only a few, relatively low ranking, government officials were invited. One
of the first speakers, however, was a representative of the Beijing Labour
Bureau, Cao Yongsheng. Throughout his talk, Cao spoke almost solely in
terms of 'managing', 'controlling' and 'restricting' migrants in the city. The
antagonism in the air was palpable. Xie Lihua, the chief editor of *Nongjianü
Baishitong* interrupted him twice to tell him to cut his rambling talk short
and to stick to the point, but he continued to read his paper till the bitter
end. I felt a little sorry for him. After all, the pressures on city officials to
restrict the influx of migrants are immense. It is also probable that Cao felt
himself to be under surveillance and was therefore being careful to say only
what would be expected of an official in his position. However, none of the
other speakers, I reflected in hindsight, appeared to be constrained in this
way. Indeed, the Forum was a fascinating example of 'civil society' at work
in contemporary China.

In stark contrast to Cao, Liu Guanghua, from the Huaguang Women's
College in Nanning, gave a passionate talk about social and health problems
amongst prostitutes, the majority of whom are rural migrant women. She
was highly critical of the fact that the illegality of prostitution and the

perceived criminality of women sex workers mean that they have no-one to turn to for help, and no means by which to protect themselves or to seek redress when their rights are violated. In Vietnam and elsewhere, Liu pointed out, concern about the spread of AIDs has led government women's organisations to establish education and other services for sex workers, but in China, despite a rapid spread in AIDs, the Women's Federation had done nothing of this kind, and a prostitute who sought help from the Women's Federation was much more likely to be arrested than given support.

In the afternoon, Qiao Xiaochun, a male professor from the Population Research Institute of the Chinese People's University, and Ma Xiaoduo, a migrant woman who had worked as a housemaid in Beijing, spoke about China's household registration (*hukou*) system. As Professor Qiao pointed out, there is nothing 'natural' about the hierarchical divisions that exist today between rural and urban China, and the discrimination and contempt that peasants and migrant workers receive from urbanites. In fact, these are social constructions with a peculiar and very 'modern' history. Myron Cohen has argued that present day conceptions of 'the peasantry' (*nongmin*) in China go back only as far as the first half of the twentieth century, when Chinese intellectuals, trying to define what was wrong with China's 'old' society and from there to forge a path toward a new, more 'modern' one, adopted Western constructions of a rural-urban divide, and of the peasantry as being the backward 'other' holding back modernisation.[3]

3. Myron Cohen, 'Cultural and political inventions in modern China: The case of the Chinese "peasant"', *Daedalus*, no.120 (2), 1993, pp151-170. See also, Yi Tsi Mei Feuerwerker, *Ideology, Power, Text. Self-Representation and the Peasant "Other" in Modern Chinese Literature*, Stanford University Press, Stanford, California 1998, pp9-35.

4. Andrew Kipnis, 'Within and against peasantness: Backwardness and filiality in rural China', *Comparative Studies in Society and History*, vol.37, January 1995, pp110-135.

Under Mao Zedong, the Communist Party countered this image of the backward peasantry holding China back, and through its designations of individuals and families as belonging to the 'good' poor peasant and worker classes and the 'bad' landlord, capitalist classes, etc., it accorded people with a poor peasant background a high level of status and moral standing.[4]

At the same time, however, it did two things that were to have devastating consequences for those dependent on the land. First of all, it implemented industrialisation policies which, far from pulling the countryside out of 'backwardness', squeezed it dry. Second, it introduced the household registration system, which, as Qiao notes, has done more than any other institution to cement into place a caste-like hierarchical divide between rural and urban citizens. Under this system, which was introduced in the mid-1950s as a means to regulate the population and to restrict rural to urban migration, citizens are registered as either agricultural or non-agricultural residents. Household registration is inherited from the mother and it is extremely difficult to transfer one's registration from agricultural to non-agricultural, or even from a small town to a larger city. Combined with central planning, this system once acted as a very effective brake on rural-urban migration, for in the city it was usually not possible to buy grain or to find housing, without a local, non-agricultural household registration card. In a market economy, the state has no longer been able to control the allocation of goods in this way, however, and has therefore found it much harder to control rural-urban migration. All the same, household registration is frequently used as a basis for discrimination against outsiders, especially peasants, and in favour of locals, by local governments, employers and others. For example, as had been pointed out to us earlier by Cao Yongsheng, in Beijing people without local registration are banned from a number of occupations and workplaces, including banks and high class hotels.[5]

Throughout the 1990s, the state came under a great deal of pressure to reform the system of household registration, both from those who were concerned at the inadequacies of the system for controlling population movement, and from those who felt it to be inequitable. Some changes have occurred. For example, some small towns no longer make the distinction between agricultural and non-agricultural household registration. Qiao, however, was pessimistic about the chances of this reform being implemented in larger cities in the new future. In 1998 it was also announced that in principle, children would now be able to inherit their father's household registration, rather than their mother's, if they so wished. However, specific regulations are drafted by individual localities, and at least in Beijing, according to Ma Xiaoduo, there has, as yet, been no change in regulations on this matter.

Ma Xiaoduo has worked in Beijing and Shenzhen for the past seventeen years and is now married to a Beijing resident and has a pre-school age daughter. Ma began her talk by saying that she was very moved and excited - never had she heard so many people express their concern for migrant women. For a while, she was so overcome by emotion that she could not speak. Then she gave a very passionate and disturbing account of her efforts to change her household registration. Without Beijing household registration, not only she and her family face enormous practical difficulties, but, she said bitterly, they are treated with contempt at every turn. For this reason, Ma has spent the last seventeen years trying to get Beijing household registration. She has spent large sums of money and tried all manner of tricks to get through the red tape, but to no avail. Last year, when she made enquiries about enrolling her daughter in a nearby school they told her she would not be accepted because she did not have local household registration. Then, when she heard of the new policy enabling children to inherit their father's household registration, she went to enquire at the Public Security Bureau, but they sent her away, denying knowledge of any changed policy.

Apart from the general discrimination and contempt faced by rural migrant women in urban areas, and the barriers they face in employment and in the education of their children as a result of the household registration system, the exploitation and mistreatment of migrant workers by their employers was highlighted in the Forum. Zhou Litai is a lawyer working on behalf of injured migrant workers in joint ventures and foreign owned factories in the Shenzhen Special Economic Zone. Here, more than 70 per centof all workers are rural migrant women.[6] As Zhou pointed out, China's Labour Law, and other laws covering migrant workers' rights, are very good by international standards. The problem is that the law is continually

5. For a discussion of the origins and social consequences of the household registration system, see Tiejun Cheng and Mark Selden, 1994, 'The origins and social consequences of China's *hukou* system', *China Quarterly*, no.139, pp644-668.

6. For analyses of the situation of migrant women working in Shenzhen, see Ching Kwan Lee, *Gender and the South China Miracle: Two Worlds of Factory Women*, University of California Press, Berkeley 1998; and Pun Ngai, 'Becoming Dagongmei (Working Girls): The politics of identity and difference in reform China', *China Journal*, no.42, July 1999.

violated, especially in the non-state sector. Consequently, as Dorothy Solinger has written, 'migrant peasant labourers employed in foreign-funded firms - like those throughout the third world - struggled in conditions reminiscent of the gruesome scenes in Charles Dickens's accounts of early Western industrialisation'.[7] Zhou claimed in his talk that the most serious problems are caused by employers restricting workers' physical freedom and destroying their self-integrity through abuse and authoritarian discipline, and by demanding long working hours from workers. Despite the fact that the Labour Law stipulates an eight hour working day, with a maximum of three hours overtime in any one day or thirty six hours per month, it is quite common for workers to be required to work 10 to 14 hour days on a regular basis. One young Sichuanese woman, whom Zhou was representing, had been required to work 78 hours of overtime within the space of nineteen days. She was so exhausted that she collapsed one day, falling onto the machine she was operating. Both her arms got caught in the machine and were mashed to a pulp.

In order to prevent such tragedies, Zhou suggested, first of all, that migrant women workers need a much better understanding of their rights and the laws under which they were protected. A large proportion of the women working in Shenzhen come from poor, inland, mountainous areas. They are poorly educated and have little idea of their rights under the law, or else do not know how to protect those rights or what to do if they are violated. In addition, Zhou stressed that local level governments need to do a better job of educating employers as to their legal responsibilities, and of enforcing the law. Too many, he said, turn a blind eye to instances in which employers act illegally and against the interest of workers, because of their concern not to discourage foreign investment or to reduce enterprise profits. Finally, Zhou argued, China's labour dispute arbitration system needs to be strengthened, the relevant laws and legal processes need improving, and the National People's Congress (i.e., China's legislature) needs to play a greater role in supervising legislative work at the local level.

On the second day of the forum, two thought provoking papers were presented by Zhang Ailing and Chen Ying, who run primary schools for the children of rural migrants in Beijing and Wuhan respectively. According to survey data, the majority of the floating population are single and unmarried and they generally return home to the village to 'settle down' rather than remain in the city to marry and have children. However, there is also a substantial number of rural couples who migrate with their children, or who give birth in the city, sometimes in order to evade the one child family policy. Furthermore, with large scale rural urban migration now entering its second decade, there is also a number of migrant women, like Ma Xiaoduo, who have married in the city and have had children with an urban resident. According to China's Education Law, all children have equal rights to an education, but, as Ma Xiaoduo had told us, migrant children are frequently barred from urban schools, or else are charged exorbitant fees,

7. Dorothy J. Solinger, *Contesting Citizenship in Urban China. Peasant Migrants, the State, and the Logic of the Market*, University of California Press, Berkeley 1999, p219.

so a large proportion of them receive no education and end up on the streets. In Beijing, according to Zhang Ailing, there are approximately 80,000 migrant children of school age, of whom 87 percent are not enrolled in school. For this reason, some schools are now being set up solely for migrant children, but they are having to fight long and hard for legal recognition. Chen Ying, the head of the Chun Miao primary school in Wuhan, the largest school for migrant children in China, told us that it took two years before the school achieved legal standing, and Zhang Ailing said that the Taoyuan primary school she set up last year for the children of migrants in the Haidian district of Beijing remains illegal.

Apart from Zhang Ailing and Chen Ying, most of the speakers on the second day were Women's Federation representatives. They included both provincial and municipal cadres concerned with the abuse of the rights of migrant women in the cities and towns in their jurisdiction, and county-level cadres speaking about the situation in the migrant women's places of origin. Many feminists, both outside and within China, are very critical of the All-China Women's Federation, seeing it as little more than a mouthpiece of the Party, incapable of truly furthering women's interests. I myself was glad that no representatives of the national or Beijing municipal Women's Federation were participating in the Forum, because based on my past experience I expected little more than meaningless platitudes from officials at those levels. However, the women who did participate once more impressed upon me the fact that grass roots Women's Federation activists are quite a different story, and in some cases, are truly awe inspiring in their dedication to improving the situation of the women around them.[8]

As I listened to the speakers, I noted two characteristics of their discourse. The first was that, whilst the concerns of women were the focus, gender was not discussed. The fact that in three days of talks not a single person felt it necessary to question, explain or justify the foregrounding of women was, for me, a refreshing change from conferences I had been to in Australia. On the other hand, it was worrying that the particular ways in which gender contributes to migrant women's exploitation and marginalisation were not raised. In her analysis of migrant women workers in Shenzhen, Pun Ngai points out that:

> Mao's China highlighted the category of class while negating sexual differentiation. Deng's China, on the other hand, is marked by the proliferation of gender discourses and female bodily images. Capitalist production in Shenzhen relies on gender as a basic constituent in developing a new system of work-place hierarchy. The rural women were recruited because they were not only migrant peasant-workers, but also females, considered to be cheaper and easier to regulate.[9]

She notes that when labour control was at stake, management often invoked the regulation of gender, castigating the workers for being 'unfeminine'

8. The work of the Women's Federation in rural areas is discussed in Tamara Jacka, *Women's Work in Rural China. Change and Continuity in an Era of Reform*, Cambridge University Press, Melbourne 1997, pp90-100.

9. Pun Ngai, *op. cit.*, p18.

when they were not sufficiently submissive. 'Those who controlled regulatory power tried hard to create anxieties among the targets of their condemnation - they would be shamed if they, as girls, behaved like boys ... Gender became a means of discipline and self-discipline, invoked so that they would learn to police themselves'.[10]

10. *Ibid.*, p.15. See also Ching Kwan Lee, *Gender and the South China Miracle: Two Worlds of Factory Women, op. cit.*, 1998.

The other aspect of the talks that I personally found disturbing was the recurrence of the claim that in order to prevent the abuse of migrant women's rights, it is necessary, first of all, to raise the women's 'quality' (*suzhi*), that is, their level of education, their knowledge about laws and legal processes, and their levels of cultural, social and political consciousness. References to the 'low quality' of the population, and in particular, of women, peasants, migrant workers and ethnic minorities, and efforts directed at 'raising the quality of the people', figure in a range of discourses that are central both to the Communist Party's efforts to reconstitute 'social stability' and above all, its own hegemonic control over the populace, and to the popular construction of notions of modernity and national identity, especially amongst urban intellectuals and cadres. These 'low quality' (*suzhi di*) groups are the flies in the ointment, the troublesome others that the elite would prefer to have nothing to do with, but upon whom, precisely because of their troublesomeness, an inordinate amount of discursive attention is focused.

The question of nationhood and of modernity, or more particularly, of China's lack of modernity and its supposed weakness as a nation, has been debated obsessively by intellectuals and political activists for most of the twentieth century. However, whilst there have been considerable continuities and overlaps between different political periods, there have also been disjunctures and changes. To put it most simply, one could say that the primary locus of blame has shifted from 'tradition, backwardness and imperialism', to 'imperialism, feudalism, capitalism and bad class elements' to 'population (and imperialism)'. As Ann Anagnost has written:

> ... with the announcement of the one-child family policy in 1978, population has insistently been raised not just as a problem but as a principal causal factor in China's failure to achieve its national destiny. However, the 1980s witnessed a subtle but profound shift in China's discourse on population from an emphasis on quantity to quality ... Here we see that the issue of population becomes the means to express the persistent problem of how to produce a modern citizenry out of undisciplined masses ... Implicit in this project is the discourse on the quality of Chinese labor that must be contextualized beyond national borders to acknowledge the evaluative gaze of global capital. Given the opening of China's borders to transnational capital flows, the success of the economic reforms becomes contingent on the selling of Chinese labor on a global market, with its more rigorous norms of discipline and skill.[11]

11. Ann Anagnost, *National Past-Times. Narrative, Representation, and Power in Modern China*, Duke University Press, Durham and London 1997, pp119-123.

Increasingly in the last half-dozen years, the issue of low quality has come to signify the root cause of China's 'historic failure of the nation to come to its own'. As such it betrays a curious doubleness, in which an elite subject somehow becomes detached from the mass to view the 'inappropriate other' critically, as from a distance.[12]

12. *Ibid.*, p77.

On the afternoon of the second day of the Forum, Xie Lihua asked me and Arianne Gaetano, a doctoral candidate from the University of Southern California, to give a short talk. (Arianne and I were the only non-Chinese participants in the Forum). I tried to convey my discomfort with the way in which some people explained migrant women's problems in terms of their 'low quality', saying that, whilst it might well be true that they are in need of education, for example about their legal rights, by far the greatest problems they face are social and structural. To say that they are due to the women's 'low quality' is akin to blaming the women themselves for their situation, which will only add to the pressures on them, not help them. I added that if an urbanite put to me that peasants or migrants were 'low quality', I would respond that no, it was urbanites who were 'low quality' - for was not discrimination against others a sign of 'low quality'? Perhaps it was urbanites, not migrant workers, who needed educating. Arianne then went on to make the comparison between urban denigration of rural people as 'low quality' and imperialist representations of China as 'backward'. In private conversation Arianne added that what is disturbing about the '*suzhi di*' discourse is not only that it places responsibility for social ills on the poor quality of 'others' themselves, thus seemingly absolving the Party and urban residents of any responsibility to address the social conditions that create otherness. By explaining social inequalities merely in terms of superior/inferior character, it also naturalises these inequalities, undermining any critique of them as being socio-structural. Finally, to be seen as sincere, calls to improve quality must be accompanied by financial investment and concrete plans to do so. Otherwise, they can all too easily be used by cadres as a convenient excuse to do nothing.

It was only later that I realised how seriously we, especially I, had transgressed the boundaries of what was acceptable coming from (imperialist white western) outsiders, particularly just then, with the memory of the Nato bombing of the Chinese consulate in Belgrade fresh in people's minds. Xie Lihua did not speak to me after that session, and I felt, with a sinking heart, that she was displeased. In hindsight, Arianne and I believe that she had probably expected a degree of kudos to flow from her role as a recruiter of 'foreign friends'. To be seemingly attacked by those 'foreign friends' was not what she had anticipated. Of course, it had not been our intention to attack, but perhaps we should not have expected her to see it in any other way. For one thing, 'raising the quality' of women is a central aim of the Women's Federation, of which she is a leading cadre. For another, we were all implicated in precisely the kind of 'us and them' imperialist discourse that Arianne and I were criticising. Thus, Xie Lihua, and, I suspect, many in the audience, had cast us as external onlookers and advisers with a position of superiority because (but only because) of our experience of the 'more advanced' west. And in that context, our critical remarks could only be read as denigrating our Chinese hosts.

On the other hand, some women later told me that they had been inspired by what we said. Others challenged me, saying that I could not deny that a lot of the migrant women workers did have very low levels of education and that presented serious difficulties. Then the next day, one grass roots women's cadre from Shaanxi province, Chen Xiuqin, began her talk by condemning the '*suzhi di*' discourse with an emotional force that was simultaneously inspiring and shocking. 'Of course', she said, 'everyone would like to "improve their quality", but the environments in which the majority of rural migrant women from Shaanxi grow up in make that an impossibility'. 'These girls', she said, 'don't have enough food to eat, or enough money to pay for school fees. How can they possibly "enrich their lives" or "improve their quality"? And with that kind of beginning, how can they possibly avoid being exploited when they migrate to the city?' Rural women, she said, could not be blamed for their 'low quality' - this was a social issue. The sheer poverty of much of rural China caused a host of problems, and the protection of migrant women workers' rights would never be achieved before such poverty was overcome. Chen also suggested that employers needed to be educated about migrant women workers, and she was very critical of the media for romanticising these women's plight.

Other speakers took a somewhat more optimistic approach, emphasising the importance of providing services and support for migrant women and of migrant women supporting each other and organising to improve their situation. We were told about two organisations that have been established to provide support for migrant women. One in Beijing, the 'Home for Working Sisters' (Dagongmei zhi Jia), was established in 1996 by the editorial office of *Nongjianü Baishitong* and currently has about 400 members amongst rural migrant women working in Beijing. It has quite a spacious office that women can visit any time, and it runs regular activities and classes. In Shenzhen, a similar organisation, called the Nanshan District Women Workers' Service Centre (*Nanshanqu Nüzhigong Fuwu Zhongxin*) was set up three years ago by the Nanshan Trade Union and the Hong Kong Women's Network. In her talk about the centre, Guo Xiuying said that one of its main aims was to increase women workers' sense of self respect, self confidence and independence (zizun, zi'ai, ziqiang, zili) and she emphasised the degree to which the centre was run by migrant women themselves.

In the last session of the Forum, the aim was to establish a dialogue between migrant women and other conference participants. This session, however, was characterised by a curious spatial and interpersonal awkwardness. Rather than the audience being seated in rows facing the speakers at the front of the room, for this session the organisers arranged the tables into two large concentric squares. This had the participants from Hong Kong and me quite amused and perplexed, and despite a Beijing journalist telling me that in Beijing this kind of session was always arranged like this, even the locals seemed confused about where they should sit.

In the end, the migrant workers - four women and one man from Beijing, and four women who had travelled up from Shenzhen - all sat along one side of the inner square, and took it in turns to briefly tell their stories to the rest of us, who were arranged on the remaining three sides of both squares. Unlike in the other sessions, the speakers had not been asked to address any particular theme, but rather to just talk about whatever they felt was most important. The result was a mix of stories, some highly structured around a single point, some only very loosely structured life histories. Some were more positive than others, but overall, the impression was of suffering. I found this amongst the most interesting of the sessions, but I also felt uncomfortable. There was a degree of tokenism and of voyeurism in the way in which the migrant workers had been incorporated in this part of the Forum.

Afterwards, there was an opportunity for questions, and then the session, and the Forum, were brought to a close with a quite powerful, and empowering, speech by Xie Lihua, in which she placed China's rural-urban migration and urbanisation in historical and global perspective, and portrayed rural migrant women as pioneers in the development process. For me, this last session highlighted a tension that had run through the entire forum, between an effort on the part of the organisers to break down the distinction between the 'experts' and the migrant women, and a kind of maternalism on the part of 'us', the conference organisers, the 'experts' and the 'concerned audience', toward 'them' the migrant women workers. Ultimately, it was the latter maternalism that dominated the proceedings. Nevertheless, the Forum was a vital first step toward overcoming the marginalisation of rural migrant women, and toward bringing together (post)modern, urban China and its 'others'.

POSTSCRIPT

Since I drafted this report, Xie Lihua herself has published an editorial in *Nongjianü Baishitong* in which she says that by the end of the Forum, it was generally acknowledged by participants that the *'suzhi di'* epithet must no longer be applied so indiscriminately to migrant women workers. The editorial gives a very good summary of some of the problems associated with the *'suzhi di'* discourse. However, it also provides a thought provoking and poignant outline of 'the other side of the coin', that is, of the dilemmas faced by those, like herself, who seek to empower and assist rural women who, however, are unable to run income generating projects, for example, because they are illiterate and because they lack the cultural inclination and the skills to take charge of such matters.[13]

I am grateful to Arianne Gaetano for sharing her views on the Forum with me, and for her critical comments on the first draft of this report.

13. Xie Lihua, 'Zhubian de hua: Daodi shei de suzhi di' (Editorial: Whose quality is low?'), *Nongjianü Baishitong*, no.8, August 1999, pp4-5.

Avant-Garde Dissent after Tiananmen Square

Craig Clunas

Geremie R Barmé, *In the Red: on contemporary Chinese culture*, Columbia University Press, New York 1999, 512pp; $20.95 cloth.

Written before the US Air Force, 'losing its way' in the skies over Belgrade, made such an unpredicted but in retrospect almost inevitable intervention into the dynamics of contemporary Chinese cultural nationalism, *In the Red* opens with a different, if less fatal, example from its roster of its grievances. This is the failure of a contemporary Chinese writer, indeed any Chinese writer this century, to land a Nobel Prize for literature. However, in their refusal to oblige, the inscrutable Norwegians arguably simply reflect the common agenda of their European and American constituency, whose unawareness of and lack of curiosity about the culture of the world's largest state is striking. Although *putonghua* (so-called 'Mandarin' Chinese) now mingles increasingly with the Turkish, Kurdish, Greek, Somali and English spoken on the streets of the part of North London where I am writing this, Chinese writers are less read than South Asian ones, Chinese artists of the diaspora remain corralled in a pen marked 'Chinese artists', and Zhang Yimou's lush costume dramas remain almost the lone success among the global audience for film. Why this should be so is in no sense the central topic of Barmé's dense and excellent volume, but the book's very existence, and the sharpness of its analysis, ought to terminally damage lingering excuses about 'not knowing what is going on' in China. If we don't know, it's because we choose not to.

What Barmé does do is cast an acute and sceptical eye on a wide range of the cultural formations which have accompanied China's transition from Mao Zedong's revolutionary line, which died with its originator in 1976, to the current phenomenon of 'socialism with Chinese characteristics' where, as he puts it, 'the rule of ideology [often] won the day in the centre, the laws of the market were victorious in the highly competitive periphery' (p141). He traces over the last twenty-five years a parabola from an authoritarianism of a high Stalinist kind to the 'velvet prison' of the present or near-present moment, using Miklòs Haraszti's formulation in a highly self-conscious way, designed to undercut the expertise of 'China hands' inside and outside the country, whose authority to speak is attested by their concentration on China alone, as utterly non-understandable in anything but its own terms. Barmé who knows more about China than most, is having none of this, insisting on the contrary that:

> In considering Chinese culture after the 1970s, the writings from the once fraternal socialist states, as well as works by authors who have lived

under the strictures of official censorship, can be a valuable aid in understanding the predicament of urban elitist and popular culture in mainland China (p4).

He sees the traumatic events of 1989, subsumed today under the location 'Tiananmen Square', as provoking among at least some of China's elite intellectuals a consideration of 'the devastating effects of socialism on the cultural life of the nation'. This is a process he sees as still 'slow and reluctant', compared to the lacerations handed out by many of the same commentators of 'the Chinese tradition'. It is 4 June 1989 which is the inescapable pivot of much of the book's argument, or rather arguments, for one of its many merits is its refusal of any of the great narratives of Chinese culture, whether those promoted by the (still) great, glorious and correct Chinese Communist Party, or by any of the other proponents of a single solution to China's predicaments.

This is a book densely packed with detail, detail of who wrote or filmed or painted or printed what, when, and who said what about it (thank goodness it has such a good index, an increasing rarity even in academic publishing). It has an exceptionally confident grasp of the politics involved, the key players in the key ministries, the critics who were listened to, and what their agendas might have been at different moments. One of those key players is none other than Barmé himself, as the author of important cultural criticism published in Chinese in pre-handover Hong Kong, work which was read and appreciated and attacked elsewhere in China. Barmé is a participant-observer in much of what he writes about, though scrupulously careful never to flourish his presence on the scene as a guarantee of ethnographic or orientalist authority. The book's overlapping narratives and looping chronology make serious demands on the reader; it is no primer, and will, I suspect, be relatively little used as a textbook by the small but expanding group of academics attempting to teach cultural studies or the cultural politics of modern China. That does not have to be a criticism, although something as banal as a chronology in an appendix might have been helpful to many readers, including me.

One of the deft case studies through which the argument is constructed, is the case of the T-shirt entrepreneur Kong Yongqian, whose 'cultural shirts' caused a great furore in the summer of 1991 with their sardonic messages. These shirts form the centrepiece of a useful 'Photo Insert' in the middle of the book, which I for one could have done with more of. Barmé has a great ear for language, but native speakers of British English need to be aware that his translation of one of the most popular of the T-shirt slogans as 'I'm pissed, leave me alone' relies on American /Australian usage. Many of its wearers may well have drunk like fish in the macho style of the Beijing *liumang* (hooligan), but in British English, it says 'I'm pissed off, leave me alone.' Either way, it definitely annoyed the police and the party, who described the shirts to Kong on his detention as the most serious political incident in Beijing since that of June 4, 1989, just before letting him go without charges. The limits of the state's tolerance were seen very starkly later that year when one of Kong's many imitators, a labour activist named Zhou Guangqiang, got three years in a labour camp for producing T-shirts carrying slogans advocating workers' rights. The T-shirt craze ran right through the first half of the 1990s, one of the most visible manifestations of a non-establishment (if not anti-establishment) form in Chinese popular culture. Barmé has written of it before, but never at such length and with such perspicuity, and this chapter is for me one of the most successful in the book.

Alongside it I would place the immediately following chapter on 'Packaged Dissent', looking at Beijing's 'unofficial' but highly commercialised art scene, dependent on the increasingly large foreign community for patronage. This patronage in turn allowed the party to deploy its classic strategy of demonising the Western Other in order to repress political and cultural opponents on the home front. It was always easier, and politically safer, to blame the canker of US cultural values, for example, than to confront the systemic problems behind the deleterious social impact of economic reform (p189).

Barmé shows how the censure by official cultural organs of Zhang Yuan's 'underground' movie *Beijing Bastards* was an essential part of the film's marketing strategy, almost necessary to land it a couple of awards in European film festivals, and a slot at London's Institute of Contemporary Arts and on Channel 4 television (albeit in the middle of the night). The theme of marketing, an obsession with Beijing's chattering classes, is taken up again in the next chapter on 'Artful Marketing', where Barmé compares the deployment by Chinese artists of the avant-garde of the once sacrosant image of Mao, with the way Madonna had ten years earlier used the iconography of Catholicism, at one and the same time 'both culturally powerful and commercially exploitable' (p219).

If one had a criticism of this subtle and powerful book, which combines an admirable grasp of a huge amount of empirical data with a refusal to make that data the sole explanation in itself, it would be that the 'contemporary Chinese culture' it treats of so well is (by the author's own admission) the culture of the big cities, above all Beijing, and of a literary/artistic elite in that city. The culture of what used to be called 'the masses' and still is called 'the people' is harder to read. If Barmé does not anticipate the rise of the Falungong, the 'Palace of the Revolution of the Dharma', a mass movement which seems to refuse western categories of political/cultural analysis just as much as it refuses to play the games at which the Beijing elite is so adept, then neither did the Communist Party, or anyone else for that matter. Whether its exiled leader Li Hongzhi turns out to be a defining figure of Chinese culture in the next century remains to be seen. What his influence suggests is that class distinction in cultural forms, whatever the Communist Party may say, has not entirely had its day in modern China, and that the 'popular' part of Chinese culture may yet prove to be richer and stranger than anyone imagined. I have no doubt that even now Geremie Barmé is turning his supremely well-tuned antennae to this new phenomenon. On the basis of this excellent book the outcome of his thoughts on the matter are to be anticipated with relish.

A TREASURE BOX OF POSSIBILITIES

Tseen Khoo

Michael Dutton (ed), *Streetlife China*, Cambridge University Press,Cambridge 1998; 304pp; £13.95 paperback.

Streetlife China is an enthusiastic and important offering in the currently limited field of Chinese popular cultural studies. Michael Dutton has helpfully included a select bibliography and it only takes a quick survey to realise that the past decade's publications about contemporary Chinese culture are relatively few. This book is unique for pulling together many disciplines in the humanities, including sociology, cultural studies, literature, anthropology, and history. A lecturer in Political Science at the University of Melbourne and thrice holder of research fellowships in China, Dutton presents a far-ranging collection of disparate articles which has as its key themes 'the emergence of a market-driven consumer culture, and how this intersects with social outsiders; state strategies and the street's response' (pi). Excellent and appropriate use of photographs and other graphics complements this pioneering collection of critical and descriptive articles, as well as interviews.

The editor has organised the articles (some of which are only a page long) by nesting them neatly into sections within the six larger parts. One of these sections, 'Defining Outsiders, Labelling *Liumang*', spans three topics: the semantics of Chinese characters that designate hooligan, vagrant, or drifter; the social stigma of criminal 'reform' and the meagre options for these 'second-class citizens'; and the under-representation (and, indeed, non-representation) of homosexuals in Beijing. Dutton's juxtaposition of language issues alongside those of sexual identity and ingrained Chinese social hierarchies operates skilfully in presenting the diversity of research being undertaken in this area, as well as opening reader's minds to the myriad topics about contemporary Chinese culture and society which have not yet been explored. The common thread of 'outsider-hood,' and what this can mean politically and socially, remains consistent through the three contributions.

I was particularly drawn to the part titled 'The Architecture of Life' which included consideration of the physical aspects of space and construction with research about Beijing city as a compound (Zhao Dongri) and Confucian hierarchy in traditional Chinese architecture (Yang Dongping), as well as the community and other social interactions which follow on from these spatial restrictions. An intriguing conclusion is offered by Yang Dongping who refers to contemporary China as a 'walled culture': 'the difference between rural and urban space (unlike the internal urban landscape) was never a sign of a social or hierarchical division'. The modernity of the rural-urban dichotomy for China contrasts strikingly with the almost constantly preoccupied 'Western' criticism on this issue.

A couple of the articles did seem somewhat simplistic, and I can only assume that Dutton intended them also as items of cultural interest in themselves. For example, Jin Ren's item about 'Homosexuals in Beijing' features prose such as 'How many homosexuals are there in Beijing? No one is able to accurately calculate, but one gay guy who is pretty familiar with the scene and a frequent visitor to Dongdan park, says he can recognise about 1000 regulars' (p70). The lack of research about homosexuality in China is undeniable and these generalisations, scattered throughout the four-and-a-half page item, do not provide much enlightenment about, or development of, the issue. Admittedly, Jin Ren's piece is reproduced from the *Economic Evening News* and is not intended as an 'academic article'. I found it very interesting to read it as representative of the awkward depiction of gayness in China (lesbianism is not mentioned at all), with its strongly anthropological perspective.

This initial foray into these formerly taboo topics is certainly a starting point. The primary sources suggested by the authors are importantly brought to light and topics seldom discussed in open forums are addressed. Dutton himself has commented that *Streetlife China* 'is like a treasure box of possibilities. Possibilities both for Chinese society and for those of us in the business of making sense of it' (pxii). Other sections in the book include 'Social Relations and the Architecture of Life,' 'Subaltern Tactics, Government Response', and 'Stories of the Fetish: tales of Chairman Mao'. This latter series of articles is accompanied by great shots of Mao clocks, fans, cakes, and statuettes. Dutton foregrounds each section judiciously with editorial commentaries which serve the articles well. The breadth of theoretical work that is represented in the book, and that which will certainly take place because of the book, signals a field of study which is becoming less populated by 'China specialists' but drawing more generally on cultural studies in contemporary Asian societies. This expansion of theoretical perspectives on contemporary China partners well the increasing work being performed on issues of globalisation and the influence of international media and 'world values' on local communities. These transitional phases, viewed from a cluster of cultural studies perspectives, would appeal to a wider audience than purely historical, empirical, or anthropological studies.

Beyond the 'browse appeal' of the collection, Streetlife China integrates several over-arching concerns in contemporary life for Chinese communities and individuals. In particular, the exploration of the present rural-urban split and emerging class issues for the increasingly mobile population is made more complex and intertwined. This is more specifically represented in the articles by Gong Xikui's 'Household Registration and the Caste-like Quality of Peasant Life'; Zhang Quingwu's 'The Resident Identity Card and the Household Register'; and Dutton's own compilation of 'Beggars, Prostitutes, and Undesirables: The Internal Rules of the State'. The integration of official Chinese government documentation as primary material for future researchers is an aspect of this collection which deserves noting. I would have also appreciated a 'List of Contributors' to gauge the range and experiences of authors in the book.

The usefulness of this collection to a wide range of academics and also to the general public is testament to Dutton's talent for balancing the provision of specialist and background segments. Its refreshing viewpoints and styles, and its scope of topics and theoretical groundings, should ensure that *Streetlife China* remains a valuable resource for quite a few years.

COLONISED INTO ADMISSION

Sarah Stevens

Lisa Lowe, *Immigrant Acts: on Asian American cultural politics*, Duke University Press, Durham and London 1996; 252pp; US $16.95 paperback.

Immigrant Acts investigates Asian American cultural productions in relation to the material history of Asian immigration to the United States and the exclusion of Asian Americans from US national culture. Lowe argues that the US national culture attempts to assimilate individuals and particularities into a system of representation which erases the historical specificity of the Asian American experience. She creates a richly textured work which theorises the racialisation of US citizenship, the flawed concept of multiculturalism, and the ways in which Asian American cultural products use techniques of displacement, decolonisation, and disidentification to critique cultural institutions.

Lowe's critical first chapter deals with the material history of Asian immigration and the racialisation of the American citizenry. She elaborates on the historical treatment of Asian immigrants, Asian Americans, and Asian nations, mapping a genealogy of racial formation. Lowe argues that national culture is the vehicle through which citizens are created and that the US national culture in particular posits the citizen against the immigrant, the American against the Asian. The development of Asian American culture must be seen in light of the historical contradiction between political and economic acceptance of Asian immigrant labour and the exclusion of Asian immigrants from US citizenry and national culture.

Lowe urges an analysis of Asian American cultural politics which pays strict attention to the reality of economic, racial, and gender inequities which have emerged as a result of the material history of Asian Americans. She points out that an emphasis on issues of legal equality or identity politics obscures the divisions within the broad term 'Asian American' by ignoring important material factors such as gender and class, in addition to the individual's specific historical context of immigration, level of English-speaking ability, and location within the US. The benefits and drawbacks of appealing to Asian American identity echo the debates between nationalist and feminist concerns, between the politics of identity and difference.

In addition, Lowe criticises the belief that an increase in 'multiculturalism' and the inclusion of Asian American material in academia will result in a re-making of US national culture. She observes that the use of the university as a grounds for establishing Asian American studies can lead to formalised ethnic/area/racial studies departments and an 'ethnic canon,' thus reifying the same hegemonic institution which excludes Asian Americans. Through a close analysis of the 1990 Los Angeles Festival of the Arts, Lowe also critiques the current drive for 'multiculturalism' as a movement 'that aestheticises ethnic differences as if they could be separated from history' (p9). In this context, Lowe shows how the documentary *Sa-I-Gu* by Christine Choy, Elaine Kim, and Dai Sil Kim-Gibson contests the panacea of pluralist inclusion, both through the layered testimonies of various speakers and through the visual form of the video.

Lowe's alternative to the approaches of the 'ethnic canon' and multiculturalism is to examine Asian American cultural products as the site of contradictions which critique US nationalist domination. Her discussion of literary works includes Thereesa Hak Kyung Cha's *Dictée*, Jessica Hagedorn's *Dogeaters*, and Fae Myenne Ng's *Bone*. Lowe contends that the form of the novel stands as a symbol for dominant, colonial culture. The novel (along with the historical narrative) is a cultural institution which privileges a realist aesthetic, an obsession with linear progress, and the narration of a single unified subject. National culture uses 'the formal devices of the novel as a means of situating Asia and narrating the incorporation of Asian immigrants into the US nation' (p101). Lowe draws a parallel between the novel form and the colonial use of language, both of which are used to coerce the colonised into an admission of their inferiority and to assimilate heterogeneous groups into a single representational system. Both, however, can also provide a means for the colonised to fight against this dominant schema. Lowe argues that Asian American writing can be read as a product of decolonisation. Asian American cultural products use the novel form to displace 'representational regimes,' by showing the limits and the breakdowns of the realist aesthetic. Such writings focus on the cracks in the dominant discourse, centralising concepts of displacement, decolonisation, and disidentification.

As one example of this de-centring of dominant culture, Lowe discusses the role of gossip within Hageborn's novel *Dogeaters*: 'Extravagant and unregulated, gossip functions as an "unofficial" discursive structure - or perhaps we might better characterise it as an antistructure or a destructuring discourse - running distinctly counter to the logic of verisimilitude and the organised subordination of written narrative' (p113). Blood, as a symbol of dismembering the body-as-unified-subject and refusing official representation, is utilised as another means to sever dominant discourse in *Dictée*. The limits of official narrative structures can also be revealed through an emphasis on mapping spaces, instead of creating a linear narrative which fetishises progress. Such cultural products which resist realist assimilation and universal representation are 'immigrant acts', attesting to the historical and political reality of the Asian American experience.

Lowe's clever textual references prove that these cultural products can be better understood by situating them within the historical context of colonial reality and the process of decolonisation. In so doing, however,

Lowe tends to essentialise colonialism and its generic effects on the Asian American experience. This aspect of her work could be strengthened if she paid more attention to the material reality of particular colonial situations - as she does so brilliantly when investigating the historical reality of immigration. Lowe's discussion of *Dictée* benefits from a discussion of the Korean experience with Japanese colonialism and the history of the US political involvement in Korea. Her other references to decolonisation and Asian American cultural products would profit from similar detail. Do the cultural products of Chinese Americans and Indian Americans reveal similar attempts to disrupt colonial cultural politics, even though China was a semi-colonial nation under the dominance of several colonisers and India was a long standing colony of the British Empire? Lowe's investigation of colonialism - and her contribution to colonial theory - would be enriched by more attention to such historical specifics.

In Lowe's defence, however, she is generally very careful not to essentialise the category of Asian American. She continually shows that Asian American cultural products are full of 'heterogeneity, hybridity, multiplicity' and criticises simplistic understanding of themes like generational conflict and filial piety in the works of Maxine Hong Kingston and Amy Tan. Lowe emphasises the importance of differentiation and examining the particularities of Asian American experience. Along this vein, her study would further benefit from more attention to the work of South Asian Americans. Since Lowe defines Asian American in a way which includes countries like India and Pakistan, including South Asian American cultural products in her analysis would explain the logic of this choice and broaden her study. The majority of her discussion focuses on East Asian American cultural products. A quick browse through the index reveals very few references to South Asia or even Southeast Asia (in contrast, references to China, Japan, and Korea are numerous enough that East Asia does not appear as an index term). If Lowe wishes to continue to use the umbrella term 'Asian American' to encompass all of these heterogeneous, hybrid, and multiple identities, she should justify her choice by expanding her selection of visual and literary texts.

Lisa Lowe's greatest strength lies in her ability to reveal the ways in which Asian American cultural products are linked to both the historical treatment of Asian immigrants and the treatment of Asian nations under the linked systems of imperialism and capitalism. *Immigrant Acts* encourages differentiation between the various experiences of Asian Americans and complicates our understanding of this vital arena of cultural politics. Her work has important implications for understanding the racialised foundations of the United States, the relationship between former imperial systems and modern Asian nations, and the racial implications of the global reorganisation of capitalism. In addition, Lowe proves that Asian American cultural products engage in a process of decolonisation, by showing the limits of the grand narrative and representational politics.

BOOKNOTES

James Boon, *Verging on Extra-Vagance: anthropology, history, religion, literature, art ... Showbiz*, Princeton, Princeton University Press, 1999, 351pp; £33.50 cloth, £14.95 paperback.

Verging on Extra-Vagance? Only that? James Boon takes his title and one of his epigraphs from Thoreau, who spoke of his fear 'lest my expression may not be *extra-vagant* enough, may not wander far enough beyond the narrow limits of my daily experience, so as to be adequate to the truth of which I have been convinced'. I may not be the only reader of Boon's new collection of essays - a work of immense learning, originality, and wit - who will want to assuage whatever Thoreauvian qualms the author maybe feeling on this point. Intellectually omnivorous, disarmingly self-aware, dashingly insouciant, perkily polymathic, he has turned a batch of occasional essays and reviews into a Great Big Postmodern Roller-Coaster of a Book whose idiom, when all is said and done, seems plenty extra-vagant indeed - and then some.

Boon may claim Thoreau, and Kenneth Burke, as the guiding light for his forays into 'AnThoreaupology' (see Preface), but one might be forgiven for thinking that certain modernist (proto-postmodernist?) figures - Jocoserious Joyce, or the protean-ventriloquist Pound, of 'Kulchur' fame - also inform the tone of this seemingly speed-enhanced Cook's tour of 'disputatious paths of interpretive theory, semiotics, area research, fieldwork, media studies and cultural critique' (pxvi). Each chapter, or 'essay-*étude*', as Boon prefers to call them, 'offer[s] nondogmatic ruminations that twist, dart, and swerve with the subject studied' (pxiv); reading through several in a row can induce feelings similar to those brought on in childhood (or even after?) by too-strenuous sessions of the American floor-game *Twister*.

So short a review can do little more than indicate that this volume contains three so-called 'Rehearsals' (on Burke, on Opera, and on Melville, Cavell, commodities, and other matters), followed by thirteen chapters divided into three parts. Part One, a more or less anthropological section, treats of Ruth Benedict, of Montaigne, foreskins, and a good deal else, and of Bali, Bateson, Jane Belo, and disciplinary development. Part Two ranges more broadly, giving us 'Cosmopolitan Moments: As-if Confessions of an Ethnographer-Tourist (Echoey "Cosmomes")', 'Why Museums Make Me Sad (Eccentric Musings)', and 'Litterytoor'n'Anthropolygee: An Experimental Wedding of Incongruous Styles from Mark Twain and Marcel Mauss.' Part Three packs in seven smaller chapters, mostly reviews and lectures, slightly reworked and repackaged and attending to various subjects in and around anthropology. In a final 'Encores and Envoi', Boon, acting rather like Keats'

'Joy, whose hand is ever at his lips, bidding adieu', revisits Burke, Cavell, Thoreau *et al*.

Boon admits '[i]t would be idle to claim for [his] anecdotal episodes any rigor beyond what ultraobjective readers may be generous to credit in uneasy vergings on extra-Vagance' (p99). His book does not advance anything so 'ultraobjective' as a thesis but rather provides repeated instances or embodiments of an attitude, a 'relatively relativist' bearing toward a world of 'manifold cultures, diverse disciplines, and rival critiques - identifying with none, friendly toward many, wary of some' (p278). Truly amazing in his scope, seldom less than 'brilliant' (but oh! the awful wearisomeness of 'brilliance'!), the profligately neologising Boon invites from his reader an answering attitude of *adexaspmiration, enthusenniusiasm,* even (sometimes) *contraviction*. Yet in the end one wants to render the same verdict on this challengingly playful, playfully challenging writer that Boon himself renders on Derrida, at the end of a painstaking review of *Given Time*: 'OH, WHAT THE HELL. Just take the thing; pay the guy; let him get away with it' (p220).

James Buzard

Ian Burkitt, *Bodies of Thought: embodiment, identity and modernity*, Sage, London 1999, 163pp; £45 cloth, £14.99 paperback

At work in much recent theory has been the desire to overcome the perceived deficits of the post-structuralist project. These deficits centre around the issue of a concrete and grounded analysis that takes questions of differential embodiment and embeddedness seriously, rather than as another layer of signifiers. In this light, we can begin to understand the corporeal wave that has swept across the contemporary theoretical landscape, in feminist theory, philosophy, social theory, post-colonial theory, geography and so on.

Bodies of Thought is another such attempt at a more existentially nuanced approach to thinking embodiment and embeddedness. What is distinctive and fresh in his text is the lucid overview and critique Burkitt provides of some of the key sources in this growing field, enabling the different thinkers to complement, dialogue and provoke each other as they are threaded together. Among the theoretical cast we find the usual suspects: René Descartes, Michel Foucault, Friedrich Nietzsche, Mikhail Bakhtin, Maurice Merleau-Ponty, Judith Butler, Iris Marion Young and Norbert Elias, as well as those less well trodden in this particular arena, for instance Evald V. Iyenkov, A.N. Leontyev and Richard Dawkins.

Burkitt's central thesis is to move beyond the legacies of Cartesian dualism by arguing for the experience of human reality that is derived from and transformed through the body and its relationship to the environment, as well as material and symbolic systems. Unlike 'discursive constructionism', where the body is always reduced to (passive) forms of significational content, Burkitt's body is multi-dimensional and is as capable of modifying the world as it is of being modified by it. As such, Burkitt emphasises the body's capacity as a productive, communicative, powerful and thinking being and therefore the core of possibility for a transformative praxis.

The most effective and thought-provoking argument in the book is Burkitt's strong rejection of the view shared by Nietzsche and Foucault on the primacy of violence in the formation of ordered society, which amounts to a self-fulfilling prophecy in that stories of origins project self-images of society with necessarily futural portent. In its stead, Burkitt develops a much more participatory and creative model which stresses the significance of artefacts and exchange in the transmission and transformation of culture. A constant theme of the text is the stress placed on the dynamic relationship between humans and non-humans, objects and subjects, artefacts and the body to show how they fold and animate each other in the birth of meaning.

There are only two minor disappointments in an otherwise thoroughly stimulating book. Firstly, the text omits a sustained treatment of race and class, which is odd considering the attention Burkitt places upon the body's multi-dimensional complexity. Secondly, a deeper and more penetrative reading of Merleau-Ponty's *Phenomenology of Perception* would, for instance, have supplied him with many resources on the way to conceptualising an active and creatively embedded account of bodily being. Burkitt's book is however a welcome contribution to this field.

Bibi Bakare

Anke Glebe, *The Art of Taking a Walk: flânerie, literature, and film in Weimar culture*, Princeton University Press, Princeton 1999, 283pp; £35 cloth, £13.50 paperback.

The Art of Taking a Walk takes us on a guided tour of some of the familiar and not so familiar landmarks in the culture of flânerie. For Gleber, flânerie is a primarily visual (or visualising) art of uncovering different temporalities within urban space. By being 'out of step', by refusing to 'keep to the path', flânerie reveals memories, fears and pleasures that are the less apparent aspects of urban modernity.

Focusing on Weimar Berlin, Gleber gives a detailed reading of the work of Franz Hessel - a novelist and essayist (his flâneur essays were collected in the appropriately titled *Spazieren in Berlin*) and a close and influential friend of Walter Benjamin. Via Hessel, Gleber offers a dialectical understanding of flânerie as being both outside the instrumental movements of the planned city while still being caught in the visual web of the spectacle. For Gleber, Hessel's work is exemplary of the attitude of flânerie: distanced, potentially critical, politically ambivalent and 'cinematic'. Indeed a meta-theory of flânerie is supplied through a work on cinema: Siegfried Kracauer's *Theory of Film* with its provocative subtitle 'the redemption of physical reality'. If flânerie is to be found in cinema's ability to apprehend actuality through its scrutiny of insignificant details, by its constant slowing down and speeding up of the urban flow, then a theory of flânerie is not limited to the physical actuality of 'being in the street.' *The Art of Taking a Walk* works to destabilise a separation between urban modernity as illusion or representation and as experienced reality.

The benefits of this approach are clearly visible in her discussion of the gendering of flânerie. Instead of rehearsing arguments about the impossibility of the (female) flâneuse, or arguing for a different, feminine urban modernity, Gleber resuscitates a tradition of female avant-gardist flânerie through the work of Irmgard Keun and Charlotte Wolff.

While at times the book seems to mirror the slow ambulatory attention of flânerie, the impression it leaves is not of a culture consigned to history, but of a cultural potential that is far from exhausted.

Ben Highmore

BACK ISSUES

1 **Peter Wollen** on fashion and orientalism / **Denise Riley** on 'women' and feminism / **Dick Hebdige**'s sociology of the sublime / **Laura Marcus** on autobiographies / **John Tagg** should art historians know their place? / **Franco Bianchini** on the GLC's cultural policies / **Homi K Bhabha**, **Stephen Feuchtwang** and **Barbara Harlow** on Fanon

2 **Mary Kelly, Elizabeth Cowie** and **Norman Bryson** on Kelly's Interim / **Greil Marcus** on subversive entertainment / **Georgina Born** on modern music culture / **Geoffrey Nowell-Smith** on popular culture / **Ien Ang** on 'progressive television' / **Alan Sinfield** on modernism and English Studies in the Cold War / **Tony Bennett** on Eagleton.

3 *TRAVELLING THEORY* – **Julia Kristeva** on the melancholic imaginary / **David Edgar** on carnival and drama / **Kobena Mercer** black hair – style politics / **Jacques Ranciere** on journeys into new worlds / **Peter Hulme**'s Caribbean diary / **Bill Schwarz** on travelling stars / **Ginette Vincendeau** on *chanteuses realistes* / **Steve Connor** on Springsteen / **Christopher Norris** on Gasché's Derrida.

4 *CULTURAL TECHNOLOGIES* **Out of print**

5 *IDENTITIES* **Out of print**

6 *THE BLUES* – **Jacqueline Rose** on Margaret Thatcher and Ruth Ellis / **James Donald** how English is it? / **Benita Parry** on Kipling's imperialism / **John Silver** on Carpentier / **Mitra Tabrizian** and **Andy Golding**'s blues / **Barbara Creed** on *Blue Velvet* / **Joseph Bristow** on masculinity / **Graham Murdock** on Moretti's *Bildungsroman* / **Edmond Wright** on post Humptydumptyism.

7 *MODERNISM/MASOCHISM* – **Victor Burgin**'s Tokyo / **Linda Williams** on feminine masochism and feminist criticism / **John Tagg** on criticism, photography and technological change / **Geoff Bennington** *l'arroseur arrose(e)* / **Emilia Steuerman** on Habermas vs Lyotard / **Paul Crowther** on the Kantian sublime, the avant-garde and the postmodern / **Mark Cousins** on Levi Strauss on Mauss / **Iain Chambers** being 'British' / **Adrian Forty** on lofts and gardens / **Lisa Tickner** on Griselda Pollock.

8 *TECHNO-ECOLOGIES* – **Peter Wollen** cinema: Americanism and the robot / **John Keane** on the liberty of the press / **S.P. Mohanty** on the philosophical basis of political criticism / **David Kazanjian** and **Anahid Kassabian** naming the Armenian genocide / **Paul Théberge** the 'sound' of music / **David Tomas** the technophilic body / **Felix Guattari** the three ecologies / **Margaret Whitford** on Sartre.

9 *ON ENJOYMENT* – **Slavoj Zizek** the undergrowth of enjoyment / **Peter Osborne** aesthetic autonomy and the crisis of theory / **Rachel Bowlby** the judgement of Paris (and the choice of Kristeva) / **Joseph Bristow** being gay: politics, identity, pleasure / **Gail Ching-Liang Low** white skins black masks / **Christine Holmlund** I Love Luce / **Line Grenier** from diversity to indifference / **Mark Cousins** is chastity a perversion? / **Simon Critchley** review of Christopher Norris.

10 *RADICAL DIFFERENCE* – **McKenzie Wark** on the Beijing demonstrations / **Paul Hirst** on relativism / **Cindy Patton** African AIDS / **Anna Marie Smith** Section 28 / **Tracey Moffatt** something more / **Susan Willis** Afro-American culture and commodity culture / **Hazel V. Carby** on C.L.R.James / **David Lloyd** on materialist aesthetics / **Peter Redman** Aids and cultural politics.

Back issues cost £14.99 each
Make cheques payable to *Lawrence & Wishart* and send to:
Lawrence & Wishart, 99a Wallis Road, London E9 5LN

Why not Subscribe?

New Formations is published three times a year. Make sure of your copy by subscribing.

SUBSCRIPTION RATES FOR 2000 (3 ISSUES)

Individual Subscriptions
UK £35.00
Rest of World £38.00

Institutional Subscriptions
UK £70.00
Rest of World £75.00

Please send one year's subscription
starting with Issue Number ———————————

I enclose payment of ————————————————

Please send me ———— copies of back issue no. ——————

I enclose total payment of ——————————————

Name ——————————————————————

Address ————————————————————————

——————————————————— Postcode ——————

Please return this form with cheque or money order (sterling only) payable to *Lawrence & Wishart* and send to:
Lawrence and Wishart, 99a Wallis Road, London E9 5LN

ARENA *journal*

A twice-yearly, internationally oriented scholarly periodical, *Arena Journal* will continue a commitment of the first series of *Arena* to publishing material which reflects on a renewed left critical practice. It is a place for theoretically and ethically concerned discussion on the prospects for co-operation within contemporary life.

Arena Journal will respond to the challenges of the last twenty years to the 'classical' accounts of social life which have emerged from theories of subjectivity and the sign, challenges which have affected the status of figures such as Marx, Weber and Durkheim, as well as post-classical theorists such as Habermas and Giddens. A central focus of the *Journal* is upon the interpretive and technical intellectual practices and their relation to the reconstruction of social processes: class relations, forms of selfhood and community life. We welcome contributions from various perspectives which engage with the *Journal's* special concerns.

ARENA *journal* No. 14, 1999/2000

Subscribe to *Arena Journal*

Rates (in Australian dollars please)

	1 year	2 years	3 years
Individuals	-	40	57
Organizations	44	83	125

Overseas: add $14 pa (air only)

Send to:
Arena Journal
PO Box 18
North Carlton
Australia 3054
Telephone: 61-3-9416 0232
Fax: 61-3-9416 0684
Email arena@vicnet.net.au